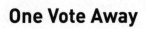

One Vote Away

ONE VOTE AWAY

AWAY

How a Single
Supreme Court Seat
Can Change History

TED CRUZ

REGNERY
PUBLISHING
A Division of Salem Media Group

Regnery® is a registered trademark of Salem Communications Holding Corporation

ISBN 978-1-68451-134-1
eISBN 978-1-68451-135-8

Library of Congress Control Number: 2020938901

Published in the United States by
Regnery Publishing
A Division of Salem Media Group
300 New Jersey Ave NW
Washington, DC 20001
www.Regnery.com

Manufactured in the United States of America

10 9 8 7 6 5 4 3 2 1

Books are available in quantity for promotional or premium use. For information on discounts and terms, please visit our website: www.Regnery.com.

*This book is dedicated to William Hubbs Rehnquist,
the sixteenth Chief Justice of the United States and my friend.*

CONTENTS

INTRODUCTION

Huddled in a modern, all-glass conference room in Greenville, South Carolina, with afternoon sunshine streaming through every window, a dozen of us were preparing for the presidential debate that evening. Our campaign had just shocked the world by winning Iowa. We placed third in New Hampshire, and South Carolina was the next primary coming up. My debate-prep team consisted of hardened political operatives, policy experts, and seasoned Supreme Court advocates.

Into the room walked Bruce Redden, my body man. Bruce had played football at Oklahoma State; he was the field-goal kicker, the team's second leading scorer whose college nickname was "Sunshine" because of his (then) long, bleached-blonde hair. He's charming, utterly trustworthy, and I love him like a brother.

Gesticulating with his right hand, Bruce interrupted our strategy session to ask, "You know about the thing?"

"What thing?"

"The Scalia thing."

"What Scalia thing??" I replied, puzzled.

"He died," Bruce answered.

"What?!?"

That morning, February 13, 2016, the great Antonin Scalia was found dead in his sleep at the Cibolo Creek Ranch hunting lodge near Marfa, Texas. After nearly thirty years on the Court, after ushering in a profound restoration in judicial fidelity to the Constitution and becoming one of the greatest justices in the history of our Nation, Justice Scalia had moved on to meet the Good Lord. The news was not yet public. Nobody knew.

But the local Texas sheriff, whose office had discovered the body, called me and my fellow Texas senator, John Cornyn, to let us both know what had happened. The sheriff got Bruce on his cellphone, and Bruce had just informed me.

Immediately, that became the sole topic of our debate-prep session. President Obama, of course, would try to rush through a replacement in the waning months of his presidency. Replacing Scalia with a liberal would flip the Court and create a five-justice left-wing majority that would produce lasting, fundamental damage to our constitutional liberties. And there was a real risk that Republicans in the Senate—far too often faint of heart, worried about press criticism—would roll over and let him.

Together, we drafted a statement calling on the Senate to hold the seat vacant. To let the voters decide. It was an election year—we were already well into the presidential primaries—and for the past eighty years, no Senate had confirmed a Supreme Court vacancy that had occurred in a presidential election year. We should not be the first.

As soon as the news broke publicly, we released my statement. I sent out a tweet, "Justice Scalia was an American hero. We owe it to him, & the Nation, for the Senate to ensure that the next President names his replacement." And, remarkably, in the hours that followed, my statement was echoed by many other Senate leaders, including Judiciary Chairman Chuck Grassley and Majority Leader Mitch McConnell. Later, McConnell's former chief of staff told a *New York Times* reporter that Mitch had rushed his statement out that afternoon because he knew that I would call for keeping the seat vacant in the debate that evening, and he didn't want to be seen as being pressured to follow my lead.

Regardless of how or why, to the astonishment of everybody, Senate Republicans held firm. Every one of us. Instead of letting Obama dictate the outcome, we together argued that the 2016 election should be a referendum on what type of nominee should replace Justice Scalia. We the People should decide.

That vacancy became a central—perhaps the deciding—issue in the 2016 presidential campaign. For many Americans, myself included, it was the single most important reason we voted for Donald Trump over Hillary Clinton.

◆   ◆   ◆   ◆

This book is about the Supreme Court. It's about the critical cases before the Court and the imperative for us to defend our constitutional liberties. But to understand how central the Court was to my own decision-making in 2016, this introduction will take a brief detour through the tumultuous months immediately following my presidential campaign.

I ended my presidential campaign on May 3, 2016. At that point, our campaign had defied all expectations. When we entered the race—in a crowded, diverse, and talented field of seventeen different Republicans—the media immediately dismissed me as having no chance whatsoever. Instead, we went on to earn nearly 8 million votes and win 12 states; our campaign amassed over 326,000 volunteers, and we raised over $92 million, the most raised in the history of Republican presidential primaries—more than Bush, McCain, or Romney—from over 1.8 million contributions. Other than Trump and myself, no other Republican won more than a single state. (Kasich won Ohio, and Rubio won Minnesota; Trump and I won every other state.)

There was a time when it looked like we were going to win. In March and April of 2016, we had a three-week period where I won five consecutive primaries, *all by double-digit margins*. We won Utah, Colorado, North Dakota, Wyoming, and Wisconsin, each one right after the other. But then the phenomenon that is Donald Trump took over. The mainstream media, which claim to hate the man, would only run stories about Trump, around the clock. Each of our primary victories was largely ignored—the media basically pretended they didn't happen—and altogether the media gave Trump $3 billion in free media coverage. That was, and is, utterly unprecedented in the history of presidential politics.

And it became too much to overcome. Throughout 2016, whenever primary voters actually heard our message, we won, over and over again. But then the tsunami of free media coverage drowned everything else out, and we could no longer be heard. The only events that consistently broke through the media fire wall were debates, and the GOP stopped holding debates on March 10 (while the field was still crowded). Therefore, during the two months when it was basically a two-man race, Trump and I never had even a single one-on-one debate. Even though the media made millions on every debate, they didn't care about making money on more debates; they had decided they wanted Trump to be the nominee because many of them cynically believed he'd be the easiest for Hillary to beat. (It is rich irony that many of these same media figures now incessantly bemoan the Trump presidency, given that their deliberate actions played a decisive role in his election.)

Trump won New York (his home state), and the media immediately treated the race as if it were over, repeating that message 24/7. And it worked. The nonstop media coverage ("It's over. It's over. It's over.") moved the numbers, and in states where we had been leading or tied (like Maryland, Pennsylvania, Indiana, and California), our numbers plummeted, dropping 10–20 points in thirty-six hours.

On the night of May 3, after Indiana, the numbers showed there was no longer a viable path to victory, and so I ended my campaign. Doing so wasn't easy. We had thousands of activists who had traveled from state to state to state, knocking on doors for us and making phone calls. They had poured their lives, their energy, their passion into the campaign. When I said we were suspending the campaign, one woman in the crowd let out a wail of pain that pierced me deeply; I could barely finish speaking.

Afterwards, I desperately wanted to stay and hug and thank every single volunteer. But I just couldn't do it. Tears were streaming down my face, and I lacked the strength to stop them. With a battery of TV cameras watching, I damn sure wasn't going to let the media try to turn "Lyin' Ted" (Trump's false but brutally effective nickname) into "Cryin' Ted." And so I went backstage to grieve with my family and closest advisors. Remarkably, Heidi stayed out with the crowd, spending over an hour thanking every single person there. I was immensely grateful that she did.

For the next couple months, I withdrew from politics. I spent a week down in Mexico, lounging in the pool with close friends, zip lining with my girls, playing hoops, and enjoying more than a few margaritas. And then I just let the political process play out.

Remember, in May of 2016, it wasn't at all clear what type of general election campaign Trump was going to run, much less what kind of president he would be. On policy issues, he'd been all over the map: At various times, Trump had advocated for gun control, higher taxes, and the Gang of 8 amnesty bill. He'd been a Democrat, he'd supported and contributed to both Chuck Schumer and Nancy Pelosi, and he had described himself as "very pro-choice" and an enthusiastic supporter of partial-birth abortion.

All of those positions changed dramatically in the 2016 campaign, but campaign conversions have a way of not sticking very long. Especially since most Republican political consultants believe you should run to the middle in a general election and run away from any conservative positions you might have taken in the primary.

So I just watched and waited. At the time, I was deeply conflicted. I was certain I didn't want Hillary to win; her policies, I had no doubt, would be a disaster for the nation. But there were also massive uncertainties as to what Trump would actually do as president. Too many Republicans had failed to deliver in the past; after eight years of Obama, we desperately needed a real conservative in the Oval Office, and we needed conservative policies to turn our country around. I wanted to do everything I could to maximize the chances of that.

Contrary to the media perception, my hesitancy wasn't personal. For most of the campaign, on a personal level, Trump and I had gotten along quite well. At my invitation, we participated in a rally together on the steps of the Capitol. We both went out of our way to be nice to each other, to praise each other, and we were appealing to the same core voters: working-class Americans fed up with the Washington swamp.

Then, when the campaign clearly came down to just the two of us, we beat the living daylights out of each other. "Politics ain't beanbag," as the famous saying goes.

The next month, Trump asked to see me in D.C. I of course agreed, and we sat down at the National Republican Senatorial building. It was a friendly meeting, a little stiff, but Trump was relieved (and surprised) that I had suspended the campaign when I did. By not fighting to the bitter end—by suspending once it became clear there was no longer a realistic path to victory—we allowed his campaign to pivot to the general three months earlier than they would have otherwise.

At that meeting, Trump asked me if I'd be willing to give one of the prime-time speeches at the RNC national convention. I said, "Sure, I'd be happy to." He didn't ask for my endorsement, and I didn't offer it.

I thought long and hard about that speech. At the time, I wasn't yet ready to endorse. The reason was not that Trump had attacked my family, as the media later supposed. Both my wife and my dad, who were the targets of Trump's ire, are strong, fiercely independent, and love our country. They had both laughed off his attacks at the time. The reason I wanted to hold back was that I had real doubts about what Trump actually believed, how he would campaign, and, if elected, how he would govern. Trump's history had been all over the map—on virtually every policy issue under the sun—and we were in a moment in time when the stakes of getting it wrong were massive. I believed I was in a position where I could have a meaningful, positive influence on how he would campaign and what policies he would actually support.

I wanted to use the speech to encourage Trump to be more conservative. To lay out a path for him to reassure conservatives that he really meant to keep the promises he had made. As a model, I looked to two prior convention speeches: Ronald Reagan's speech in 1976 when Gerald Ford was nominated and Ted Kennedy's speech in 1980 when Jimmy Carter was nominated. Both had fought tough primaries and lost. And, critically, *neither* had endorsed the nominee in the speech. Instead they laid out a vision they hoped the nominee would follow.

I endeavored to do the same thing. Indeed, much of the language about the nominee I copied almost word-for-word from Reagan's and Kennedy's speeches. Here's what I said, in the critical part: "To those listening, please, don't stay home in November. Stand and speak and vote your conscience, vote for candidates up and down the ticket who you *trust to defend our freedom and to be faithful to the Constitution.*"

That was the vision of how I wanted Trump to campaign and to govern, defending our freedom and being faithful to the Constitution. I wanted him to be a conservative.

But there was a difference in how the speech was received. When Reagan said largely the same thing, Ford treated it as an endorsement. When Kennedy said it, Carter treated it as an endorsement. I assumed Trump would do the same.

The Trump campaign had a written copy of my speech hours before it was given. They loaded it onto the teleprompter. They knew exactly what I was going to say.

Before I walked out on the stage, Paul Manafort—the Washington lobbyist briefly turned Trump campaign chairman and today an imprisoned felon—pulled me aside and threatened me. He said I needed to explicitly endorse Trump, or else. The "or else" wasn't clear, but it sure sounded menacing. I told him I was giving the speech as written.

Right before I walked out, my campaign strategist Jason Johnson said to me, "now we'll find out if they're rational." What he meant is that it is overwhelmingly in the interest of any nominee to unify the party to win in November. But, given Manafort's threats, it wasn't clear that was what they wanted.

When I went out on stage, I didn't know how the crowd would react. It had been a hard-fought primary, and there were a ton of Trump delegates in the front rows. I didn't know if they'd boo me the moment I stepped on stage.

Instead, they stood and gave me a rousing two-minute standing ovation.

For most of my speech, the reaction was enthusiastic, as I traced the history of our party as the Party of Lincoln—as the defender of equal rights for all and the champion of working-class Americans—and as I extolled protecting our freedom and defending the Constitution.

What I didn't know is that Manafort had instructed his whips—the campaign staff wearing brightly colored baseball caps interspersed among the delegates—to quietly wait for me to say the words "vote for candidates up and down the ticket who you trust to defend our freedom and to be faithful to the Constitution." And then to whip the delegates to boo ferociously.

And they did. It wasn't organic; it was staged by the campaign chairman. I guess that was the beginning of the "or else."

The whips were effective, and thousands of delegates followed the instructions and booed energetically. I've got to say, it's a unique experience facing the angry roar of a stadium of 20,000 people. Not all were booing, but a lot were.

I hadn't anticipated that reaction because it was so against the political interests of the campaign. Eight million voters had supported my campaign, and Trump needed everyone unified to have a chance at winning in November. But I had underestimated the thuggish instincts of Manafort and his crew. It's simply who they were. And that mattered more to them than beating Hillary.

What got a lot of attention afterwards was the phrase "vote your conscience." That had been a last-minute addition, and it evoked a strong reaction in the convention hall because it had also been the slogan of those contesting Trump's delegates in the preceding week at the convention. I hadn't been there for that battle and wasn't involved in the delegate fight, and so I didn't appreciate the raw emotion that phrase had taken on with many delegates.

Regardless, my purpose was to lay out a path for Trump to win and then to govern as an actual conservative. I viewed the speech as putting forth what I wanted to see in order to vote for him—and for conservatives to be able to trust that he'd defend freedom and the Constitution.

Hillary Clinton obviously was not going to do so, but I wanted to do everything I could to ensure that the Trump campaign (and later, the Trump administration) would follow through and be genuinely conservative.

And, much to the happy surprise of many (myself included), after the election the administration's policies ended up being remarkably conservative. Far beyond anything we could have reasonably expected.

As the summer of 2016 proceeded, my top priority became getting a solid commitment from Trump on judicial nominations, and on Supreme Court nominations in particular. I was very worried that, if elected, Trump might make really bad nominations, and I wanted to do everything possible to prevent that.

At the time, remember, Trump had put out a pretty good list of eleven potential nominees for the Scalia seat, but the list wasn't exclusive. He had said these were "the kind of nominees" he would choose—those eleven, or presumably anybody else on earth. Contemporaneously, he also said in February 2016 that he thought his sister would make a "phenomenal" Supreme Court justice. His sister was a sitting federal appellate judge appointed by Bill Clinton who had already voted to strike down New Jersey's partial-birth abortion law. So there was reason to be concerned. (Trump later said he was joking about naming his sister.)

In the two months after the convention, Trump continued to campaign as a conservative. Unlike prior nominees, he didn't run away from his early campaign promises. He didn't embrace the liberal policy positions he had advocated a few years earlier. And Hillary's campaign kept going further and further left.

In September, I made the decision, and my team began negotiating with the Trump team for me to officially endorse him. The price of my endorsement was explicit: I wanted a clear, unequivocal commitment that he would nominate Scalia's replacement from a specified list, and *only* from that list. And I wanted Senator Mike Lee added to that list. The campaign agreed to both conditions. On September 23, 2016, the Trump campaign put out a revised list, adding ten more names, taking it from eleven to twenty-one; among those new names was Mike Lee.

Then-candidate Trump explicitly committed in writing that Scalia's replacement would come *only* from that list, that nobody else would be considered. For me, after dropping out of a hard-fought presidential race, securing a conservative jurist to replace the great Scalia was paramount.

We were closely coordinating with the Trump campaign, and within minutes of their announcement, I put out my endorsement in a lengthy Facebook post that I had written explaining why I believed conservatives should support Donald Trump. Judicial nominations were the number-one reason. Here's what I wrote that day:

> First, and most important, the Supreme Court. For anyone concerned about the Bill of Rights—free speech, religious liberty, the Second Amendment—the Court hangs in the balance. I have spent my professional career fighting before the Court to defend the Constitution. We are *only one Justice away* from losing our most basic rights, and the next President will appoint as many as four new Justices. We know, without a doubt, that every Clinton appointee would be a left-wing ideologue. Trump, in contrast, has promised to appoint justices "in the mold of Scalia."

For some time, I have been seeking greater specificity on this issue, and today the Trump campaign provided that, releasing a very strong list of potential Supreme Court nominees—including Senator Mike Lee, who would make an extraordinary justice—and making an explicit commitment to nominate only from that list. This commitment matters, and it provides a serious reason for voters to choose to support Trump.

◆   ◆   ◆   ◆

Over the next two months, I campaigned for Trump, and I energetically urged conservatives to come out and support him. And they did, in record numbers.

The week after the November election, I flew to New York, went to Trump Tower, and met with the president-elect and his team. I spent four and a half hours with them that day and had dinner with his team that evening.

I told him, "Mr. President, we've been given an historic opportunity. This happens very, very rarely: unified control of the House, the Senate, and the presidency. We can't waste it. I want to do everything humanly possible to lead the fight in the Senate for us to actually deliver on the promises we made."

The conversation then shifted to whether I would consider a job in the administration. The president asked if I would be interested in secretary of Homeland Security. Although I care deeply about securing the border, I said no. I thought I could have significantly more impact in the Senate.

I told him the one job I might consider was attorney general. Frankly, I made what I'd characterize as a half-hearted play for the position. I said, "Mr. President, there are a lot of people who were on board way before I was. And so if Sessions or Giuliani or Christie want it, it should probably go to them. But if you wanted me as AG, I'd be willing to discuss it." We did discuss it for some time, but it seemed clear to me even then that he wanted Jeff Sessions in that slot, which was his prerogative. Sessions is a good man, but, unfortunately, we saw over the next two years that he was not at all prepared for the job of attorney general.

Instead, Trump pressed me in a different direction. He asked if I was interested in the Supreme Court vacancy. I paused for a second, and then said no. I told him I didn't want it. He pressed me further on the matter, as did his senior team that afternoon. But I told them flat no, I didn't want to be on the Court.

That may seem surprising to some folks. But it was not the first time I had passed on the judiciary. When I was Texas solicitor general a decade earlier, the Bush administration had inquired if I was interested in the Fifth Circuit Federal Court of Appeals. I told them I was flattered by the interest, but I didn't want to be a judge.

Though I hold judges in the highest esteem, there's a simple reason why I don't want to be a judge: principled judges stay out of policy and political fights. If I were ever a judge, that's exactly what I'd do; I would follow the law, no matter what.

But I don't want to stay out of policy and political fights. I want to lead them. I want to fight for lower taxes and regulations, for more jobs, for economic growth, for individual liberty, for a strong national defense. And, in our constitutional system, the Senate is the right place to do that. I care deeply about having principled judges on the bench—and I want to be part of nominating and confirming hundreds of them hopefully for many years to come—but I don't particularly want to be one of them.

Nevertheless, when I returned home to Texas after visiting Trump Tower, the discussion weighed heavily on me. I don't want to overstate matters; Trump didn't offer me a seat on the Court. But he and his team made it clear that it was a real possibility. And, politically, you could see why they considered it. At a time when there was still significant perceived tension between us, having me safely ensconced and permanently silenced in a lifetime judicial appointment no doubt appealed to the Trump team. If things between the incoming administration and the Senate fell apart, I would be sidelined as a potential critic or challenger.

I had said no, but the thought lingered; this was Justice Scalia's seat, a man I'd revered for my entire adult life. To even imagine occupying his chambers and trying to continue his legacy was breathtaking.

For the next couple of weeks, I continued to think about it, and I wrestled with it and prayed about it. Most of my close friends and family thought I was nuts for saying no to the Court. Heidi understood, and so did my parents, but just about everyone else said, "Are you sure?" The next weekend, I invited my pastor to come over to our house to pray with me about the choice. He had an interesting perspective. He said, "I understand your choice. For me, I imagine if someone offered me the chance to become one of the leading theologians in the world, which could have a profound impact on millions for decades to come. If doing so meant that I had to give up being a pastor, no longer be a shepherd to our congregation, I would pass on the opportunity because it's not my calling."

The more I considered it, the more certain I became in the choice. And, I knew I had to make the decision irrespective of any future run for the presidency. I've run once, and we came incredibly close to winning, and it's no secret that I hope to run again in the future. But the only right way to make this decision and not second-guess myself for the rest of my life was to assume that a viable path to the presidency would never materialize, that the last meaningful public position I would ever hold would be where I am right now, in the Senate.

I came to the conclusion that I could add greater comparative value in the Senate. There are a number of good, principled people who very much want to be judges and who would stay faithful to the Constitution. There are depressingly few principled leaders in electoral politics. It's a brutal, ugly game. You have to raise money constantly, and you get demonized on a daily basis. Most people with any sense say forget it and choose to do something else. Stop and think, in fight after fight—the public policy battles that really matter—who consistently steps forward and leads when it's hard? Because we desperately need political leaders who will charge into battle, who will make the public case for liberty, who will work to move people's hearts and minds to embrace our constitutional freedoms.

That's why I spent 2017 doing three CNN town-hall debates with Bernie Sanders on Obamacare and on taxes. Those debates were among the highest rated programs on CNN the entire year. And that's also why I launched a podcast (*Verdict with Ted Cruz*) during impeachment that at the time became the number one–ranked podcast in the world. That podcast continues every week, and to date, we've gotten over 15 million downloads.

Reagan inspired a generation of young conservatives dedicated to Liberty, and I want to do all I can to do the same. For decades on the other side of the aisle, in the Senate, Ted Kennedy mentored and launched hundreds of committed liberals who went on to have an extraordinary (and unfortunately harmful) impact on our nation; I resolved to do precisely the opposite, and I've worked hard to mentor scores of young conservatives and libertarians, who in turn have gone on to serve in Congress, as Texas solicitor general, as journalists, as federal judges and U.S. attorneys, and in dozens of senior roles throughout the Trump administration.

And so I came to a real peace with saying no to the Court. Perhaps at a different phase in life I might think differently, but the Court is not where I personally believed I could make the biggest difference.

The question was briefly revisited in June of 2020. While vacationing with my family near my in-laws' home in California, I received a call on my cellphone from President Trump. While I stood in flip-flops and my girls water skied on a pristine lake behind me, Trump told me he was expanding his list of potential Supreme Court nominees and asked if he could include me on the new list. I told him, "If it's helpful, sure, you can add me to the list. But I don't want the job, and I wouldn't take it." Unlike our conversation four years earlier, this time I didn't hesitate.

◆　◆　◆　◆

Two weeks into his presidency, on January 31, 2017, President Trump nominated Judge Neil Gorsuch—one of the twenty-one judges on the list—to fill Justice Scalia's seat. Democrats fought passionately against his confirmation, going so far as to launch the only partisan filibuster of a Supreme Court nominee in our nation's history. I helped lead the fight to confirm him, making the case both on the Senate Judiciary Committee and on the Senate floor, where we ultimately had to change the rules to overcome the Democratic blockade. The Senate confirmed Justice Gorsuch, 54–45.

Why was the two-year battle to fill Scalia's vacancy so hard-fought? Because today, the Supreme Court has become the preeminent arbiter of our constitutional rights. And the type of justice who serves has a profound impact on public policy and our fundamental liberties.

This would have surprised the Framers of our Constitution. In *Federalist* No. 78, Founding Father Alexander Hamilton famously described the judicial branch as the "least dangerous" of the three branches of the federal government because it "may truly be said to have neither force nor will, but merely judgment." That is true—in theory, at least. But history has not always borne out Hamilton's prognostication.

Starting in the 1960s, America saw the rise of activist judges. Under our constitutional system, judges are not supposed to decide policy matters. They are not supposed to make decisions based on their own political preferences. Instead, contested questions of public policy are meant to be left to the elected branches of government so that the voters can hold them accountable.

Judges are supposed simply to apply the law. As Chief Justice Roberts rightly put it at his confirmation hearing, a judge's job is like a baseball umpire, merely to "call balls and strikes" (sadly, a standard he has not always lived up to).

Americans have sharply different views on many policy issues, from abortion, to marriage, to religious faith, to the death penalty, to immigration, to the fundamental divide between socialism and free enterprise. In a democracy, those decisions should be made by the voters, not by unelected judges with life tenure.

But decades ago, activists on the far left decided that democracy was too cumbersome. It was too slow. And it was too difficult to persuade their fellow citizens that their policy prescriptions were sound and wise. So instead, they resorted to litigation, trying to get judges to mandate the public policy outcomes they wanted—even if the voters disagreed.

To be sure, judges should strike down laws that violate the Constitution. Some journalists and commentators have tried to define judicial activism as any time that a court strikes down any law. And, in an embrace of moral relativism—a justification that "everybody does it"—they have argued that Republicans want conservative judicial activists just like Democrats want liberal activists.

For anyone principled, that is not the case. It is "activist" any time a judge disregards the law to follow his or her own policy preferences. That means it is activist whenever a judge creates a new legal "right" not found in the Constitution. And it is also activist whenever a judge tries to erase an actual right protected in the text of the Constitution.

I don't want Republican judges or Democratic judges. There are many policy issues about which I personally am passionate (e.g., low taxes, low regulations, lots of jobs, school choice, securing the borders, a strong national defense). But it's not the role of a judge to mandate policy outcomes with which I happen to agree. Instead, I want constitutionalist judges who will honor their oaths to follow the Constitution.

The Court was right in *Brown v. Board of Education* (1954) when it struck down segregated public schools because they violated the Fourteenth Amendment's guarantee of "equal protection of the laws." The Court had been wrong in *Plessy v. Ferguson* (1896)—which *Brown* overruled—when it previously upheld segregated schools because the Justices personally supported the policy of segregation.

The Court was also right when it struck down the District of Columbia's draconian laws prohibiting gun ownership in D.C., in *Heller v. District of Columbia* (2008) because it violates the Second Amendment right "to keep and bear arms."

Conversely, the Court was wrong in *Roe v. Wade* (1973) when it created a brand new "right" to abortion found nowhere in the text of the Constitution. For two centuries, state legislatures, elected by the people, had decided questions of abortion policy. The justices took that power away by fiat.

For the same reason, the Court was wrong in *Obergefell v. Hodges* (2015) when it mandated same-sex marriage laws nationwide. You may personally agree or disagree with gay marriage, but, for two centuries, marriage laws had been policy decisions for elected legislatures—which meant different states could come to different conclusions about the proper standards. Instead, a majority of justices decided to strike down every state marriage law with which they disagreed.

All of us know that the Supreme Court is supposed to protect our constitutional rights. It is also charged with securing our Constitution's defining structural features, federalism and the separation of powers. Both doctrines protect Liberty by dividing power, by establishing checks and balances to prevent any branch of government from becoming too powerful. The alternative, unchecked government power—while commonplace in dictatorships across the globe—would fundamentally alter the nature of our nation and what it means to be an American.

Over the past six decades, the Court has arrogated to itself far too much power—well beyond what it is entitled to under the Constitution. It has seized this power at the expense of Congress, the executive branch, the states, and We the People alike.

While it has grown in power, the actual functioning—the how and why—of the Court remains a mystery to many. They don't understand just how precarious our constitutional liberties and core constitutional structures can be when they fall into the hands of rogue judicial activists. This book aims to explain what really happens at the Supreme Court—by relying on my own experience as a longtime Supreme Court advocate.

One doesn't need to be a lawyer to enjoy this book. Or, I hope, to learn something meaningful from it. All you need is to have is an interest in preserving the constitutional liberties we enjoy as Americans. Or to have an appreciation for federalism, separation of powers, and national sovereignty. If you're interested in the Constitution, or in Liberty, or in your own fundamental rights, then this book is for you.

This book will discuss fundamental rights and contentious policy issues that go to the heart of our Republic: free speech, freedom of religion, the right to keep and bear arms, abortion, U.S. sovereignty and international law, the death penalty, race, and democratic control over our elections.

It will examine eight critical constitutional issues and landmark Supreme Court cases that every American should know. Some of these decisions were good, and some of them were bad. Most of them were decided by just one vote. Almost all of them I helped litigate.

It gives the back story behind these vital cases. What was really going on. Why they matter. What the Court did. How it changed America. And how so many of our precious liberties and freedoms hang so precariously in the balance.

The reader will understand why judicial selection matters so much—and how to make sure we get our Supreme Court picks right going forward.

◆   ◆   ◆   ◆

Before I was elected to the Senate, I made my career as a Supreme Court litigator, and I had the blessing to play a part in defending many of our foundational liberties. I had the opportunity to defend many of our foundational constitutional structures.

In 1996, just a year out of law school, I began as a law clerk on the Supreme Court, clerking for Chief Justice William H. Rehnquist. "The Chief," as we called him, was one of the greatest justices ever to serve on the Court. The sixteenth person to serve as chief justice of the United States, he sat on the Court for thirty-three years.

Each of the nine justices hires law clerks, typically four per year. The clerks spend almost every waking moment with their justices, helping them read the briefs, study the case law, prepare for oral argument, and draft their opinions. For a young lawyer, there is no better opportunity to learn and understand the real inner-workings of the Court.

The Chief hired just three clerks per year rather than four. He had a staggering intellect, with a near-perfect photographic memory. He was deeply conservative, and he had spent decades trying to lead the Court away from the activist path it had set out on in the 60s and 70s.

Rehnquist became a teacher, a mentor, and a close friend. I was immensely fortunate to work for him. The Supreme Court was a world I hadn't known before. I didn't come from a family that had access or influence. There were no lawyers in my family, and nobody had ever gone to an Ivy League school. My dad came as a penniless immigrant from Cuba, and my mom was the first in her Irish-Italian working-class family ever to go to college. When I was in high school, the small business they had started went bankrupt. We lost our home and all our savings, and I took out large student loans and worked two jobs to make it through college and law school.

Getting the opportunity to clerk for the Chief helped launch my career before the Court. When the Chief offered me the job, my father wept (one of only two times I've ever seen him cry). I was being given the opportunity to see the Court from the inside, to get to know the justices personally, to learn and to see how they decide the cases before them. Over the next year, I worked sixteen-hour days, typically from 9:00 a.m. till 1:00 a.m., broken up only by basketball games three times a week with fellow clerks, police officers, and staff at the Court. There's actually a basketball court above the courtroom where the Court sits, immediately atop the twenty-four carat gold–gilded ceiling of the courtroom. The roof is low, and you have to develop a low-arching jump-shot to avoid being blocked by the ceiling. They call it "the highest court in the land."

After my clerkship, I went into private practice, to Cooper & Carvin, a small six-person litigation firm in D.C. specializing in constitutional and Supreme Court advocacy. It was founded by two senior lawyers from the Reagan Department of Justice, Chuck Cooper and Mike Carvin. Both are extraordinary lawyers; together they taught me how to practice law. Mike is a brilliant litigator who would go on to play a major role in helping us win *Bush v. Gore.*

Chuck is also a former Rehnquist clerk, and he's an incredible strategist, a beautiful and elegant writer, and a very dear friend. During the presidential campaign, Chuck took a leave of absence from his firm to come to Houston full-time and help lead the campaign. He was an integral part of my debate-prep team, and had I won the election, he would have been my nominee for attorney general.

I left Cooper & Carvin in 1999 to join the George W. Bush presidential campaign, working as a young policy staffer in Austin. On the campaign, I met my wife, Heidi, my best friend and the love of my life.

From there, I joined the Bush administration, as an associate deputy attorney general at the Department of Justice and then as the head of policy at the Federal Trade Commission.

And then, in 2003, I was appointed the solicitor general of Texas, the chief appellate lawyer for the State of Texas. My boss was Greg Abbott, then the Texas attorney general and a close friend. I served in that role for five and a half years, litigating major constitutional issues before the state and federal courts. Then, I returned to private practice, for the next five years leading the Supreme Court practice at Morgan Lewis, one of the largest law firms in the country.

Over those ten years, I authored over eighty U.S. Supreme Court briefs and argued before the high court nine times, more than any other lawyer in Texas and more than any other member of Congress. My job was to win—to try to get five justices to agree and to rule for my client.

And, in case after case, we won major victories. This book tells you the inside story of those constitutional battles—most of which were decided by just a single vote.

We start with *Van Orden v. Perry*, a landmark religious liberty case, where the Court upheld as constitutional the public display of a Ten Commandments monument on the Texas State Capitol grounds. The Bill of Rights begins by protecting our religious liberty, and it is a cornerstone of the rights we hold dear. *Van Orden* was decided by a 5–4 vote, and every year religious liberty challenges are among the most contentious issues before the Court.

After that, we turn to school choice, which I believe to be the most pressing civil rights issue in the nation. Millions of children are trapped in schools that deny them access to a quality education. For a child's hope in life to be dictated by his or her race, ethnicity, wealth, or zip code makes a mockery of equal protection. In *Zelman v. Simmons-Harris*, the Court, 5–4, upheld Ohio's school choice program, allowing scholarships for low-income kids to give them a much better chance at the American dream.

From there, we move to *Heller v. District of Columbia*, another case I helped litigate, which affirmed our individual Second Amendment right to keep and bear arms. The right to self-defense is one of our most cherished inalienable rights, foundational to our right to life. In *Heller*, also 5–4, the Supreme Court for the first time ever established that the Second Amendment text means what it says, and the government cannot take that individual right away.

Then to *Medellín v. Texas*, a case I argued and won twice, upholding U.S. sovereignty and striking down both the World Court's and the president's authority to intervene in our criminal justice system. Our right to be a sovereign and free Republic is at the very core of the American experiment, and I was privileged to defend the sovereignty of both Texas and the United States against the attempted usurpation by the United Nations. For a host of reasons, it was the single most fascinating case I ever litigated.

In *Gonzales v. Carhart*, where the Supreme Court upheld the federal ban on the gruesome practice of partial-birth abortion, I led the States in defense of the federal law, and we prevailed 5–4, the exact opposite outcome that the Court had reached just seven years earlier in striking down a nearly identical Nebraska law, 5–4. The principal difference? Justice Alito had replaced Justice O'Connor, and that one vote was the difference as to whether partial-birth abortion would be deemed required by the Constitution.

We then turn to *Citizens United v. Federal Election Commission*, a case much reviled by the left and which they desperately seek to overturn. *Citizens United* upheld the free-speech rights of citizens to engage in the political process, to speak out, and to criticize candidates for federal office. Free speech is indispensable not only to our First Amendment but also to our functioning democratic process. By a vote of 5–4, the Supreme Court properly held political speech to be at the heart of the First Amendment's free speech protection. In response, Senate Democrats introduced a constitutional amendment *to repeal the free speech protections of the First Amendment.* I led the fight against that foolhardy amendment, which thankfully failed, but not until after every single Senate Democrat had voted for it.

We continue with *Kennedy v. Louisiana,* an unfortunate case, where five justices deemed it unconstitutional to impose the death penalty for the reprehensible crime of child rape. I argued the case in defense of state laws allowing the death penalty for the most egregious and violent child rapists. Capital punishment has long been controversial politically, and different states have reached different policy judgments about whether and when it should be allowed. The text of the Constitution repeatedly refers explicitly to the death penalty, but that didn't stop five justices from prohibiting the death penalty altogether from 1972 until 1976. In the decades since, the Court has added more and more arbitrary constraints on capital punishment, resulting in decades-long delays in the carrying out of sentences. And just one additional justice could shift the Court back to banning the death penalty altogether.

We then turn to two more cases that I helped litigate at the intersection of judicial authority and democratic control of elections: *Bush v. Gore* and *LULAC v. Perry.* The former, of course, resolved the 2000 presidential election after thirty-six roller-coaster days in which the nation and the world waited for the results to be determined. The latter involved a challenge to the Texas redistricting plan, where plaintiffs argued that the Constitution prohibits state legislatures from taking politics into account in drawing congressional districts. In both instances, the Court was asked to substitute its preferences and judgment for that of the voters—to put courts instead of the people at the center of elections—and in both cases, the Court voted 5–4 to decline that invitation.

And finally, we'll examine past Supreme Court nominees and look at how we can make sure we get our Supreme Court picks right moving forward. On this front, the two parties do not perform equally. Democrats have a nearly 100 percent success rate; in major hot-button cases, their nominees vote exactly as they're supposed to vote almost without exception. They vote consistently for the policy outcomes favored by liberals, regardless of the law or the Constitution. Republicans, on the other hand, have a much worse record.

Many of the worst liberal judicial activists were appointed by Republicans. Earl Warren, William Brennan Jr., John Paul Stevens, David Souter, Harry Blackmun—the author of *Roe v. Wade*—were all Republican appointments.

In terms of justices' actually following the law and following the Constitution, Republicans have gotten it right 50 percent of the time at best. We'll examine the pattern of differences between those nominees who honored their oath and those who did not. And we'll lay out what to look for in future Supreme Court nominees.

Every single vote on the Court matters in every major case the Court hears. There is no room for error. On too many issues, we are one vote away.

Every American should understand what was at stake in these crucial cases and what is at stake in appointing Supreme Court justices. Every American who loves and cherishes the Constitution should be profoundly concerned about what losing the Supreme Court would look like—about what that would mean for these pivotal issues and for so many others. But every American who loves and cherishes the Constitution should also be inspired by the prospect of what securing the Supreme Court for a generation will look like.

This book is not intended just for academic or historical or legal purposes. Every one of these issues—every one of these rights and bedrock structural provisions—will be discussed, debated, and very much at stake in the 2020 election this fall. Judicial selection, especially for the Supreme Court, will also be very much at stake in the 2020 election. The Supreme Court will be on the ballot. And all of these issues will be at stake in elections after that of course.

The Supreme Court hangs in the balance. Five justices on either side can preserve our liberties or destroy them. Five justices on either side can secure our cherished structural freedoms or destroy them. Five constitutionalist justices can ensure the American experiment continues to thrive, but five liberal activist justices could fundamentally transform our Nation.

And far more often than we should be comfortable with, we are just one vote away from losing these fundamental rights and freedoms. For ourselves and our posterity, we have a solemn obligation not to let that happen.

CHAPTER 1

RELIGIOUS LIBERTY AND VAN ORDEN V. PERRY

Cecil B. DeMille. Catholic nuns. Schoolchildren. World War I veterans. All are directly implicated in the ongoing battles before the Supreme Court concerning religious liberty. This is the inside story of the battles before the Court to protect our First Liberty.

No right is more precious than the right to religious liberty. There is a reason that the Framers of the U.S. Constitution protected religious liberty in the very first clause of the very First Amendment of the Bill of Rights. The right to seek out and worship God, with all your heart, mind, and soul, according to the dictates of your own faith and your own conscience—to believe or not to believe—is fundamental to who we are.

There is no moral and just government that does not respect the religious liberty protections of its people. True political liberty, free speech, social stability, and human flourishing all depend upon a robust and durable protection, under the rule of law, of our fundamental right to choose our faith. And, on the flip side, efforts to undermine religious liberty and to persecute religious minorities are a telltale sign of tyrannical government.

Many who founded this nation were themselves fleeing religious persecution, and they came to form a country where the government could not take away that fundamental liberty. When the Pilgrims left Plymouth, England, aboard the *Mayflower* in 1620 and subsequently landed in Massachusetts, they were fleeing religious persecution. The Pilgrims were Puritans and were deeply pious men and women (as the Mayflower Compact shows in no uncertain terms).

More than a century later, the Declaration of Independence, the document that gave birth to our nation, declared, "We hold these truths to be self-evident, that all men are created equal, that they are endowed by their Creator with certain unalienable Rights, that among these are Life, Liberty and the pursuit of Happiness."

Thirteen years later, the language used by the Framers of the First Amendment reflected this robust commitment: "Congress shall make no law respecting an establishment of religion, or prohibiting the free exercise thereof...." The constitutional text does not say religious faith shall be tolerated or accommodated where convenient; it says "Congress shall make *no* law."

The two religion clauses that follow are referred to as the Establishment Clause and the Free Exercise Clause. And the intersection of the two has been a source of confusion and the vehicle for many of the more extreme lawsuits and decisions by judicial activists undermining religious liberty.

The Establishment Clause prohibits government from using government power to coerce people to believe one particular religious faith or denomination. Having declared independence from England and fought a bloody war to achieve it, the Framers did not want the United States to have an official Church like the Church of England. Rather, they sought to protect our individual right to choose our own faith.

The left reads its own hostility to faith into the Establishment Clause, arguing that the clause implies the notion of an absolute "wall of separation of church and state." But the phrase "separation of church and state" is found nowhere in the Constitution. It's not in the Bill of Rights, and it's not in the Declaration. Instead, that phrase comes from personal correspondence that Thomas Jefferson wrote the Danbury Baptist Association in 1802.

In that letter, Jefferson was not arguing for a wall to protect government from any acknowledgment of faith, but rather a wall *against government interference with* churches to protect the church from government. In other words, Jefferson thought that the American people needed a one-way wall stopping government from controlling churches to protect their most basic right.

How do we know this? Well, the purpose of the religion clauses was to protect our "rights of conscience," as Jefferson put it. They were to protect faith, not to require government to be affirmatively hostile to the acknowledgement of faith.

As the Supreme Court long understood, government cannot "show a callous indifference to religious groups" because "[t]hat would be preferring those who believe in no religion over those who do believe." *Zorach v. Clauson* (1952).

But, starting in the 1960s, the Supreme Court began reading the Establishment Clause as doing something much more: requiring the removal of God from the public square.

In 1962, in *Engel v. Vitale*, the Court banned the public recitation of prayer in public schools, and the next year, in *Abington School District v. Schempp*, the Court banned reading the Bible in public schools.

The consequences of those decisions were far-reaching, and at the time even some of the more liberal justices expressed caution. In *Abington*, Justice Arthur Goldberg warned that "brooding and pervasive devotion to the secular" and "hostility to the religious" would violate the constitutional rights of believing Americans. Regrettably, the anti-religious sentiment Goldberg noted all the way back in 1963 would become a strong, persistent trend in Supreme Court cases.

And it is contrary to two centuries of our nation's history and practice. Indeed, there are countless illustrations of the government's acknowledgment of our religious heritage, including the statutorily prescribed national motto "In God We Trust," and even the cry before every single proceeding of the Supreme Court: "God save the United States and this Honorable Court."

All throughout American history, our political and civil leaders have publicly pointed to their faith in God Almighty. They have appealed to God, they have looked to God, and they have implored their fellow Americans to appeal to and look to God alongside them. When President George Washington issued his famous Thanksgiving Proclamation in 1789, he told his fellow citizens that it is "the duty of all Nations to acknowledge the providence of Almighty God, to obey his will, to be grateful for his benefits, and humbly to implore his protection and favor."

John Adams, who succeeded Washington as America's second president, captured in a succinct manner our Founding Fathers' view of the role religion was meant to play in America. "Our Constitution was made only for a moral and religious people," Adams wisely observed in a 1798 letter. "It is wholly inadequate to the government of any other."

The Great Emancipator, Abraham Lincoln, was a religious and biblically literate Christian. Our sixteenth president, famously dedicating and consecrating that bloody Pennsylvania battlefield, put it this way: "We here highly resolve that these dead shall not have died in vain, that this nation under God shall have a new birth of freedom, and that government of the people, by the people, for the people shall not perish from the earth."

Two years later, he repeatedly invoked and relied upon appeals to our Creator during what was perhaps our nation's darkest and bloodiest hour, encapsulated by the captivating denouement of his magisterial Second Inaugural Address:

> With malice toward none, with charity for all, with firmness in the right as God gives us to see the right, let us strive on to finish the work we are in, to bind up the nation's wounds, to care for him who shall have borne the battle and for his widow and his orphan, to do all which may achieve and cherish a just and lasting peace among ourselves and with all nations.

The next century, as the United States led the World War II effort to defeat the existential evil that was Nazi Germany, President Franklin D. Roosevelt contrasted America and our genocidal foe in a starkly religious juxtaposition:

> Our enemies are guided by brutal cynicism, by unholy contempt for the human race. We are inspired by a faith that goes back through all the years to the first chapter of the book of Genesis: "God created man in his own image." ... We are fighting, as our fathers have fought, to uphold the doctrine that all men are equal in the sight of God.

In the 1960s, the Civil Rights Movement in America arose from the churches. Its greatest leader, Dr. Martin Luther King Jr., of course, was also *Reverend* King. He was a Baptist preacher who held an undergraduate degree in Bible studies and a Ph.D. in theology. His speeches and writing constantly appealed to America's Judeo-Christian religious and moral tradition.

For the past two years, I have twice had the privilege of joining several other bipartisan senators in reading aloud the entire text of Dr. King's magnificent "Letter from a Birmingham Jail" on the Senate floor. That missive was addressed to "My Dear Fellow Clergymen," and was a powerful call to action to the church to defend civil rights. He called the church to be not simply "a thermometer that recorded the ideas and principles of popular opinion," but rather "a thermostat that transformed the mores of society."

And Dr. King's historic "I Have a Dream" speech, given on the steps of the Lincoln Memorial, is as powerful a Christian sermon as ever delivered, worth quoting at length:

> I have a dream that one day this nation will rise up and live out the true meaning of its creed: "We hold these truths to be self-evident: that all men are created equal."

I have a dream that one day on the red hills of Georgia the sons of former slaves and the sons of former slave owners will be able to sit down together at the table of brotherhood....

I have a dream that my four little children will one day live in a nation where they will not be judged by the color of their skin but by the content of their character....

I have a dream that one day every valley shall be exalted, every hill and mountain shall be made low, the rough places will be made plain, and the crooked places will be made straight, and the glory of the Lord shall be revealed, and all flesh shall see it together.

This is our hope. This is the faith that I go back to the South with. With this faith we will be able to hew out of the mountain of despair a stone of hope. With this faith we will be able to transform the jangling discords of our nation into a beautiful symphony of brotherhood. With this faith we will be able to work together, to pray together, to struggle together, to go to jail together, to stand up for freedom together, knowing that we will be free one day.

This will be the day when all of God's children will be able to sing with a new meaning, "My country, 'tis of thee, sweet land of liberty, of thee I sing. Land where my fathers died, land of the pilgrim's pride, from every mountainside, let freedom ring."

And when this happens, when we allow freedom to ring, when we let it ring from every village and every hamlet, from every state and every city, we will be able to speed up that day when all of God's children, black men and white men, Jews and Gentiles, Protestants and Catholics, will be able to join hands and sing in the words of the old Negro spiritual, "Free at last! free at last! thank God Almighty, we are free at last!"

Read those words again, dwell upon them and hear Dr. King's powerful cadence echoing through history, and then try to imagine arguing that it is the Supreme Court's job to ensure that we keep God out of the public square. In doing so, we deny our country's profound history and legacy of protecting religious liberty, diversity, and faith.

◆   ◆   ◆   ◆

Our story begins with a landmark religious liberty case that I had the privilege of litigating before the Supreme Court: *Van Orden v. Perry*. And, curiously enough, it begins at the movies.

Cecil B. DeMille was one of the founding fathers of American cinema. In inflation-adjusted terms, he is the most commercially successful producer-director in Hollywood history. In 1956, his epic Charlton Heston film "The Ten Commandments," which was nominated for an Academy Award for Best Picture, opened across the country. It was DeMille's final film, and perhaps his best known.

In an odd twist of fate, the fallout of this film, released fourteen years before I was born, led to one of my most meaningful Supreme Court cases.

Nearly a decade earlier, in 1947, Minnesota state juvenile judge E. J. Ruegemer was presiding over the case of a troubled young man who had stolen a car and struck and injured a priest walking alongside the road. The prosecutors argued for sending him to the boys' reformatory in nearby Red Wing, but the judge decided instead to sentence the boy to studying and learning the Ten Commandments. That, in turn, sparked an idea for the judge, who was dismayed by what he saw as the deterioration of morals and character among young people at the time. (It's amazing how some things never seem to change.)

Judge Ruegemer teamed up with the Fraternal Order of Eagles, a national service organization of which he was a member. Over the decades, the Eagles have had seven members who went on to serve as president: Teddy Roosevelt, Warren G. Harding, Franklin D. Roosevelt,

Harry S Truman, John F. Kennedy, Jimmy Carter, and Ronald Reagan. Judge Ruegemer suggested the Eagles work to post the Ten Commandments in public spaces across the nation, so that young people might read and reflect upon them. As the judge put it, "it does society good to have reminders of right and wrong in public places."

In 1951, the Eagles began distributing framed copies of the Ten Commandments to courthouses and schools in Minnesota. By 1953, the program had expanded nationally.

Then, Cecil B. DeMille got wind of it. A consummate marketer, DeMille called Judge Ruegemer and suggested that the Eagles produce more permanent monuments, bronze plaques of the Ten Commandments. Ruegemer raised the ante, suggesting that they instead use Minnesota granite to produce giant tablets, modeled after the stone tablets Moses (and later Charlton Heston) carried down from Mount Sinai.

DeMille was thrilled. If the Eagles would raise the money and distribute the monuments, DeMille and Paramount Pictures would provide Hollywood glamour, sending Heston or Yul Brynner (Rameses) or Martha Scott (Moses's mother) to speak when the monuments were erected.

Initially, the exact text of the monument posed some challenge. The precise wording of each commandment depends on the one's faith. So the Eagles brought together a committee composed of a Protestant minister, a Catholic priest, and a Jewish rabbi to collaborate and agree on the language to be used.

The Eagles presented their first Ten Commandments monument to the City of Chicago at its 1954 Grand Aerie Convention. Over the course of the next five decades, they erected hundreds of Ten Commandments monuments all over the nation, in parks and libraries, at courthouses and state capitols and city halls. Virtually all of the monuments were identical, standing six foot, three inches tall, and three foot, six inches wide; their last monument was erected at Vergennes, Vermont, in 2010.

In Texas, our Eagles Ten Commandments monument was erected in 1961. The Eagles dedicated it "to the Youth and People of Texas." It stands just outside the State Capitol, as one of the seventeen monuments and twenty-one historical markers on the twenty-two-acre grounds that com-memorate the "people, ideals, and events that compose Texan identity."

For over four decades, the monument stood and caused no discern-ible fuss or consternation. For over forty years, Texas legislators, state employees, and civilian passersby alike enjoyed the monument while meandering across the idyllic Capitol grounds.

Enter Thomas Van Orden, a bright man who went to college and graduated from SMU Law School. After falling on hard times and becoming homeless, Van Orden spent considerable time walking the Capitol grounds in Austin. One day, he spied the Texas monument, and a lawsuit was born.

Van Orden, you see, is an atheist. He believes there is no God, and it offended him to see the Ten Commandments acknowledged on public grounds.

Van Orden was hardly unique in his alleged grievance. Across the country, for decades, there has been concerted litigation against the public display of the Ten Commandments. Over and over again, indi-vidual litigants, often coordinated or funded by the ACLU, have brought cases seeking to remove the physical display of the Ten Commandments from public view.

And, unfortunately, in 2001 at the time of Van Orden's lawsuit, most of these Ten Commandments–monument challenges had been successful. Typically, when state or local governments defended these monuments, they lost. This was the manifestation of years of liberal judges' being appointed to the bench and adopting a jurisprudence deeply hostile to public acknowledgements of America's Judeo-Christian religious tradition.

In Texas, thankfully, our litigation record was different. The Texas attorney general's office was charged with defending the lawsuit and, in the federal district court, we won: the court rejected Van Orden's claims.

On appeal, before the New Orleans–based Fifth Circuit Court of Appeals, I argued the case before the three-judge panel. And, during the course of argument, I committed one of the cardinal sins that, when I was teaching Supreme Court litigation at the University of Texas Law School, I would regularly urge my students never to commit.

I attempted humor in the course of the argument. As I described the history of drafting the text of the monument, I explained that the Eagles' committee had consisted of a priest, a minister, and a rabbi. Judge Edward Prado interrupted and said, "this sounds like the beginning of a joke." To which I responded, "Yes, your honor, but in this case no one walked into a bar."

There's a reason you don't tell jokes at oral argument. As a general rule, it's the province of the judges to tell jokes and the province of the lawyers to try to make their case. But I got lucky: the judges took mercy on me and laughed nonetheless.

The Fifth Circuit ruled, and we won unanimously. Van Orden then filed a petition for a writ of certiorari with the Supreme Court. A "cert petition," as it is commonly called, is a formal request for the Supreme Court to review the decision of the lower court. Because the Supreme Court has what's called a discretionary docket, it gets to pick most of the cases it will hear (there are only a handful of mandatory exceptions). To grant cert and hear the case requires the affirmative vote of four of the nine justices.

At that point, we had a strategic decision to make. And the decision tree we were facing was fraught with peril. Normally, the default position for anyone in our litigating position would be to oppose cert, for a simple reason: If the Court denies cert and you won below, then the case is over. You can take your victory home. And usually, the odds are with the side who opposes cert. Every year, the Supreme Court receives about 8,000 cert petitions, and it only grants about 80 (roughly 1 percent) of them.

But we were in a unique situation. I sat down with my boss, Texas Attorney General Greg Abbott, and we discussed the state of First Amendment law as it relates to these public displays of the Ten Commandments. Both of us were well aware that liberal activist judges across the country had been ruling against Ten Commandments monuments over and over again.

Whenever the Supreme Court considers a cert petition, the primary thing the justices look for is a "circuit split," where multiple federal courts of appeal have considered the same question of law and ruled differently. The idea is that, to the extent possible, the law in the federal courts should be uniform across the country. So when there's a split, that is a major reason for the Supreme Court to grant cert and resolve the issue for all the federal circuits.

On the issue of these Ten Commandments–monument displays, and on the issue of the Fraternal Order of Eagles monuments in particular, there was a real and live circuit split, which meant that if we succeeded in getting the Court *not* to take our case, the odds were high they would choose to grant cert on another Ten Commandments monument case shortly thereafter.

Given the depth and breadth of the split, I thought that the Court was on the verge of taking a Ten Commandments case. Moreover, I thought our case had the best facts to win. We had litigated the case carefully, with an eye toward ultimately prevailing before the Supreme Court. We did not have many of the "bad facts" that many of the other cases had, which amounted to politicians saying stupid things on the record that made defending the monument much harder.

Since our fact pattern was so much better, I believed that our case was the best case to reach the Court. If a worse case made it to the Supreme Court, those bad facts would potentially produce a binding national result, and the bulldozer would not be far behind in coming for our own Ten Commandments monument in Austin.

So I urged General Abbott to do something unusual: acquiesce to the cert petition. We told the Supreme Court we agreed that the split was real, wide, and deep, and that the issue was important. So we said that, if the Court were inclined to grant a case on Ten Commandments monuments, then this case presented an ideal situation to grant cert and affirm a permissible display of the Ten Commandments.

This course of action entailed risk because if the Supreme Court took the case and we lost, both Attorney General Abbott and I would have faced considerable criticism for acquiescing to the Court's granting cert to begin with.

But I thought about what the great ancient Chinese military general Sun Tzu once taught: every battle is won before it's fought. It's won by choosing the terrain on which it will be fought. And our case presented the best terrain on which this particular legal issue could ever be fought.

The Supreme Court did end up granting cert. And at the same time, it granted cert in another Ten Commandments–monument case, *McCreary County v. American Civil Liberties Union*, coming out of Kentucky. The Court scheduled both cases' oral arguments for the same day.

As it turned out, the lawyer representing Van Orden at the Supreme Court was one of the most acclaimed liberal constitutional scholars in the country, Erwin Chemerinsky. Chemerinsky is the current dean of the University of California, Berkeley School of Law, and he was formerly the founding dean of the University of California, Irvine School of Law. He represented Van Orden *pro bono*, which means for free. Over the years, I've gotten to know Chemerinsky quite well, and he and I have debated each other on questions of constitutional law multiple times. He's brilliant and very much a man of the left.

The Supreme Court's jurisprudence on religious displays in public is complicated, to say the least. As discussed, the Court has applied multiple and often conflicting standards, and for more than twenty years the Court's religious-liberty jurisprudence often seemed to hinge on whatever Justice Sandra Day O'Connor deemed appropriate on any given day. On religious liberty, she was the quintessential swing vote, capable of going in either direction in almost any case. It was very hard, sometimes impossible, to reliably predict how she would rule.

In writing our Supreme Court brief, I spent hundreds of hours poring over Justice O'Connor's Establishment Clause jurisprudence. Throughout our brief, we incessantly cited O'Connor and the standard(s) she had advocated. Indeed, I joked that I wanted "O'Connor, J." to be the most frequent words in our brief—more common than "and" or "the." A lawyer in my office asked if it was possible to be too obsequious to

O'Connor in this case, and I replied, tongue in cheek, "No—if we could possibly put an oil painting of Justice O'Connor on the cover of the brief, we should do it."

Context and case-specific facts clearly mattered a great deal in O'Connor's jurisprudence. But Chemerinsky, for all his academic renown, did not put in the legwork necessary to accurately describe the facts of our case. Chemerinsky's brief described the monument as towering before the Capitol and as the "lone" religious symbol to be found on the Texas State Capitol grounds. He described a "large," "uniquely prominent" religious monument, "in front" of the Capitol "on the Great Walk," situated "by itself" so that "no other monuments [are] visible when standing before it."

Every element of that description was false. The monument is one of the smallest on the Capitol grounds, is in back of the Capitol, and is surrounded by six other visible monuments. Numerous other monuments contain religious references, and what Chemerinsky erroneously described as "the Great Walk" (which leads to the main entrance found on the front side of the Capitol) is, in fact, a driveway on which Capitol staff park their cars.

Religious references on other monuments on the grounds include a statue of a young girl wearing a Cross in the Tribute to Texas Children, the words "God - Country - Peace" on the Veterans of World War I memorial, and the Aztec symbol of the eagle on a cactus. The latter is part of the Mexican flag, which appears multiple times across the Capitol grounds. In the center of the Mexican flag is a brown eagle eating a serpent, while perched on a prickly-pear cactus growing from a rock surrounded by water. The Aztecs believed that their leaders were given this image in dreams by the Sun God Huitzilopochtli, as the site where they should found their theocratic capital Tenochtitlán. Founded in 1325 A.D. on a marshy island in Lake Texcoco, the city is the present-day site of Mexico City.

And, almost directly above the Ten Commandments monument, atop the Capitol dome, is the Goddess of Liberty. She stands nearly 16 feet tall and weighs 2000 pounds, and she likely represents Pallas Athena, the

Greek goddess of wisdom and justice, who served as the protectress of the democratic city-state of Athens.

Close attention to detail is a hallmark of any good lawyer. But sometimes, when law professors litigate cases, they don't put in the mundane effort to understand the facts on the ground. As I responded in our brief, Professor Chemerinsky's brief was so far removed from the actual state of affairs at the monument that it could only have been written by someone who had never physically been there.

In our brief, we corrected those misrepresentations, which helped the Court get a fuller and more accurate assessment of the context of the monument.

Then we began preparing for oral argument. As solicitor general, it was typically my job to argue our cases before the Supreme Court. But my boss, Texas attorney general and future Governor Greg Abbott—a strong mentor and a good friend to this day—had made clear when I started that he wanted to argue a Supreme Court case.

Over the past century, some state attorneys general argued all of their state's cases before the Supreme Court. Others would allow whatever career attorney happened to litigate the trial case to argue the Supreme Court case. Neither approach has proven a good one. Most attorneys general are politicians first, not appellate lawyers. And many line lawyers in AG offices are trial lawyers with little or no appellate experience. Either way, Supreme Court advocacy for the states suffered badly, and in the last couple decades that led to the rise of state solicitors general across the country.

State SGs are typically appellate specialists. Often, they are former Supreme Court clerks who know the Court well. And they lead offices of extremely talented appellate lawyers. In 2002, when the newly elected Abbott offered me the SG position, I was only thirty-one years old. I thought (hoped!) I could do the job well, but at the time I had only ever argued two cases in court, neither of which was before the Supreme Court. Abbott took a chance on me, offering to make me the youngest SG in the country.

I asked my old boss Chief Justice Rehnquist if I should take it. At the time, Heidi was working in the Bush White House, she loved her job, and taking the appointment would necessitate our commuting cross-country, not an easy proposition. The Chief was emphatic that I should take the post. States are the second most frequent litigants before the Court, behind only the U.S. government. The Chief told me that the rise of state SGs had dramatically improved the quality of appellate advocacy at the Court. Previously, much of it had been quite shoddy; "California is just terrible," he observed.

Fortunately, Abbott was a much more skilled appellate lawyer than most state AGs, and he was committed to excellent appellate advocacy. Abbott himself had spent over a decade as a judge, both as a state trial judge and as a Texas Supreme Court justice. Abbott is not a micro-manager; he set broad objectives, but he didn't try to run the day-to-day operations of Texas's Office of the Solicitor General.

All that being said, Abbott had made clear when he appointed me that he wanted to argue one Supreme Court case and that I should be on the lookout for the best one for him to argue. When the Supreme Court granted cert in *Van Orden*, I went to Abbott and said that this was the one. It was an area of immense importance, with a discrete area of juris-prudence, and we would likely have the United States Solicitor General Paul Clement arguing alongside us.

Abbott agreed, and in the weeks before oral argument, he cleared his calendar of the myriad commitments that typically fill an attorney general's day. He spent hour after hour after hour reading Supreme Court cases, reading the briefs, and talking with me and my team of lawyers about the issues and about our strategy in the case.

I organized several moot courts for General Abbott. One that I remember particularly well was in Washington, D.C. Around the table sat a murderer's row of Supreme Court advocates. Paul Clement, the U.S. SG and one of the most experienced advocates in the country, was there. Also at the table was Jay Sekulow, recently President Donald Trump's lawyer during the impeachment trial and, before that, one of the most highly regarded Supreme Court religious-liberty advocates in the country. Several other very experienced Supreme Court lawyers joined us, as well.

The moot lasted over an hour. Everyone had withering questions for Abbott—so much so that I was nervous that my boss would be annoyed at me for having arranged such a bare-knuckles moot. Fortunately, as a consummate professional, he was thankful that the rigorous questioning had ensured he was fully prepared for the main event.

The argument came on March 2, Texas Independence Day. The night before, I advised General Abbott: if the argument started going poorly and it seemed we might not prevail, he could simply raise his fist in the air and say, "Remember the Alamo!"

That morning began with a brief moment of humor. As Abbott and I were sitting at counsel's table, Paul Clement was at the table next to us. Moments before the Supreme Court justices were to ascend the dais at 10:00 a.m. sharp, Paul leaned over to Abbott and me and whispered loudly, "We figured out a theory to win this case." Abbott and I were, of course, quite interested. Paul continued, "We're going to argue that the Ten Commandments…are international law." The joking reference, of course, was to the rising pattern of some Supreme Court justices—especially those on the left—relying on international law, wrongly in most instances, to help adjudicate constitutional cases.

General Abbott gave a very strong argument—so much so that it prompted something that rarely occurs. He was praised from the bench by the justices themselves. My former boss Chief Justice Rehnquist was gravely sick at the time, and he would live for only a few more months. He was not on the bench to preside, so the argument was presided over instead by Senior Associate Justice John Paul Stevens. At the close of General Abbott's oral argument, Justice Stevens thanked General Abbott for demonstrating that one needn't be at the podium to give an excellent argument. That reference was, of course, to the fact that Greg Abbott is confined to a wheelchair and has been for three decades, ever since he was tragically injured by a falling tree-branch while jogging and was paralyzed from the waist down.

The decision of the Court in *Van Orden v. Perry* came down on the last day of the term, and it was the last decision the Court issued that year. By a vote of 5–4, Texas prevailed.

The plurality opinion was authored by Chief Justice Rehnquist. There was a deep sense of justice and completeness in Rehnquist's authoring the opinion. As an associate justice, Rehnquist had been one of the original dissenters in *Stone v. Graham*, a 1980 case in which the Supreme Court struck down the display of Ten Commandments in public schools.

And *Van Orden*, upholding the display of the Ten Commandments, would be the last judicial opinion William Hubbs Rehnquist ever wrote. In his plurality opinion, the Chief Justice described the Supreme Court's Establishment Clause jurisprudence as "Janus-like," facing two directions at once. One line of Supreme Court cases views the public acknowledgement of faith and God with deep skepticism and sees the courts as a tool to scrub the public square of any acknowledgment of God Almighty. The other line of cases, many of which were authored by Chief Justice Rehnquist, recognizes that acknowledging faith, God, and our Judeo-Christian heritage is entirely consistent with religious liberty—and, indeed, protects every individual's freedom of conscience.

Liberal judges have long viewed the Free Exercise Clause and the Establishment Clause as in conflict with one another. In so doing, these black-robed activists have been eager to read public displays of religion as infringing upon the Constitution, and the Establishment Clause as a Lysol disinfectant for removing all faith from the public square.

There was an irony to the end result in *Van Orden*. I had told General Abbott about our extensive efforts to craft a litigation strategy targeted precisely to earn Justice O'Connor's vote. As it turned out, that plan was a dismal failure. Justice O'Connor voted to strike down the Ten Commandments monument in Texas. Every argument that I had so carefully crafted to appeal to O'Connor missed the mark, but, as it so happened, they persuaded Justice Stephen Breyer instead.

Texas prevailed in *Van Orden* because Justice Breyer, a Bill Clinton appointee and a reliably liberal jurist, made the decision to split the baby in half. In *Van Orden*, Texas won. But in *McCreary*, the accompanying Kentucky case whose opinion came down on the very same day, Kentucky lost.

As with so many Establishment Clause cases, the precise facts and context mattered (which is why we spent so much time and effort correcting petitioner's misrepresentations of the facts in *Van Orden*). And, in the Kentucky case, local politicians had made a number of foolish and ill-advised statements when their Ten Commandments display was erected that the Court deemed impermissible.

So in the end, our strategy of acquiescing to the Supreme Court on the writ of certiorari was vindicated. Had the Supreme Court taken only the Kentucky case, the result that day would have been a 5–4 loss for public displays of Ten Commandments monuments. That precedent, in turn, could have resulted in our monument and the hundreds of others across the country's being torn down.

But, instead, the *Van Orden* precedent proved the far more important of the two; the Texas monument still stands, as do other Ten Commandments monuments nationwide.

There is another note of irony to the tale of *Van Orden v. Perry*. As we stood in the Supreme Court courtroom arguing whether or not it was permissible to display the Ten Commandments on government property, the Supreme Court justices were surrounded by no fewer than forty-three images of the Ten Commandments. There are forty images of the Ten Commandments etched up and down the bronze gates running along both sides of the courtroom. There are two more images of the Ten Commandments carved onto the bottom panel of the wooden doors as you exit the Court. And above the justices' shoulders to the left is a granite frieze of great lawmakers in history, among them Moses, holding the Ten Commandments—text still in Hebrew—looking down upon them. And yet, sadly, four justices were ready to say, in effect, "bring out the chisels."

◆   ◆   ◆   ◆

The litigation against the Ten Commandments is but one example of the widespread assault on religious liberty. There are many more.

In California, for instance, another atheist named Michael Newdow filed a lawsuit seeking to remove the words "one nation under God" from the Pledge of Allegiance. And in 2002 the Ninth Circuit Court of Appeals agreed with him, ruling that the Constitution forbids schoolchildren from reciting "one nation under God."

When *Elk Grove Unified School District v. Newdow* went to the Supreme Court, Texas led the states in defense of the Pledge of Allegiance. The amicus curiae (Latin for friend of the court) brief we authored was joined by all fifty states—every Republican and every Democratic attorney general—one of very few briefs in history to get support from every single state.

At the same time as we were circulating our brief, I was helping lead the trial team defending the Texas redistricting plan that the Legislature had just adopted. I still remember well, during breaks in the trial, calling my fellow SGs urging them to join our brief in *Newdow*. The last couple of states to join, I must confess, I had some fun with, telling the SGs "you know, if your boss wants to be the only attorney general in America not to support the Pledge of Allegiance, well, that's certainly political courage...." They all joined.

In our brief, we detailed the history of the Pledge of Allegiance. The text of the Pledge was adopted by Congress in 1942, and the words "under God" were added separately twelve years later. It was the height of the Cold War in 1954, and Congress added the words "under God" to illuminate a key distinction between our government and those of communist nations. Congressional Committee Reports from the time of the 1954 amendment note that, whereas the communists were "spiritual[ly] bankrupt," our government recognized the importance of each human "endowed by [God] with certain inalienable rights which no civil authority may usurp."

We argued that acknowledging the Almighty was consistent with our "history and ubiquity," as Justice O'Connor had put it in *Lynch v. Donnelly*, a 1984 case upholding, 5–4, the town's Christmas nativity scene in Pawtucket, Rhode Island. As the majority opinion observed in *Lynch*, "[o]ur history is replete with official references to the value and invocation of Divine guidance," including official Thanksgiving and Christmas holidays, House and Senate chaplains, the national motto "In God We Trust," the Pledge of Allegiance, religious paintings in the National Gallery, and Moses holding the Ten Commandments on the frieze of the Court. *Lynch* quoted at length President Franklin D. Roosevelt's 1944 Proclamation of Thanksgiving:

> [I]t is fitting that we give thanks with special fervor to our Heavenly Father for the mercies we have received individually and as a nation and for the blessings He has restored, through the victories of our arms and those of our Allies, to His children in other lands.... To the end that we may bear more earnest witness to our gratitude to Almighty God, I suggest a nationwide reading of the Holy Scriptures during the period from Thanksgiving Day to Christmas.

Ultimately, the Court agreed with us unanimously. But it did so only on alternative procedural grounds, namely that because Michael Newdow was a non-custodial parent, he didn't have standing to bring a claim on behalf of his school-age daughter. Therefore, by an 8–0 vote (Justice Scalia recused), the Court vacated the Ninth Circuit decision below.

By avoiding the merits issue in *Newdow*, the Court avoided the sharp divides that typically accompany religious liberty cases. But that was the exception rather than the rule. In another major religious-liberty case I helped litigate, *Salazar v. Buono*—the Mojave Desert Memorial Cross case—those divisions emerged yet again.

On a barren rock in the midst of the 1.6 million-acre Mojave Desert National Preserve, in 1934, the Veterans of Foreign Wars erected a memorial for those who gave their lives in World War I. For seven decades, this simple white Latin cross—standing alone atop Sunrise Rock—stood unmolested as a quiet testament to the bravery of so many fallen heroes.

For decades, the memorial was tenderly cared for by Riley Bembry, himself a World War I veteran who helped erect it in remembrance of his fallen brothers. Shortly before Bembry died in 1984, he handed caretaking duties over to over to his friend Henry Sandoz and his wife, Wanda, who faithfully looked after the cross.

But then in 2001 the American Civil Liberties Union took notice and brought a case arguing that the Constitution prohibits ever seeing the image of a cross on public land. The ACLU prevailed in federal district court and again in the Ninth Circuit Court of Appeals. As a result, the federal courts ordered that the veterans memorial be covered up with a large burlap sack, tied with an iron chain and padlock at the bottom. Later, the sack was replaced with a plywood box.

The case went up to the Supreme Court and, along with my good friend Kelly Shackelford of the First Liberty Institute, I had the privilege of representing the Veterans of Foreign Wars, the American Legion, the Military Order of the Purple Heart, and several other veterans groups. In total, we represented over 3 million veterans nationwide, as *amici* (friends of the court), defending the constitutionality of the monument.

I was no longer Texas SG at the time. I was instead in private practice at Morgan Lewis, one of the nation's largest law firms, leading their Supreme Court and national appellate practice out of their Houston office. As a result, most of my cases were for paying clients. But this case was special. It was near and dear to my heart, and I was fighting for the veterans of our nation. And so I took the case *pro bono*—for free.

The Supreme Court, as in the Ten Commandments case, was closely divided. But ultimately, in a 5–4 decision, the Court upheld the veterans memorial. And it still stands in the Mojave Desert National Preserve today. The Court's majority opinion cited our brief a dozen times in ruling that memorials to fallen soldiers could permissibly contain religious symbols without violating the First Amendment.

After the Court's decision, I stood on Sunrise Rock with Henry Sandoz. It's barren, beautiful, and totally isolated. And, rising up silently into the arid sky—sans burlap sack or plywood box—is that simple white cross memorializing our fallen heroes.

The consequences of our victory were far-reaching. Had the plaintiffs prevailed—had the Court ordered that seventy-plus-year-old veterans memorial torn down—the next crusade to remove the thousands of crosses and Stars of David from the tombstones in Arlington National Cemetery would surely not have been far behind.

And just as with the Ten Commandments case, we were only one vote away.

◆   ◆   ◆   ◆

The legal challenges to religious liberty continue relentlessly. Before the Court today, the display of the Ten Commandments is less frequently the target of litigation—*Van Orden* settled that, for now at least. Instead, the main religious liberty issues to come before the Court today concern individuals trying to live according to their faith and facing legal persecution or punishment because of it.

The First Amendment's text protects "free exercise" of religion. But this was readily understood at the time of the American Founding as encompassing a substantially broader array of behavioral protection than more limited protections for either "worship" or "conscience." As my old friend Judge Jim Ho of the Fifth Circuit wrote in a case earlier this year:

> The broader scope of "exercise"—in contrast to "worship" and "conscience"—indicates that, at the time of the Founding, the public would have understood the right to "free exercise" to extend beyond mere ritual and private belief to cover

any action motivated by faith. Consistent with that conclusion, Congress amended the draft language that later became the First Amendment, replacing the original phrase "rights of conscience" with the "free exercise of religion."

Perhaps no case illustrates that more acutely than the story of the Little Sisters of the Poor. The Little Sisters of the Poor are an order of Catholic nuns who have taken vows of poverty and pledges to help the elderly and the needy. When Congress passed Obamacare, it included within it a so-called "contraceptive mandate" that required the Little Sisters and other religious organizations to pay for contraceptives and abortion-inducing drugs for others. If they refused to do so, they faced millions of dollars in fines.

The Little Sisters, understandably, concluded that paying for abortifacients would be inconsistent with their Catholic faith. And the Obama administration, in response, attempted to offer an alleged "compromise" by Solomonically splitting the baby. The problem is that their "compromise" did not fix the problem; it still required them to subsidize activities contrary to their faith. And so it was rejected by both the United States Conference of Catholic Bishops and the Little Sisters of the Poor.

The mainstream media loves to lionize Pope Francis any time he expresses support for economic or environmental causes that are put forward by the left. Curiously, that same media largely ignored that when he visited the United States in 2015, Pope Francis made a point to sit down and personally meet with the Little Sisters of the Poor at their residence across the street from Catholic University in Washington, D.C. The Pope spent fifteen minutes at their home and shook hands with each of the Sisters in their chapel in order to express his "support for them in their legal battle," a Vatican spokesman explained.

Nevertheless, the Obama administration's legal position continued to be that these intrepid nuns should be forced to indirectly subsidize contraception and abortifacients that directly violated their sincerely held religious beliefs.

The legal issues pertaining to Obamacare's "contraceptive mandate" first made it to the Supreme Court in the 2014 *Burwell v. Hobby Lobby Stores* case. This was a similar case in which Hobby Lobby, a privately held corporation owned by evangelical Christians, raised religious objections over being forced to pay for abortion-inducing drugs. By a vote of 5–4, the Supreme Court upheld Hobby Lobby's religious liberty rights, ensuring that the owners of that company could continue to live according to the dictates of their faith.

The Little Sisters' case was held at the Court pending the resolution of the *Hobby Lobby* case and, ultimately, the litigation against the Sisters was—thankfully—settled by the Trump administration.

When the Supreme Court decided *Hobby Lobby*, it did so not on constitutional grounds, but on statutory grounds. The Court ruled in Hobby Lobby's favor on the grounds of the Religious Freedom Restoration Act, or "RFRA," a 1993 piece of federal legislation.

RFRA was passed in direct response to the largely unpopular 1990 Supreme Court case of *Employment Division v. Smith*, which had held that enforcing neutral laws of general applicability does not violate your constitutional right to religious liberty. At the time that RFRA was enacted into law, it passed by a whopping 97–3 margin in the Senate and in the House by a unanimous voice vote. In the Senate, such liberal stalwarts as Ted Kennedy and Chuck Schumer voted in favor of RFRA. It was signed into law by Democratic president Bill Clinton.

Just three decades ago, in Congress at least, religious liberty was a bipartisan commitment. Democrats and Republican disagreed on issues of taxes, spending, and so many other policy areas. But when it came to protecting the rights of believers to live according to the dictates of their faith, whatever that faith might be, we saw widespread, bipartisan agreement in Washington.

In the wake of the *Hobby Lobby* decision, however, that bipartisan agreement crumbled. Today's Democratic Party has sadly become radicalized on questions of religious liberty, as evidenced by the 2020 Democratic debates, which featured Beto O'Rourke—my erstwhile opponent in the 2018 U.S. Senate race in Texas—saying that he would strip churches and synagogues of their tax-exempt status and forcibly regulate religious institutions.

Beto O'Rourke, of course, has since endorsed and been embraced by Joe Biden. And Biden has since praised O'Rourke as an up-and-coming star in the modern Democratic Party who would play a leading role in a Biden administration.

The radicalization of the Democratic Party was also manifest in legislation that Senate Democrats introduced in the immediate aftermath of *Hobby Lobby*, which would have gutted RFRA. It would have dramatically weakened that statutory protection for faith that had passed Congress overwhelmingly.

I spoke vigorously against that legislation on the Senate floor, citing multiple Democratic presidents and flanked by a picture of no less a Democratic presidential stalwart than John F. Kennedy:

> The bill that is being voted on this floor, if it were adopted, would fine the Little Sisters of the Poor millions of dollars unless these Catholic nuns are willing to pay for abortion-producing drugs for others.
>
> Mr. President, when did the Democratic Party declare war on the Catholic Church?
>
> Let me make a basic suggestion. If you're litigating against nuns, you have probably done something wrong, and the Obama administration is doing so right now. Mr. President, drop your faith fines. Mr. Majority Leader [Harry Reid], drop your faith fines. To all of my Democratic colleagues, drop your faith fines. Get back to the shared values that stitch all of us together as Americans.
>
> President John F. Kennedy, in an historic speech to the nation, said—quote—"I would not look with favor upon a president working to subvert the First Amendment's guarantees of religious liberty."

Mr. President, where are the Kennedys today? Does any Democrat have the courage to stand up and speak for the First Amendment today? Does any Democrat have the courage to stand up and speak for the constitutional rights of practicing Catholics? Does any Democrat have the courage to stand up and speak for the Little Sisters of the Poor? Do any Democrats have the courage to listen to the Catholic Conference of Bishops and speak for religious liberty? Mr. President, it saddens me that there are not 100 senators here unified, regardless of our faith, standing together protecting the religious liberty rights of everyone.

Sadly, protecting religious liberty got zero Democratic votes. Instead, every single Democrat in the U.S. Senate voted to nullify the Religious Freedom Restoration Act. I was heartbroken to see it, and it augers dangerous times to come.

And, in the summer of 2020, Joe Biden pledged that, if elected, he would resume the Obama administration's ongoing persecution of the Little Sisters of the Poor.

When it comes to Democratic judicial nominations, we can expect their nominees to reflect their current hostility to faith. And, on the Supreme Court, as we've seen, they're just one vote away.

CHAPTER 2

SCHOOL CHOICE AND *ZELMAN V. SIMMONS-HARRIS*

Religious liberty and civil rights intersect in the fight for school choice in America.

I believe that school choice is the defining civil rights struggle of our time. To be sure, public education in America is actually older than America itself. By the time the Declaration of Independence was written in 1776, at least five public high schools existed. The oldest school, and one which still stands today, is The Boston Latin School in Massachusetts. In the first half of the nineteenth century, Horace Mann served as a national trailblazer for education reform. And by the time the Fourteenth Amendment was ratified in 1868, public education was ubiquitous throughout America.

There are countless outstanding public schools in America today. These are the public schools that have talented and committed teachers, that develop well-rounded curricula across academic disciplines, and prepare students for successful careers—whether that means college, graduate school, trade school, or direct entrance into the workforce. The teachers and administrators at these schools deserve praise, support, and our gratitude.

But not every child has access to an excellent education. Sadly, the caliber and quality of public education in America varies dramatically from school to school. Far too often, it is the public schools in the more affluent, suburban neighborhoods that are most able to attract and retain dedicated teachers who are skilled in pedagogy and deeply committed to the success of their students. Conversely, far too often, it is the public schools in the poorer, struggling neighborhoods of America that have difficulty attracting and retaining qualified teachers and enforcing discipline and high academic standards.

For too many low-income children, especially inner-city African-American and Hispanic children, their public-school options are severely limited. Kids unable to get a decent education see their prospects for future success dramatically limited. Education is, in most circumstances, the gateway to the American dream. It certainly was in my family when my mom became the first in her family to go to college and when my dad came from Cuba with nothing. For both, education opened the door for them to experience the promise of America.

I support school choice across the board. Scholarships, vouchers, charter schools, tax credits—all of the above: whatever gives parents and children the maximum choice for their own education and their own future.

Education is antecedent to most of our other public policy concerns. From poverty to crime to healthcare to substance abuse, if kids don't get an education, we know that those other challenges are far more likely to follow; conversely, if children do get an excellent education, each of those problems is much more likely to be overcome.

It is a damning stain on America's conscience that a child's chances of life success are so heavily influenced by—perhaps dictated by—the zip code in which he or she is raised. It is a profound civil-rights crisis, about which every single American of every political or partisan stripe should be on the same page. Whether one is a conservative or a liberal, or a Republican or a Democrat ought not matter in the slightest when it comes to the urgent need to secure access to a quality education—and access to educational choice, in particular—for every young American.

Yet today's Democratic Party is passionately opposed to school choice. The reasons are simple: teachers unions massively fund the Democratic Party and provide many of its hardest working foot soldiers. As a result, very few Democratic politicians are willing to give up the millions of dollars that flow from union support.

In a just world, teachers unions would enthusiastically support school choice. After all, the vast majority of teachers go into education because they want to help children, and teachers see firsthand the maddening bureaucracy, red tape, and barriers to quality teaching that today's system often creates. But the union bosses who lead the teachers unions have decided that school choice is an existential threat to their power, and so they demand partisan fealty above all.

I became active in the school-choice movement twenty-five years ago. When I had just finished my clerkship at the Court, the Federalist Society (a national organization of conservative and libertarian students, lawyers, professors, and judges) asked me to serve as the first-ever chairman of their school choice and education reform committee. I agreed, but with one caveat: although I was passionate on the issue, I didn't yet have a demonstrated record, so I told them I needed a co-chair. I signed on alongside my friend Nicole Garnett, who was then a lawyer for the Institute for Justice, a libertarian non-profit law firm that was litigating many of the school-choice cases across the country.

Nicole and I became the first two co-chairs, and then, when she went to be a law clerk for Justice Clarence Thomas, she stepped down and was replaced by her husband Rick Garnett, who had been my co-clerk with the Chief. Both Nicole and Rick are amazing, and today they're both law professors at Notre Dame.

In the late 90s, we hosted a national school-choice conference in Ohio, which was ground zero for school-choice battles at the time. We brought in conservatives and even some liberals to consider and debate the key issues of choice.

Shortly thereafter, I was invited to speak to the national convention of the ACLU. You read that right. In 1999, long before I had been elected to anything, the ACLU asked me to participate in an hour-and-a-half-long one-on-one debate on school choice before their national convention in San Diego. My opponent was liberal columnist Juan Williams, and the supposed "neutral" moderator was Barry Lynn, head of Americans United for Separation of Church and State.

It remains the most hostile audience I've ever addressed. But, I hope, in the course of the debate, at least some of the arguments I presented made them think. The one argument that seemed to resonate even slightly was the following: "The ACLU has a long and venerable history of standing up to paternalism, to government making decisions for you the individual. Survey after survey of African-American and Hispanic parents show overwhelming support—60 percent, 70 percent, or more—for school choice. Why do you, the ACLU, feel so comfortable substituting your own paternalistic view for their own view of what's best for their children?"

In the 90s, the main policy argument against choice was that allowing some students to receive scholarships to private schools would destroy the public schools. At the time, choice programs were nascent, so that argument had theoretical plausibility. And, had it been true, it would have been a compelling reason to oppose choice; the public schools are and will remain the backbone of our education system for the vast majority of children.

But now, as dozens of jurisdictions across the country have implemented various forms of school choice, we know three facts empirically: (1) Kids and parents in failing schools desperately want out, as choice programs are regularly over-subscribed by large margins. (2) Kids who exercise choice predictably do better, achieving better reading and math scores and much better rates of college admission. And (3) the data demonstrate conclusively that not only does choice *not harm* the public schools, it actually *helps* the public schools because the competition improves the quality of education for the kids who stay in the public school.

This third point is foundational. Before I was Texas solicitor general, from 2001–03 in the Bush administration, I was the head of policy planning at the Federal Trade Commission. The FTC's statutory mission is to protect consumers and to promote competition. Roughly seventy-five Ph.D. economists work at the FTC, and I asked two of them to study in depth the impact of competition on education. In particular, I asked them to take seriously the argument that school choice harms public schools and to examine the data. They framed the question more generally, as economists are wont to do: "What is the impact on a regulated monopoly when competition is introduced, and, specifically, what is the impact on quality for those who remain with the incumbent providers?"

They published the results in a formal FTC report. First, they looked to several other industries, previously oligopolies, where competition had been introduced: surface freight transportation, telecommunications, and air transportation. Not surprisingly, their empirical examination found that competition was good; in all three, quality increased for those customers who never switched to the new providers.

Then, they examined every empirical study that had been done on school-choice programs. The data from those were entirely consistent: when students trapped in failing schools are given options, it helps those students and, overall, *it helps the public schools.*

As of today, EdChoice, a leading national school-choice advocacy organization, observed the following: "Of the 26 studies that examine the competitive effects of school choice programs on public schools, 24 found positive effects, one saw no visible effect and one found some negative effects for some kids."

And for many children, whether at Jewish day schools or Catholic parochial schools or small Christian schools like my alma mater, Second Baptist High School in Houston—or homeschooling, for those parents able to commit the time required—school can also help nurture an important faith component in their lives. That is a choice for parents to make, a fundamental and precious liberty.

Sadly, parental rights frighten those who want government to have total control over what children are allowed to learn. A recent article in *Harvard Magazine* entitled "The Risks of Homeschooling" demonstrates just how extreme this elitist condescension can get. It quotes Harvard Law School professor Elizabeth Bartholet arguing for banning homeschooling because she "thinks [it's] dangerous" for parents to "have 24/7, essentially authoritarian control over their children from ages zero to 18." According to Bartholet, "it's always dangerous to put powerful people in charge of the powerless, and to give the powerful ones total authority."

That view, however, is contrary to two centuries of constitutional precedent protecting parents' fundamental rights to raise and educate their children. As the Court held in *Pierce v. Society of Sisters* (1923),

> The fundamental theory of liberty upon which all governments in this Union repose excludes any general power of the State to standardize its children by forcing them to accept instruction from public teachers only. The child is not the mere creature of the State; those who nurture him and direct his destiny have the right, coupled with the high duty, to recognize and prepare him for additional obligations.

And for those parents who make the choice to give their children a religious upbringing, that is a choice that substantially benefits society; as President George Washington exhorted his fellow citizens in his Farewell Address of 1796, "let us with caution indulge the supposition that morality can be maintained without religion. Whatever may be conceded to the influence of refined education on minds of peculiar structure, reason and experience both forbid us to expect that national morality can prevail in exclusion of religious principle."

The urgency of school choice is all the more important—vital—for parents, often single mothers, trapped in poverty. And for too many kids trapped in failing schools, frightened and without options.

In my eight years in the Senate, the legislation I'm most proud of passing was legislation to expand school choice. In 2017, as a part of the historic tax cut we passed, I offered an amendment that became the only amendment to pass on the Senate floor that added anything to the bill. The amendment concerned college 529 plans, tax-advantaged savings plans that allow parents and grandparents to save for the college expenses of their kids and grandkids. My amendment expanded 529 plans to include K–12 as well.

It was after midnight when we voted. At the time, there were fifty-two Republicans in the Senate. As the votes came in, two Republican Senators voted no. At that point, Senate floor staff picked up the phone and called the vice president, who was at the residence at the time. They told him it looked like we needed his vote to break the tie, and he began to head to the Capitol.

Then, Joe Manchin, a Democrat from West Virginia, voted yes. An audible gasp could be heard in the well of the Senate. At which point, Senate floor staff called the vice president and told his staff, "We got Manchin; it looks like we don't need the vice president's vote." So he turned his motorcade around and began heading back to the residence.

When Manchin returned to his desk, Democrats surrounded him. They were upset—the teachers-union bosses were going to be upset—and they upbraided him for daring to vote against them. A few minutes later, Joe sheepishly walked down to the front and changed his vote to a "no."

So the Senate floor staff called the vice president's office again…and for a second time, he turned his motorcade around. It takes about twenty minutes to get from the Naval Observatory (the vice president's residence) to the Capitol. Twenty minutes later, Vice President Pence walked onto the floor, took the presiding chair, and said, "the ayes being fifty, the nays being fifty, the chamber being equally divided, the presiding officer votes in the affirmative, and the amendment is adopted."

And with that, in the very early hours of the morning, the Senate passed what remains the most significant federal school-choice legislation ever passed. President Trump signed it into law, and today it allows parents and grandparents to save in a tax-advantaged account and then spend up to $10,000 per student, per year on tuition for public school, private school, religious school, parochial school—whatever the parent and student chooses. More than 75 percent of the families with 529 plans earn $150,000 per year or less, and my amendment potentially benefits up to 50 million school kids nationwide.

But still, far too many low-income students remain trapped in schools where they have little hope of learning. The solution of most Democratic Party politicians (and the teachers union bosses to whom they defer) is inevitably just more taxpayer money for the public schools. That can help, but, as the facts demonstrate, more money alone does not solve problems. For example, in the District of Columbia, taxpayers pay over $27,000 *per student* to fund public schools, and yet too many of the D.C. public schools produce dismal results. The kids and parents understand this; that's why 14,000 more students have applied for the D.C. Opportunity Scholarships (perennially underfunded by Congress) than there are scholarships available, and that's why more than 11,000 D.C. students are currently stuck on the charter-school wait-list.

Add to that rampant crime, drugs, and violence in too many inner-city schools, and the desperate situation children face can be overwhelming. In the Cleveland public schools, in the 1990s—staggeringly—a student entering ninth grade was statistically more likely to be a victim of violent crime *at school* than he or she was to graduate on time in four years. Thanks to heroic leadership by local leaders, that led the State of Ohio to establish a ground-breaking voucher program. Of course, it was immediately challenged in court.

The Ohio Pilot Project Scholarship allowed low-income students in failing schools to qualify for a scholarship of up to $2,250 that could be used for local private schools. The scholarships were awarded based on financial need, and—because the number of students applying was much greater than the number of scholarships made available—they were awarded by lottery. Even though the $2,250 scholarship was substantially less than the per student funding for public schools, fifty-six private schools in Cleveland agreed to participate in the program.

Parents chose which schools their children attended. But because forty-six of the fifty-six participating schools were religious, plaintiffs argued that the Constitution prohibited the scholarships from going to them. The federal district court agreed and struck down the scholarship program. The Sixth Circuit Court of Appeals did as well.

The Supreme Court reversed that decision, 5–4, in *Zelman v. Simmons-Harris.* Chief Justice Rehnquist wrote the majority opinion, upholding the Ohio scholarship program. The Court described the crisis facing the schoolchildren in Ohio in no uncertain terms, pointing to the failure of Cleveland public schools to meet the most basic educational standards. The few students who managed to graduate were often barely literate, while two thirds of students didn't even make it to their senior year.

The Ohio scholarship program was designed to give a lifeline to those students and to help save the public schools. More than 3700 students participated in the scholarship program, and 60 percent were from families at or below the poverty line.

Nevertheless, the litigation onslaught the Ohio school-choice program faced was based on the notion that the Constitution prohibits even a penny of public money from ever going to a religious school. It's an odd notion, given the long legacy of scholarship programs allowing university students to choose religious institutions. Pell grants are federal student-aid awards given to low income students to be used at the college of their choice. Nobody seriously contends that students cannot use Pell grants to attend the University of Notre Dame or Brigham Young University, even though those are religious institutions.

Yet somehow, the argument goes, a scholarship that is entirely permissible for an eighteen-year-old college student is suddenly unconstitutional for a seventeen-year-old high-school senior. That's what the federal district court held, as well as the federal court of appeals. The majority in *Zelman* rejected that claim, ruling that the Ohio statute was "neutral in all respects towards religion" and "part of a general and multifaceted undertaking by the State of Ohio to provide educational opportunities to the children of a failed school district."

As a matter of constitutional law, an individual parent or student making the choice to attend a religious school and to use scholarship funds to do so is not the government establishing a religion. It is a neutral program allowing individual choice. The *Zelman* Court concluded that "the program is therefore a program of true private choice. In keeping with an unbroken line of decisions rejecting challenges to similar programs, we hold that the program does not offend the Establishment Clause."

Justice Clarence Thomas joined the majority opinion in full, but he separately wrote a soaring concurrence. He opened by quoting abolitionist hero Frederick Douglass:

> Frederick Douglass once said that "[e]ducation...means emancipation. It means light and liberty. It means the uplifting of the soul of man into the glorious light of truth, the light by which men can only be made free." Today many of our inner-city public schools deny emancipation to urban minority students. Despite this Court's observation nearly 50 years ago in *Brown* v. *Board of Education*, that "it is doubtful that any child may reasonably be expected to succeed in life if he is denied the opportunity of an education," urban children have been forced into a system that continually fails them.

Justice Thomas, having grown up in abject poverty in Pin Point, Georgia, understands firsthand the urgency of school choice as a civil-rights issue. Raised by his grandparents, and against extraordinary obstacles, Justice Thomas poured himself into his academic studies and graduated from Holy Cross University and then Yale Law School.

He is a brilliant jurist and the leading conservative on the Supreme Court today. Few people attract more contempt and derision from the left than do African-American conservatives, and Justice Thomas has faced decades of belittling insults from the press, law school professors, and other hardened "liberals." Hollywood director Spike Lee was shamefully quoted as saying that Malcolm X would call Justice Thomas "a handkerchief-head, a chicken-and-biscuit-eating Uncle Tom."

That venom, it seems, is never directed at liberals and rarely even at white conservatives. Justice Scalia, somehow, never had his brilliance questioned; for decades, leftists have wrongly ridiculed Justice Thomas's intellect. And yet, every term on the Court, he will pick one or two opinions to fundamentally reassess a line of jurisprudence, laying out careful analyses about the extent to which the recent (or not so recent) precedents comport with the text of the Constitution, the original understanding of its meaning, and first principles.

As a person, Justice Thomas is extraordinary. No member of the Court is more beloved by the Court's janitors, electricians, guards, and support staff with whom he connects on a genuine, personal level. He's down to earth and real, with a deep, booming laugh—imagine Santa Claus bellowing "ho, ho, ho!"

Two vignettes capture Justice Thomas in person. First, when I was clerking, I brought my college and law school roommate, David Panton, by the Court to meet him. For thirty years, David has been (other than Heidi) my closest friend in the world. He was the best man at our wedding. He's from Jamaica, was a Rhodes Scholar, and has a doctorate from Oxford. Barack Obama, famously, was the first black president of the *Harvard Law Review*; David was the second. (Obama, then an unknown community organizer who had graduated a few years earlier, called David to congratulate him after he was elected.) I told Justice Thomas about David, and he wanted to get to know him.

He and David talked for over an hour; I mostly listened. At the end, Justice Thomas wanted David to come clerk for him, but David said he didn't want to pursue law (today, he's a private-equity investor instead).

"Don't you want to be a lawyer?" Justice Thomas asked him.

"No, no," David responded, "I leave that to the smart people."

"So do I," Justice Thomas quipped in response.

I laughed so hard my ribs hurt, and Justice Thomas's booming laugh echoed throughout his chambers. Two of the smartest men on the planet, both black conservatives, having the humility to make self-deprecating jokes spoke volumes about who they were.

A second Justice Thomas story involved my co-clerk, Rick Garnett, who had worked the previous year as a law clerk in Little Rock, Arkansas. There, he and his wife Nicole had befriended and tutored a young African-American boy named Carlos. The boy had never left Arkansas before, but Rick and Nicole paid to fly him up to D.C. Rick emailed all nine chambers at the Court, saying that this young boy would be in town and asking if any of the justices would be willing to meet with him. Two offices responded—those of Justices Ruth Bader Ginsburg and Clarence Thomas.

Ginsburg is an incredibly talented lawyer and jurist, and it was very kind of her to meet with Carlos, but her prim demeanor is that of a legal librarian, and so it was difficult for her and the young boy from rural Arkansas to connect. Clarence Thomas understood the world that Carlos had come from.

At the end of their two-hour conversation, Carlos observed that Thomas was a Dallas Cowboys fan. (Thomas had a framed picture of himself with quarterback Troy Aikman in his office.) The kid was impressed—that was way cooler than the Supreme Court—and Thomas noticed. So Thomas rose from his chair, walked to his desk, and showed the boy a Super Bowl ticket, encased in Lucite, and signed by Cowboys running back Emmitt Smith. He handed the ticket to the young man.

"I'm going to give you this," Thomas said. "But I want you to promise me that you will get A's in school next year."

The young man, astonished and wide-eyed, nodded in agreement.

It was one of countless stories of random acts of kindness by Justice Thomas that the media never reports. But it's who he is, because he remembers where he comes from.

Returning to his *Zelman* concurrence, Justice Thomas elaborated on why no civil rights issue is more pressing than school choice:

While the romanticized ideal of universal public education resonates with the cognoscenti who oppose vouchers, poor urban families just want the best education for their children, who will certainly need it to function in our high-tech and advanced society. As Thomas Sowell noted 30 years ago: "Most black people have faced too many grim, concrete problems to be romantics. They want and need certain tangible results, which can be achieved only by developing certain specific abilities." *Black Education: Myths and Tragedies* (1972). The same is true today. An individual's life prospects increase dramatically with each successfully completed phase of education.

Despite the incredible stakes for schoolchildren across America and despite the fact that school-choice programs allow parents and students (not government) to make their own choices, four Supreme Court justices voted to strike down the Ohio school-choice program.

In June of 2020, the Court decided *Espinoza v. Montana Department of Revenue*, another major victory for school choice. Montana had established a tax-credit program for low-income children to be able to attend the school of their choice, and the Montana Supreme Court struck that program down pursuant to a provision of the Montana Constitution. That provision was a so-called "Blaine amendment," modeled after the failed federal amendment introduced by Speaker of the House William Blaine in 1875. In the years that followed, as a result of a virulent outpouring of anti-Catholic bigotry, thirty-eight states adopted Blaine amendments into their state constitutions, each prohibiting any tax dollars from going to "sectarian" institutions.

Writing separately, Justice Alito explained, "a wave of immigration in the mid-19th century, spurred in part by potato blights in Ireland and Germany, significantly increased this country's Catholic population. Nativist fears increased with it. An entire political party, the Know Nothings, formed in the 1850s 'to decrease the political influence of immigrants and Catholics.'" Alito detailed the sordid history of Blaine amendments and how the Know Nothing party was "in many ways a forerunner of the Ku Klux Klan." Personally speaking, since my mom's ancestors were among those Catholics fleeing the Irish potato famine and coming to America in the 1800s, that history has a particular resonance with me.

In *Espinoza*, the Court reversed 5–4, striking down Montana's Blaine amendment and upholding the Montana school-choice program. The Court ruled that states don't have to create school-choice programs, but, if they do, the First Amendment does not allow them to exclude religious schools. Government cannot single out and exclude people of faith. Tragically, just as with *Zelman*, four justices were fully prepared to dismantle the Montana program and remove that option from Montana school kids.

On the mantle in my Senate office sits a bust of Dr. Martin Luther King Jr. A few feet away, on the bookcase, is a framed picture of hundreds of Cleveland schoolchildren—mostly low-income African-American and Hispanic children—holding hand-written signs in front of the Supreme Court on the day *Zelman* was argued. As I sit at my desk, I directly face that bookcase and often look at that picture and reflect on the kids whose future school choice is all about.

Today there are sixty-five school choice programs in twenty-eight states. Over 500,000 students benefit every year from vouchers, tax-credit scholarships, and education savings accounts. We need many, many more, and I will continue to fight hard to expand choice for every child in our nation.

Four justices were prepared to strike down Ohio's program, Montana's program, and virtually every other school choice program in America, taking away the educational options and—in a very real sense—the hope of millions of kids. And, from that heartbreaking outcome, we are just one vote away.

CHAPTER 3

GUN RIGHTS AND
DISTRICT OF COLUMBIA V. HELLER

The First Amendment is first in our Bill of Rights, but it is not complicated arithmetic to observe that the Second Amendment comes second. The Framers of our Constitution created a Bill of Rights to protect the most important individual liberties we enjoy as Americans. And the right of the people to keep and bear arms was, and is, as former Supreme Court Justice Joseph Story once put it, the "palladium of the liberties of a republic."

Much that can be said about the natural right to religious liberty can also be said about the natural right to self-defense. Just as there can be no true political liberty without a robust protection of religious liberty under the rule of law, so too can there be no true political liberty without a robust protection of the right to self-defense under the rule of law. Social stability and human flourishing require the right to bear arms just as they require the right to worship.

Importantly, the Second Amendment is not about hunting. Nor is it about skeet shooting, target shooting, or other leisure activities. Rather, the Framers of the Second Amendment put that provision in the Bill of Rights to protect our lives, to protect our homes, and to protect our families. It is about the right we have, if somebody comes into our home at night to harm our children, to defend our children and to defend our lives. It is about the right we have, as God-fearing, law-abiding, conscientious, armed citizens, to hold government accountable to "We the People of the United States"—who, in our system of governance, are the ultimate sovereigns.

From time immemorial, tyrants have sought to consolidate power by robbing a free people of their ability to properly defend themselves and their families. America's Founding Fathers were well aware of this sad and sorry history. As a result, they sought to preclude the citizens of the country they were birthing from ever having to worry about their right to self-defense—whether that right applies against a petty thief or a tyrannical government.

"No free man, shall ever be debarred the use of arms," Thomas Jefferson wrote in an early draft of the Virginia Constitution. "To preserve liberty, it is essential that the whole body of the people always possess arms, and be taught alike, especially when young, how to use them," Richard Henry Lee wrote at the time. Perhaps most direct and to the point was Jefferson and Lee's Liberty-loving fellow Virginian, George Mason, who said around the time of the Constitution's ratification debates that "to disarm the people...is the most effectual way to enslave them."

The Constitution's Framers, prescient as they were, were meticulous in trying to ensure that Americans would forever remain a free people. They were adamant that Americans would always prize their Liberty. And they were passionate about securing Americans' right to self-defense so that we would never find ourselves subjugated by the rise of a would-be despot.

Ultimately, the Framers of the Bill of Rights chose to codify the natural right to self-defense in clear and unmistakable constitutional language: "A well regulated Militia, being necessary to the security of a free State, the right of the people to keep and bear Arms, shall not be infringed."

Or at least most readers would normally find that to be clear and unmistakable language. By its express terms, it protects your and my right "to keep and bear Arms," which it demands "*shall not* be infringed."

Yet for over two centuries after the Bill of Rights was ratified, the Supreme Court never affirmed that the Second Amendment means what it so plainly says. Amazingly, it wasn't until just twelve years ago that the Supreme Court did precisely that in the landmark case of *District of Columbia v. Heller.* It was a case that I helped litigate, and it is a case that highlights just how far the radical left would go to destroy the Second Amendment if it were to regain control of the Supreme Court ever again.

It is now time to tell that tale.

◆   ◆   ◆   ◆

As a political matter, not too long ago there was remarkable bipartisan agreement on at least the stated importance of protecting the Second Amendment. Outside of court rulings, both Democrats and Republicans routinely pledged to defend the Second Amendment as a matter of principle. Not everybody meant it, but they at least paid lip service to the Second Amendment, even if they strongly disagreed on specific legislative proposals and whether those proposals were consistent or inconsistent with the right protected in the Bill of Rights.

In the past two decades, that has changed. Today, the position of elected Democrats (and most of their judicial nominees) is much more radical.

Reasonable minds can differ on whether gun control measures are good policy. Many believe passionately that they are, and many others believe just as passionately that they are not. Likewise, reasonable minds could differ as to which measures are permissible under the Second Amendment. But today's elected Democrats maintain that *every conceivable restriction*—including total and complete prohibition—is permissible under the Second Amendment.

Heller powerfully illustrated the breadth and audacity of the modern Democratic position.

Dick Anthony Heller was a federal police officer who lived in Washington, D.C. He carried a firearm at work, but D.C. laws, among the most draconian in the country, made it functionally illegal for him to carry a gun at his home. The D.C. laws prohibited the private possession of any and all handguns, and they required that all long guns (shotguns and rifles) be kept "unloaded and disassembled or bound by a trigger lock or similar device" *at all times*, with no exceptions (even to defend against imminent threat of violence). In practice, this meant that neither handguns nor long guns could ever be used for home protection or self-defense in the nation's capital.

Dick Heller brought a challenge against those laws in the federal district court in the District of Columbia. He argued that a total prohibition on possessing operative firearms was inconsistent with the core protection of the Second Amendment.

The district court rejected Heller's claim. The argument of the District of Columbia, which the court accepted, was that the Second Amendment does not protect any individual right whatsoever. Instead, D.C. argued, it protects only a "collective right of the militia," a fancy legal construct that means no person can ever claim that right or have it protected in court. As a practical matter, that interpretation would read the Second Amendment out of the Bill of Rights.

When the case went to the court of appeals, I became involved. As the Texas solicitor general, I drafted an amicus brief on behalf of thirteen states that defended an *individual* constitutional right to keep and bear arms.

Our brief laid out the historical and constitutional arguments for why the "collective right of the militia" view of the Second Amendment was profoundly misguided. Starting from the constitutional text, the operative language of the Second Amendment provides that "the right of the people to keep and bear Arms, shall not be infringed." And that phrase, "the right of the people," is a term of art that the Framers used repeatedly to refer to individual rights.

"The right of the people" is found in two other places in the Bill of Rights: The First Amendment protects "the right of the people peaceably to assemble," and the Fourth Amendment protects "the right of the people to be secure...against unreasonable searches and seizures." In both instances, there is no doubt the Framers were referring to individual rights.

What does an "individual right" mean? It means the right is yours, personally, and you can raise it in court both to challenge unconstitutional laws and as a defense to unconstitutional criminal prosecutions or civil actions. Thus, if Congress were to pass a law saying that no group of communists could meet together, and you were a communist, you could challenge that law in court. Likewise, if Congress barred groups of Nazis, or Democrats, or Republicans, or the NAACP from gathering together, and you were personally affected, you individually could challenge that law as violating your right to assemble. Or, if Congress said more generally that no group of ten or more could ever gather in public to protest, and you wished to do so, you could challenge that as well. (Notably, reasonable public-health restrictions, limited in scope and duration, have long been held permissible in times of pandemic.)

In the Fourth Amendment context, an individual right means that if the police break down your door and search your house—without a sufficient basis for doing so—you can sue them for violating your rights. If, in the process of that unconstitutional search, they encounter evidence of a crime (say, a bag of marijuana in your bedroom), and they prosecute you for that crime, you have an individual right to urge the court to exclude that evidence because it was seized in violation of your rights. And, if Congress were to pass a law purporting to give government the power to monitor your location at all times using GPS on your phone—with no probable cause to believe you've committed a crime—you individually could file a lawsuit challenging that law and urging a court to strike down the law.

It is a long-standing canon of interpretation, for both statutes and the Constitution, that the same words will be understood as having the same meaning if used multiple places in the same document. Therefore, if "the right of the people" referred to an individual right in the First and Fourth Amendments, then "the right of the people" should also be understood to be referring to an individual right in the Second Amendment.

Moreover, when the Constitution uses the word "right" it means, well, "right." Put differently, what on earth is a "collective right of the militia"? Nobody knows, because it's not meant to be anything real, other than a means of erasing the Second Amendment altogether. Before the Supreme Court, the District of Columbia argued that it served "to prevent Congress, using its powers under the Militia Clauses, from disarming state militias." But that would be a protection of the states as governmental entities, and in the constitutional text (e.g., the Tenth Amendment), states have "powers," not "rights." It is individuals who have "rights" in the Bill of Rights.

But what does the Second Amendment language mean concerning "a well regulated militia"? First, the word "regulated" at the time was not understood to mean "subject to government regulation." Rather, "regulated" in that context meant "equipped," so that "well regulated" meant "well equipped," i.e., having sufficient weaponry to be effective.

Second, when the Constitution uses prefatory language—explaining why a right is important—it does not constrain the operative language that follows. Thus, when the Second Amendment says "a well regulated Militia, being necessary to the security of a free State," it is explaining one important reason why the right that follows matters. But it doesn't restrict the substantive scope of that right. The Framers used a similar formulation in the Copyright Clause, which reads "[T]he Congress shall have the power... [t]o promote the Progress of Science and useful Arts, by securing for limited Times to Authors and Inventors the exclusive Right to their respective Writings and Discoveries." And in *Eldred v. Ashcroft* (2003), the Supreme Court rightly concluded that the operative power to secure exclusive rights was not limited by the prefatory purpose to "promote the progress of science and useful arts." Although that was an important purpose for the provision, it was not the only purpose.

Third, today, "the militia" might seem a fairly limited and esoteric concept. But, at the time of the American Founding, "the militia" was understood to mean everybody (specifically, all able-bodied adults). To be sure, when the Framers referred to "able-bodied adults," they had a limited view of whom they were describing. They included in that category, unfortunately, only white males. The mandate did not extend to women, nor did it extend to African Americans. Because of our sad and disgraceful early-Republic history of slavery and racism, African Americans were far too long denied the rights protected under the Bill of Rights. Slavery was the original sin of the American Republic, and we fought a bloody Civil War that killed over 600,000 Americans to eradicate that abomination.

As I explained in our eventual amicus brief to the Supreme Court, D.C.'s argument was belied by the provisions of the Militia Act of 1792, a piece of legislation that defined "militia" as all able-bodied male citizens from eighteen to forty-five.

Interestingly, a version of the Militia Act still exists today. Title 10, section 246 of the U.S. Code today provides: "The militia of the United States consists of all able-bodied males at least 17 years of age and, except as provided in section 313 of title 32, under 45 years of age who are, or who have made a declaration of intention to become, citizens of the United States and of female citizens of the United States who are members of the National Guard."

Furthermore, by statute, there are two "classes of the militia": "the organized militia, which consists of the National Guard and the Naval Militia," and "the unorganized militia, which consists of the members of the militia who are not members of the National Guard or the Naval Militia." Thus, as a matter of law, if you're an able-bodied man between the ages of seventeen and forty-five, you're a member of the militia whether you know it or not!

All of this was widely understood by the Constitution's Framers—and by the American Founding–era generation more generally. Remember, we were just a few years removed from the Revolutionary War, in which armed American colonists defeated the British Army (the mightiest military on the face of the planet) and won our independence. The Framers considered British rule to have become tyrannical, and the ability of the people to fight back is what preserved our Liberty and created our Nation. Here's how Alexander Hamilton put it in *Federalist* No. 29:

> ...if circumstances should at any time oblige the government to form an army of any magnitude that army can never be formidable to the liberties of the people while there is a large body of citizens, little, if at all inferior to them in discipline and the use of arms, who stand ready to defend their own rights and those of their fellow-citizens.

That check on government power would be meaningless if government had the power simply to disarm the citizenry. That's why the Second Amendment prohibits doing so.

Often, when trying to understand the meaning of constitutional provisions, courts will look to the actions of the early Congress, which was populated by many of the original drafters of the Constitution. Legally, what matters is not the subjective intent of the Framers, but rather what the publicly understood meaning of the terms was at the time they were adopted.

The Bill of Rights was ratified in 1791. The very next year, Congress passed the first recorded gun legislation in our history. The Militia Act of 1792 did not prohibit or restrict the private ownership of guns; to the contrary, the statute *mandated* that every able-bodied adult male *must* own a flintlock musket and twenty bullets apiece.

Ours was a newly formed country, fresh off the heels of a revolution. And the Framers understood that an armed populace could not be easily subjugated to tyranny. Again to quote the great Justice Story, the Second Amendment "offers a strong moral check against the usurpation and arbitrary power of rulers; and will generally, even if these are successful in the first instance, enable the people to resist and triumph over them."

Justice Story understood that the men who drafted the Bill of Rights were heavily influenced by the evolution of individual rights in the English constitutional tradition. In particular, the Framers were heavily influenced by the English Bill of Rights of 1689, which provided that English Protestants "may have arms for their defence suitable to their conditions and as allowed by law."

The great English lawyer Sir William Blackstone, who had a profound impact on the Framers, later explained in his famous 1765 *Commentaries* that the right of "having" arms is among the five basic rights of every Englishman, essential to securing the "primary rights" of each individual.

That the Framers viewed the right to keep and bear arms as one of the fundamental rights of Americans is demonstrated by the fact that they enshrined its protection in the Second Amendment.

After we filed our brief in the D.C. Circuit, I called the solicitor general for the District of Columbia to inform him that Texas and the other *amici* states were going to be asking the court of appeals for oral argument time. My fellow solicitor general became angry, yelling at me over the phone, "What the hell business does Texas have interfering with the laws of the District of Columbia?"

I responded to him that the decision in this case—the decision by the D.C. Circuit—would set a national precedent that could impact every state and would be especially influential as to how similar cases were resolved in other courts of appeal across the country. The rulings of the D.C. Circuit, sometimes called the nation's second-highest court, are not binding outside of D.C., but they have historically been highly influential for federal courts across the country. The Second Amendment rights of everyone else across the country would be profoundly impacted by the D.C. Circuit's decision. And the decision of the D.C. Circuit would be very important for how the Supreme Court ultimately resolved the issue upon final appeal.

I also explained to the District of Columbia solicitor general that my boss, the Texas attorney general, believed he had an obligation to defend the Second Amendment rights of every Texan—and the D.C. Circuit's decision could directly impact those rights. And, I explained with a smile, I didn't need the D.C. SG's permission to seek argument time.

Ultimately, Texas was granted argument time in *Parker v. District of Columbia*, which was the companion case to *Heller*. So I presented oral argument to the D.C. Circuit in *Parker*, defending the individual right to keep and bear arms.

Before the D.C. Circuit, Heller prevailed. And then the case went up to the Supreme Court. The Court took the case, and once again, Texas took the lead for the states defending the Second Amendment. This time, we got thirty-one states to join us as *amici*, more than double the number of states who had joined at the D.C. Circuit level.

Our brief made many of the same historical and constitutional arguments we had made to the D.C. Circuit. But we made an additional argument that proved consequential (and controversial). In footnote six of the brief, we argued that, although it was not legally necessary for Heller's position to prevail, the states acknowledged that the Second Amendment was not merely a right that bound the federal government. Rather, we conceded that the Second Amendment also bound the state governments because it was "incorporated" against the states through the Fourteenth Amendment.

As a general matter, the text of the Bill of Rights applies only against the federal government. So, for example, in the First Amendment our basic protections of religious liberty, free speech, and a free press are explicitly directed only against the federal government. In fact, it begins with the very words, "Congress shall make no law." By its own terms, the First Amendment, as with the rest of the Bill of Rights, applies just against the federal government—and not against the states.

And for the first century of our country's history, the Bill of Rights was understood as only restricting the federal government, and not the states. But all of that gradually changed after the Civil War.

In the decades since, the Supreme Court has applied virtually all of the provisions of the Bill of Rights against state and local governments as well through a process that's known as "incorporation." So today, it's clear that a state government can't violate the First Amendment any more than the federal government can.

Heller was a curious case in that it arose in the District of Columbia, which is under the direct authority of the federal government. So the Court wouldn't have to address incorporation to resolve the case. That presented an interesting dynamic for our amicus brief: it could, in effect, be a freebie for state attorneys general because they could claim they supported an individual right to keep and bear arms, while nonetheless remaining silent on whether their own state governments would have to respect that right.

I didn't want to take half-measures or facilitate political cover for attorneys general unwilling to meaningfully protect the Second Amendment, so footnote six of our brief stated:

> Although the Court need not reach the issue of incorporation in this case, *amici* States submit that the right to keep and bear arms is fundamental and so is properly subject to incorporation.... In the judgment of *amici* States, the right to keep and bear arms is "so rooted in the traditions and conscience of our people as to be ranked as fundamental."

This had particular importance because it was what is known as a statement against interest; it constituted attorneys general explicitly acknowledging an important limitation on their own power. And, should any of those AGs subsequently try to argue in another court case that the Second Amendment should not be incorporated against the states, their explicit concession to the contrary would certainly be used against them.

That prompted an angry phone call from another state SG. He wanted to join our brief, but he argued—correctly—that footnote six was gratuitous. It was unnecessary to resolve the case, and he demanded that we delete the footnote.

I conceded the footnote was unnecessary but explained that we thought it was important (for the very reason he was dismayed at the content of the concession). His boss was an elected Democrat, and so I told him that he was welcome to take the politically courageous (but perhaps foolish) step of telling his electorate he didn't support the Second Amendment. Fuming, the SG told me his state would join the brief.

Before Supreme Court oral argument, we received good news when we heard that the Bush administration's Department of Justice was going to support us. That news turned out to be less than fully good, however, when we saw the actual brief that the United States filed. Although the Bush Department of Justice agreed with the legal proposition that the Second Amendment protected an individual right, it also argued for what in constitutional law is called an "intermediate scrutiny" standard of review. The way they defined that test was so lenient and deferential to the government that, as a practical matter, it would mean virtually any government restrictions on firearms would be permissible even if the Second Amendment were still technically deemed to protect an individual right. Indeed, they couldn't even conclude that D.C.'s total prohibition would violate their lax standard; instead, they urged the Court to vacate the D.C. Circuit decision and remand the case for the court to reconsider it.

The brief was signed by then-U.S. Solicitor General Paul Clement, a friend and a very talented lawyer who had previously clerked for Judge Laurence Silberman on the D.C. Circuit and then for Justice Antonin Scalia on the Supreme Court. Readers will remember Paul from the previous chapter, from the oral argument in *Van Orden v. Perry*.

It so happened that Judge Silberman had authored the D.C. Circuit opinion in *Heller*—a jurisprudential tour de force that carefully outlined the textual, structural, and historical reasons that the Second Amendment protections were both real and meaningful. But now, his former clerk, Paul Clement, had signed a brief advocating a standard of review that would have gutted Judge Silberman's opinion. From multiple accounts in Washington, Silberman was furious. I don't think the brief necessarily reflected Paul's personal opinion, but it was the sort of "cut the baby in half" legal reasoning that can occur when a Department of Justice is trying to make everyone happy all at once.

Texas decided to take a more conservative approach (as we often did during the years of the Bush administration). We were not only going to defend the Second Amendment as an individual right to keep and bear arms, but we were going to advocate for robust judicial scrutiny for laws infringing on that right. In other words, we argued that the Second Amendment is real and that it protects a concrete right that matters for millions of law-abiding patriots across the nation.

While the Supreme Court was considering *Heller,* I recall a conversation I had with members of the *Washington Post* editorial board. The *Post,* like the *New York Times* and most other papers, leans left—sometimes very much so. I spent about thirty minutes on the phone arguing to the *Post* editorial board that they should support Mr. Heller. The reason, I argued, is that they—along with every other journalist—should be committed to a robust First Amendment. To a First Amendment, that is, that vigorously protects freedom of speech and freedom of the press, which ensures their ability to carry out their vital function. And I argued to the editorial board that if they wanted to defend a robust First Amendment, they should be disquieted by an effort effectively to read the Second Amendment out of the Constitution. That if courts were empowered to take away one amendment, they could very well try to erase other amendments as well. And so, even if the editorial writers might support gun control as a policy matter, they should be adamantly against the Court's eliminating individual rights expressly protected in the Bill of Rights. Astonishingly enough, the *Post* agreed with me and wrote an editorial in support of the constitutional right to keep and bear arms. It was no small victory.

When the decision came down, Dick Anthony Heller prevailed by a vote of 5–4. The majority opinion was authored by Justice Antonin Scalia, and it remains perhaps the finest opinion Justice Scalia ever wrote.

The Court upheld the individual right to keep and bear arms in the Second Amendment and struck down the District of Columbia's total ban on possessing a functional firearm at home. Under the D.C. law, if a single mom kept a disassembled shotgun in her closet and a criminal broke into her apartment to attack her family, she would herself become a criminal if she assembled the shotgun in order to ward him off. In other words, the law took away the fundamental right to protect yourself in the District of Columbia. Justice Scalia, writing for the Court's majority, emphatically rejected the constitutionality of that total prohibition. The Court established an individual right to keep and bear arms for those civilian weapons "in common use" at the time. By any measure, handguns met that test, so D.C.'s total ban on handguns was unconstitutional.

The District of Columbia had criminalized the exercise of this cherished and indispensable right to self-defense. The Supreme Court rightly rejected D.C.'s blanket prohibition. Justice Scalia, writing for the Court's majority, largely adopted the test that Texas and the other *amici* states had urged—a more rigorous standard of scrutiny than the lenient standard that the Bush Department of Justice had put forward in its own brief.

Two years later, in *McDonald v. City of Chicago*, the Court finished the journey that we had urged it to begin in *Heller*. In McDonald, the Court rightly concluded that the individual right to keep and bear arms is a fundamental right that is, in turn, incorporated against the states. After *McDonald*, it is not just the District of Columbia, but also all the fifty states and every local government that is prohibited from infringing upon our fundamental individual right to keep and bear arms.

Both *Heller* and *McDonald* were decided at the Court by single-vote majorities. In both cases, four justices dissented and argued that there was not *any* enforceable individual right to keep and bear arms.

To be clear, they were not writing in favor of any particular legislation that was reasonable or permissible, or in favor of any particular gun control–policy proposal. Rather, they objected to the idea that the Second Amendment protects *any* individual right whatsoever, which means that the federal government or any of the states could ban any and all firearms and make it a felony for you personally to possess a gun.

Under the dissenters' view, you would have no individual right even to challenge these laws in court. And you could be sent to prison for violating those laws. The consequence of that truly radical view is that the Second Amendment would effectively be erased from the Bill of Rights.

Four justices support that radical proposition. Hillary Clinton, in 2016, pledged to appoint *only* Supreme Court justices who would vote to overturn *Heller*—in other words, would vote to overturn and take away the individual right of every single American to keep and bear arms. And we are one vote away from that result.

◆　　◆　　◆　　◆

As a policy matter, gun-control laws are singularly ineffective. If the objective is to stop violent crime, restricting the rights of law-abiding citizens simply does not work.

I care passionately about stopping violent crime, and gun crime in particular. I've spent much of my adult life in law enforcement, trying to stop violent criminals who prey on the innocent and working to ensure that they receive the most stringent punishments.

In Texas, I was in Sutherland Springs—the site of the worst church shooting in U.S. history—the day after that brutal mass murder. I stood in that bloody sanctuary and mourned with grieving families.

I was in the Santa Fe High School just hours after the horrific shooting that left ten people—eight students and two teachers—dead.

I was in Dallas for the funeral service of five police officers shot and killed on July 7, 2016.

I was in Odessa right after the mass shooting killed eight.

I was in El Paso right after a deranged, bigoted mass murderer killed twenty-three people in a local Walmart.

I've cried with children who have lost their parents, and with parents whose children were killed before their eyes. I've prayed with families who have just come through hell, and with those who are living with memories that will haunt them for life.

I've seen too much death and carnage and agonizing grief. And there is something profoundly wrong with the evil-doers who commit such horrific acts. The fabric of our society has been badly frayed; the civic institutions of church and family and community that used to knit us together have been tragically weakened.

Not all of the solutions are governmental. Many of them, instead, can be found in the church and in strengthening our families and our communities.

But there is an important role for government and laws too. In 2013, when I was newly elected to the Senate, we confronted these issues head on. That spring, a deranged madman shot and killed twenty-six people, including twenty young children, in Newtown, Connecticut.

President Obama had just been reelected, and Democrats had control of the Senate. They were surging politically, and Democrats responded to Newtown by introducing a series of aggressive gun-control measures. Brimming with confidence, Senator Chuck Schumer declared on one of the Sunday shows that Democrats were in "the sweet spot" on gun control and they would prevail.

Although I had only been in the Senate a couple of months, I led the fight against their misguided gun-control proposals. And, by marshaling the facts and the law, by focusing on the Constitution and also on what actually works, we defeated every one of the Democratic power grabs.

On the Judiciary Committee, I charged into the debates with enthusiasm, asking, for example, Senator Dianne Feinstein why the Second Amendment used the words "the right of the people"—the same operative language as the First and Fourth Amendments—and whether she would support limiting First and Fourth Amendment rights the way she was proposing to do with Second Amendment rights. She responded indignantly (in an exchange that went viral online), "I am not a sixth grader!"

I was puzzled by that response. Of course she wasn't a sixth grader; if she were, I wouldn't have been asking her substantive constitutional questions. No, she's a senator serving on the Judiciary Committee, and she was proposing legislation to significantly restrict constitutional rights. It was a demonstration of respect—not disrespect—to ask her to engage in the substance. But, such things are rarely done in the Senate.

Virtually all of the Democratic proposals were directed at restricting the constitutional rights of law-abiding citizens. That may be a political objective for Democrats, but it is singularly ineffective for reducing violent crime.

If you look to the data, virtually all of the jurisdictions with the strictest gun control laws have among the highest crime rates and murder rates. Conversely, most of the jurisdictions with the most permissive gun laws have among the lowest crime rates and murder rates. Many more rural states, such as Idaho, Montana, New Mexico, North Dakota, and West Virginia, have among the highest gun ownership rates and the lowest murder and manslaughter rates, according to recent data.

Economist John Lott, then a professor at Yale, wrote a groundbreaking book in 1998 called *More Guns, Less Crime*. In it, he examined the effects of changing gun laws. He looked to what happened to crime rates, before and after, and, he concluded that the empirical data demonstrate that disarming law-abiding citizens *increases* violent crime, and allowing law-abiding citizens to defend themselves *decreases* violent crime. As Lott wrote:

> Criminals have ways of getting guns even when guns are banned. For example, drug gangs will get their guns to protect their drugs just as easily as they get their drugs to sell. Thus, gun control primarily disarms the citizens who obey the laws....
>
> But there is another side, one rarely mentioned in the media. Concealed weapons in the hands of good people can be used to save lives and stop attacks. The prospect of a criminal encountering a victim who may be armed will deter some attacks in the first place. Carrying a gun is also the safest course of action when one is confronted by a criminal.

This should not be surprising because firearms are often used to stop violent crimes. Indeed, the Obama administration estimated that, across America, firearms are used defensively to stop crime *over 1 million times per year.*

Instead of undermining the rights of law-abiding citizens, what is actually effective in stopping violent crime is targeting the violent criminals.

When it comes to legislation, it is often true that you can't beat something with nothing, so in the Spring of 2013 I introduced legislation along with Iowa senator Chuck Grassley (the senior Republican on the Judiciary Committee) to prevent gun crime. The Grassley-Cruz legislation targeted violent criminals, and it worked to prevent them from getting guns in the first place and to lock them up if they violated the law. It authorized $300 million in additional funding for school safety, for things like installing bullet-proof doors and windows, purchasing metal detectors, and—most importantly—increasing the number of armed police officers on campus to keep our children safe.

The mass shooting at the Sutherland Springs church in Texas illustrates how we can be more effective stopping gun crimes. There, it was already illegal for the murderer (as a point of principle, I refrain from ever repeating the names of these mass murderers, to help deny them the fame that they crave) to own a gun, in fact doubly so. He was a felon, and federal law prohibits felons from buying or owning guns. And he had a domestic violence conviction; federal law likewise prohibits individuals with domestic violence convictions from buying or owning guns.

So how did he get his guns? Well, during the Obama administration, the Air Force failed to report his felony conviction and his domestic violence conviction to the national database. Therefore, when he went to buy his guns, he passed the background check.

Grassley-Cruz would have fixed this problem. Specifically, it mandated the Department of Justice to conduct an audit of federal agencies to make sure that there are not felony convictions that they haven't reported to the database. Presumably, had the law passed, it would have caught the Sutherland Springs murderer's convictions.

Furthermore, when the Sutherland Springs perpetrator filled out his background check form, he lied twice. He checked the box that said he did not have a felony conviction, and he checked the box that said he did not have a domestic violence conviction. Both of those lies were themselves felonies, punishable by up to five years in prison.

Unfortunately, the Department of Justice rarely prosecutes these cases. For example, in 2010, there were over 53,000 felons and fugitives who tried to illegally purchase a firearm; of those, the Obama DOJ prosecuted just 44. *Forty-four out of fifty-three thousand.*

Grassley-Cruz mandated that these criminals be prosecuted. It created a gun-crime task force at DOJ specifically to prosecute felons or fugitives who try to buy firearms illegally.

Grassley-Cruz came to a vote on the Senate floor, and fifty-three senators voted yes, including nine Democrats—the most bipartisan support of any of the comprehensive measures. So why did Grassley-Cruz not pass into law? Because Harry Reid and the Democrats filibustered it—they demanded sixty votes for it to pass. Even though a majority of Senators voted for it, the Democrats blocked it. (To date, I don't know of a single reporter who has ever asked a single Democrat why they blocked bipartisan gun-violence legislation that would have made a real difference saving lives.)

Had Democrats not filibustered Grassley-Cruz, there is a very real possibility that the Sutherland Springs shooting never would have happened. The DOJ audit presumably would have caught the shooter's felony conviction, and, when he lied on the background check, DOJ would have prosecuted him. Which means he would have been in a federal prison cell instead of that beautiful country church murdering twenty-six innocent people.

◆　　◆　　◆　　◆

As with many other issues, on the question of gun control, Democrats have become more and more radicalized. Not that long ago, President Bill

Clinton credited congressional Democrats' 1994 passage of the so-called "assault weapons" ban with Newt Gingrich's Republican landslide that took over Congress the following year. Clinton likewise considered Al Gore's support for gun control as the key reason he lost the 2000 presidential election to George W. Bush.

There was a time, politically, when Democrats sought to assure rural voters, working-class voters, and other types of voters that they were not plotting to away take their guns. To be sure, there were always Democrats who were open about their hostility to gun rights. In 1995, Democratic senator Dianne Feinstein of California said, "If I had 51 votes in the Senate for, 'Mr. and Mrs. America, turn in all of your guns,' I would do it." That sentiment might work in bright blue California, but many other Democrats from across the country used to think differently.

But that has changed now.

In my U.S. Senate re-election campaign in Texas in 2018, I faced Beto O'Rourke. Beto ended up raising over $80 million. He out-raised our campaign three to one, swamped the state with advertising, and more than doubled Democratic turnout in the state of Texas over what it had been in 2014—from less than two million all the way up to four million. The money differential between our campaign and his was so stark that my campaign had a total of 18 paid campaign staffers, while O'Rourke's campaign had 805.

Our 2018 campaign ended up being the most expensive Senate race, in terms of hard money, in the history of the U.S. Senate. The last six weeks of the campaign, I went on a bus tour, barnstorming the state and doing fifty rallies and town halls all across Texas. And, thankfully, we turned out 4.2 million voters to defeat Beto's historic 4 million.

The day that Beto won the Democratic primary, I put out a humorous, satirical song on the radio. It was entitled, "If You're Gonna Run in Texas, You Can't be a Liberal Man." It was set, of course, to the tune of, "If You're Gonna Play in Texas (You Gotta Have a Fiddle in the Band)." One line of the song said that "Beto wants them open borders, and he wants to take our guns." PolitiFact, the biased and frequently dishonest journalistic outfit that routinely attacks Republicans and declares liberal bromides to be unassailable fact, rated my statement that Beto "wants to take our guns"—in a satirical song—as objectively "false."

Well, fast-forward to the 2020 presidential election and, standing on the debate stage as a candidate for the Democratic Party's presidential nomination and trying to energize the far-left activists in his party, Beto O'Rourke declared, "Hell yes, we're going to take your AR-15s!"

Shortly thereafter, on his campaign website, Beto's campaign began selling T-shirts emblazoned, "Hell yes, we're going to take your AR-15." When that happened, I couldn't resist tweeting: "Just a reminder, when I said it, PolitiFact (a wholly-owned subsidiary of the DNC) rated 'Beto wants to take our guns' as 'FALSE.' Maybe they should buy one of his new T-shirts."

PolitiFact issued an unusually personal response to my tweet, fitfully declaring that they're not "a wholly-owned subsidiary of the DNC." As the Bard put it, methinks she doth protest too much. PolitiFact further asserted that O'Rourke had recently "partially changed his position" and that its 2018 fact-check of O'Rourke remained accurate as of the time it was conducted. Of course.

Later in the 2020 Democratic presidential primary, well after Beto had dropped out and Joe Biden had won Super Tuesday in March, Biden stood alongside Beto O'Rourke in Dallas and pledged that Beto might well be in charge of gun policy in a Biden presidential administration.

That's not surprising because Biden's own views are just as radical. In August 2019, a television interviewer asked Biden the following question: "So, to gun owners out there who say, well, a Biden administration means they're going to come for my guns?" Biden's response? "Bingo!"

Moreover, in today's Democratic Party, gun confiscation is becoming more and more central to their platform. Some candidates, like Beto O'Rourke and sometimes Joe Biden, openly talk about it. Others, like former Supreme Court justice John Paul Stevens, openly advocate for repealing the Second Amendment altogether. Indeed, in 2018, then-retired justice Stevens wrote a widely read op-ed in the *New York Times* expressly entitled, "Repeal the Second Amendment."

But of course, there were already four votes on the Supreme Court (including his own) to repeal the Second Amendment by judicial fiat—to eliminate the right to keep and bear arms from the Bill of Rights altogether. Four votes to remove any constitutional protection of our right to keep and bear arms and to empower government to confiscate every firearm in America, to make it illegal for you to defend your home or your family, and to make it a felony for law-abiding citizens to own guns. With the Second Amendment, as with so many other vital issues, we're just one vote away.

CHAPTER 4

SOVEREIGNTY AND *MEDELLÍN V. TEXAS*

Who governs America? Who has authority over our laws and our criminal justice system? Is America its own nation, or are we subject to the rule of the United Nations and the World Court? And can the president of the United States give away U.S. sovereignty? Those were the questions at the heart of the most important case I argued at the Supreme Court.

The term "sovereignty" refers to the ability of a self-governing people to exercise the ultimate authority that comes with ruling itself. Sovereignty is a hallmark of every free nation-state, especially in the modern "Westphalian" nation-state system that followed the conclusion of the Thirty Years' War in 1648. It means being able to define who you are, dictating your own rules and norms, and controlling your own destiny.

A nation is sovereign if it is able to define and control the people that constitute it, is able to make all the relevant decisions that come with day-to-day governance, and is able to hold accountable its own elected and appointed rulers. A nation is not sovereign if it lacks any of these features—especially if the nation cannot control its own borders, cannot define who constitutes its own people, or is unable to make its own governing decisions due to interference or control from either another country or a transnational institution.

America's Founding Fathers had no intention of making this country anything other than a fully sovereign Republic. As Thomas Jefferson made clear in the Declaration of Independence, sometimes "it becomes necessary for one people to dissolve the political bands which have connected them with another, and to assume among the powers of the earth, the separate and equal station to which the Laws of Nature and of Nature's God entitle them."

That is not the battle cry of a people who sought to retain formal or legal ties to the British Crown. To the contrary: attaining full sovereignty was the singular goal of the American Revolution.

So America was always intended to be fully sovereign. Indeed, the language of our Constitution's Preamble clarifies this. That Preamble establishes that they who "do ordain and establish this Constitution" are "We the People of the United States."

Dr. John Eastman, a respected constitutional law scholar and my friend and former co-clerk, is fond of noting that the Preamble does not refer to "We the People of the World" but to "We the People of the United States." That is a monumental distinction. It is a distinction that makes all the difference in the world. It is a distinction that distinguishes between national sovereignty and transnational encroachment upon sovereignty.

America's constitutional order is defined by two hallmark structural features: the separation of powers and federalism. Our tripartite separation of powers at the federal level divides power between the legislative, executive, and judicial governmental departments, a division that has direct antecedents in both the centuries-old English constitutional system and the Enlightenment-era theorizing of the Frenchman Baron de Montesquieu.

But federalism was a more uniquely American political innovation. In our federalist system, both the national government and the state governments are sovereign over their own spheres of influence and authority. Most of the day-to-day governance was meant to unfold at the state or local levels. As James Madison explained in *Federalist* No. 45:

"The powers delegated by the proposed Constitution to the federal government are few and defined. Those which are to remain in the State governments are numerous and indefinite."

In America, therefore, both the federal and state governments are themselves partially sovereign. And it is We the People who are the true, ultimate sovereigns over all levels and institutions of our government. In America, government is supposed to work for the people—not the other way around.

But over the past century, America's sovereignty has too often been chipped away by the rise of transnational institutions that run roughshod over our own internal decision-making. From the United Nations to the International Criminal Court to the World Trade Organization, there has been a dangerous growth of institutions that make purportedly binding decisions over otherwise-sovereign nation-states. To be sure, some of these institutions are better than others. Some of them, perhaps, are more justifiable than others. But, by design, all of these transnational institutions are not democratically accountable—and certainly not to the American electorate—thus undermining our most basic conceptions of sovereignty in the Westphalian nation-state system.

This is hardly a problem that uniquely afflicts the United States. On the contrary, perhaps the single most iconic sovereignty-undermining transnational institution operating in the world today is the European Union. The once mighty and distinct peoples of Europe—with rich and varied languages, culture, history, currency, and governance—all subjugated their unique diversity and the democratic authority of their citizens to a supra-national, bureaucratic central authority. And with their thunderous "Brexit" vote of 2016 and delayed successful independence earlier this year, the United Kingdom restored its own sovereignty from the European Union's bureaucrats and mandarins. Brexit was, I hope, a watershed moment in the tug-of-war between sovereignty and transnationalism.

But the sovereignty restoration movement has not been limited to Britain. All across the world, from Viktor Orbán in Hungary to Jair

Bolsonaro in Brazil to Donald J. Trump right here in the United States, many nations have recently elected national leaders who have run on an express political platform of recapturing the national interest from the unaccountable clutches of the international community. And as recent books by Israeli political philosopher Yoram Hazony and *National Review* editor Rich Lowry have both detailed, the intellectual battle between nationalism and transnationalism has perhaps never been more front and center in the public eye than it is now.

Defending U.S. sovereignty has been a deep passion of mine for decades. And of all the cases I've ever litigated at the Supreme Court, one stands out as my favorite—as the most complex, the most fascinating, and by far the most consequential.

It was a case that goes to the heart of sovereignty. In *Medellín v. Texas*, we successfully defended the sovereignty of both the United States and the great state of Texas against the United Nations and its judicial arm, the World Court. And we stood up to a president—from my own party—to ensure that no president, Democrat or Republican, can ever give away U.S. sovereignty. We turn now to that story.

◆　　◆　　◆　　◆

What started with a horrific crime of violence evolved into a case that spanned decades and drew in ninety foreign nations, the World Court, and the president of the United States.

One hot, muggy summer evening, June 24, 1993, two teenage girls in Houston, Texas, were walking home and decided to take a shortcut. Around 11:15 p.m., they encountered the "Black and Whites Gang," who had assembled to initiate a new member. As the girls walked past, José Ernesto Medellín and his fellow gang members grabbed them, assaulted them, brutally raped them, and then murdered them both.

I grew up in Houston. Houston is a big city that has seen quite a bit of violent crime. Yet this crime shocked the conscience of the city. The horror and brutality those gang members unleashed on a fourteen-year-old girl and on a sixteen-year-old girl was unspeakable.

Later that evening, Medellín bragged to the family of another gang member about how proud he was of their horrific crime. He boasted about how he and his brother had kept a ring and a Disney watch as trophies of their crime.

Five days later, Medellín and his compatriots were arrested. And hours later, he hand-wrote a detailed confession to the crime. It remains one of the most bone-chilling things I have ever had the displeasure of reading. Without remorse, without hint of human compassion, he meticulously described how each girl had pleaded for her life prior to being brutally murdered.

Given his written confession and the overwhelming evidence of guilt, Medellín unsurprisingly was tried and convicted of murder during the course of a sexual assault—a capital offense. He was sentenced to death.

Years after his conviction, Medellín raised a brand-new issue in the case. It so happened that José Ernesto Medellín was a foreign national. He was born in Mexico, illegally immigrated to the United States, and lived in the United States for most of his life. So despite the fact that he grew up in America and could speak, read, and write English, he technically remained a Mexican national.

Under a treaty called the Vienna Convention on Consular Relations, every foreign national located in a nation that is a signatory to that treaty has a right to contact the consulate of his home country if he is charged with a serious crime and to receive assistance from his home country's consulate.

At his trial, Medellín never raised this issue, so the prosecutors never afforded him his right to contact the Mexican consulate. The first time Medellín raised the issue was in federal court in what is called a habeas corpus challenge. Federal criminal cases can be complicated, and death penalty cases are notoriously long and complex.

The way our criminal justice system works, there are two parallel systems: the state systems of justice and the federal system of justice. State courts are the courts that typically try murder cases. Medellín's case was tried in Texas state court, and his conviction and death sentence were affirmed by the Texas Court of Criminal Appeals—the highest criminal court in the state of Texas. But he never raised the issue of the Vienna Convention on Consular Relations until his federal habeas challenge—which was years after his criminal conviction in state court.

Habeas challenges are common, but in this case, after Medellín was convicted, the case also took a rather strange turn. The nation of Mexico sued the United States in the International Court of Justice, otherwise known as the World Court, the judicial arm of the United Nations. Mexico sued on behalf of Medellín and fifty other Mexican nationals who had committed murder in the United States and had been sentenced to death by the various state justice systems across the United States. Mexico argued that because those individuals had not been affirmatively told of their treaty right to contact the Mexican consulate, their murder convictions and death sentences must all be set aside.

Remarkably, the World Court agreed and issued an order to the United States to reopen the convictions of fifty-one murderers across the country. This was the first time in history that a foreign court had attempted to bind the U.S. justice system—much less to overturn settled criminal convictions. Medellín, in turn, argued that the U.S. justice system should be bound by the World Court decision. He argued, in effect, that he was legally entitled to a new trial.

Ordinarily, the rules of criminal trials are that defendants are required to affirmatively raise any legal defenses they might have. And the reason the system works this way is that if a criminal defendant raises a particular legal issue or legal defense, the court can appropriately address it right there and then. We don't want criminal defendants playing games with the courts—trying the case to verdict, hoping to get acquitted, and, if they don't get acquitted, raising the issue on appeal after the fact or in a federal habeas challenge. We don't want them to subsequently raise issues that the trial judge never had an opportunity to address.

Medellín, in fact, had a lawyer representing him in his trial. But he never raised any claim under the Vienna Convention on Consular Relations during his state trial. And if he had, it would have been very easy to vindicate those rights. The trial judge could simply have said, "OK, let the defendant contact the Mexican consulate and receive whatever assistance the consulate is willing to provide." It could have been resolved right there, on the spot, during trial. But Medellín's lawyer never raised the claim.

Under ordinary U.S. criminal law, if you fail to raise a claim at trial, that claim is forfeited. And you can't come back years later with a brand-new legal claim that you never raised in your own defense. But the World Court decided that the ordinary rules of American criminal law didn't matter. It didn't matter that Medellín and fifty other convicted murderers across the country had never raised their treaty claims in their state court trials. In the eyes of the World Court, the American judicial system was required to ignore its own law—to ignore our own rules—and to throw out the convictions on the basis of a claim that was never even raised at trial.

The World Court ruled for Mexico even though most countries on earth—including Mexico—don't allow collateral attacks to convictions at all. In other words, in most other countries, if you fail to raise a claim at trial or on appeal, it's game over. There is no habeas proceeding. The United States grants more procedural protections to foreign nationals in our courts than those foreign nations provide to American citizens, but the World Court decided that still wasn't enough.

Medellín went before the U.S. federal courts and argued that, based on the World Court's decision, his conviction should be overturned. The federal district court disagreed and so did the Fifth Circuit Court of Appeals. And so Medellín appealed the case to the U.S. Supreme Court.

I was the Texas SG at the time, and I ended up arguing the case not once, but twice, before the U.S. Supreme Court. The first time it went up on appeal was in 2005, and it precipitated a remarkable battle within the George W. Bush administration.

Remember the time. This was the beginning of President Bush's second term. Alberto Gonzales had just been named attorney general, and Condoleezza Rice was now secretary of state. The Bush administration was pivoting, with its leading actors trying to distance themselves from the perception of being rogue cowboys. Indeed, Condi was in the midst of what some were calling the "we love the world tour," traveling across Europe and being fêted abroad as the glamorous new secretary of state.

Gonzales and Rice disagreed on what to do in the case. Both had spent the first term of President Bush's administration in the White House; she as national security advisor and he as White House counsel. Both were deeply trusted and respected by President Bush. It was rare for the two to disagree. And yet here they did.

I'll never forget the forty-five-minute conference call that Greg Abbott—at the time my boss and the attorney general of Texas—and I both had with Harriet Miers, who was then the White House counsel. Abbott and I argued strenuously that under no circumstances should the Bush administration side with this child rapist and convicted murderer. And, even more so, under no circumstances should the U.S. government cede our cherished national sovereignty to the World Court of the United Nations.

This should have been an easy call. As governor of Texas, George W. Bush had himself rejected similar claims from convicted murderers, and Abbott and I both argued vigorously to Miers that he should do the same now.

Miers listened, and the issue appeared to be headed for an Oval Office showdown: Condi versus Al, head to head. The Department of Justice, to its credit, argued that the United States should do the right thing—fight the World Court and resist any usurpation of U.S. sovereignty. But the State Department, looking to curry favor abroad, argued for capitulation—to grant the authority sought by the World Court of the United Nations.

But before the issue came to a head in front of President Bush, DOJ blinked. Al and Condi agreed upon a compromise.

I found out about it shortly thereafter, when U.S. SG Paul Clement called me on the phone. "Ted, are you sitting down?" he asked. That's not an auspicious way to begin a conversation. "I have good news, and I have bad news," Paul continued. "The good news is that the Department of Justice is going to participate in the case before the Supreme Court and is going to agree with Texas that the World Court does not have authority over the U.S. justice system."

That sounded good. But the bad news, Paul told me, is that the president had just signed an order—a two-page "memorandum"—that purported to order the Texas state courts to obey the World Court anyway. Not because the treaties required it—to the contrary, DOJ agreed that they did not. But out of international "comity," our desire to make our allies happier.

Paul argued that I should be very happy with this outcome because, he said, the virtue of this novel theory that Justice was putting forward was that the president kept his finger on the trigger. Under this theory, Paul said, the president gets to decide when to use this new presidential power to order the state courts to obey foreign tribunals.

My response to Paul was twofold. I said that, number one, that doesn't give me a whole lot of comfort, given how the power is being exercised today, with the Department of Justice supporting a vicious child rapist and murderer. But I said, number two, "Paul, there came a pharaoh who knew not Joseph and his children." Even if I were to agree with you, I told Paul, that George W. Bush's having the power to decide if and when to exercise this authority over state court systems might be OK, what about the next president? And the next president? And the next president? No president, I told Paul, either has or ought to have that authority.

Nonetheless, that's the position the George W. Bush administration took.

The first time I argued the case, we won 5–4. But our victory was on a narrow, technical basis. Justice O'Connor, the swing justice appointed by President Reagan who had been pivotal in so many cases over her three decades on the Court, voted against us. But, miraculously, Justice Ruth

Bader Ginsburg voted with us, and, by a 5–4 ruling, the Court essentially punted the case and concluded that Medellín should have raised his claim in the state appellate court before he raised it in the federal court.

The case then took a two-year detour, back to the state courts, and in 2007 it returned once again to the U.S. Supreme Court. At that point, Chief Justice Rehnquist had passed away and had been replaced by Chief Justice Roberts. And Justice O'Connor had retired and been replaced by Justice Alito.

The second time I argued the case before the Supreme Court, the United States argued squarely against us. Indeed, Texas found itself in an unusual place. Arrayed against us were the World Court, the United Nations, ninety separate foreign nations (which together filed an amicus brief against us), and the president of the United States. And that president, of course, was not only a Republican, but a Texan with whom I had worked closely and on whose 2000 presidential campaign I had met my wife, Heidi. As we stood against this legal assault, most observers thought we would lose.

Returning to Sun Tzu's maxim that every battle is won by choosing the terrain on which it will be fought, I believe the most important issue in any case is framing the narrative. Any time I argued a case before the U.S. Supreme Court or before any other court, I spent hours and hours thinking about how to frame the central issue: what the judge or justice, when he or she went home that evening, would say to his six-year-old grandson who asked, "What did you do today, papa?"

I wanted to own that next sentence. If you can frame the narrative— if you can explain what the case is all about on terrain that will favor your position—then much more often than not, you will win. That holds true in law, politics, business, or life.

In this case, Medellín's narrative was not difficult to follow. Medellín wished for the question to be, "Can Texas flout the treaty obligations of the United States, the laws of the United States, and the president of the United States? And by the way, you know how Texas is about the death penalty...."

If that's the question—can Texas defy international treaties?—then we held a losing position. If our whole case depended on getting Justice Anthony Kennedy's swing vote on the merits, I didn't want that to be the central question.

Most litigants in my position would have defended Medellín as a federalism case. They would have argued that the World Court's order and the president's order violated the sovereign authority of the states. The problem with that defense is that it played right into Medellín's narrative. If this is a federalism case, then it's easy for them to portray Texas as a rogue state defying America's treaty commitments.

So instead, I decided to shift the narrative of the case and to focus on whether the World Court or the president could violate U.S. sovereignty. I framed it as a separation of powers case. Indeed, the opening line of the "summary of argument" section of my Supreme Court brief was: "This is a separation of powers case." The summary continued: "It implicates every axis of the structural limitations on government: president vis-à-vis Congress, president vis-à-vis the Supreme Court, international law vis-à-vis domestic law, federal law vis-à-vis the states, and, with a Möbius twist, president vis-à-vis the state judiciary."

Because we argued it as a separation of powers case, the first argument in our brief was about how the president's "memorandum" impermissibly intruded on the power of Congress. We argued that the president didn't have the authority to do this on his own. Instead, he needed the authority of Congress, either through a law passed by Congress and signed by the president or through a treaty signed by the president and ratified by the Senate, which only then could have the force of law in our justice system.

The second argument we made is that the presidential memorandum impermissibly intruded on the authority of the judiciary—a separation of powers argument about protecting the Supreme Court's own authority. We argued that the Supreme Court had previously concluded that the World Court's decision was not independently enforceable in U.S. courts, and the president didn't have the unilateral authority to change that Supreme Court determination.

This second argument gave me the opportunity to argue something before the Supreme Court that is exceptionally rare for an oral advocate: to argue for the core holding of *Marbury v. Madison*, one of the foundational cases of the Supreme Court in the early nineteenth century. In *Marbury*, Chief Justice John Marshall famously wrote—and I got to argue at oral argument—that it is "emphatically the duty of the Judicial Department to say what the law is."

It was only third in our brief, and very much as a tertiary concern, that we raised the federalism issue. Namely, that the presidential memorandum impermissibly intrudes on the authority of the states. But we directed the overwhelming majority of our time and force to defending the authority, under the Constitution, of Congress and the federal judiciary against presidential usurpation.

In defending the case, we also tried to assemble an unusual collection of allies. I asked my former boss Chuck Cooper, who had led the Office of Legal Counsel in the Reagan Justice Department and was considered one of the most vigorous defenders of presidential authority, to author a brief on behalf of former high-ranking officials at the Department of Justice. I asked Chuck if he would argue against the authority of the president to unilaterally bind the state courts. Chuck's willingness to take such a position, let alone the compelling brief that he crafted, conveyed a powerful message to those Supreme Court justices who might otherwise have been amenable to legal arguments for strong presidential authority.

I also sought out my old adversary in *Van Orden*, Erwin Chemerinsky, to join a separate brief of constitutional and international law scholars that also argued against the presidential assertion of power. A number of scholars joined—including not only Erwin, but also John Yoo, a former Supreme Court clerk for Clarence Thomas and now a professor of law, who had served in the Bush Justice Department and was widely considered the most vigorous academic proponent of strong presidential power.

To unify Erwin Chemerinsky and John Yoo on the same brief before the U.S. Supreme Court was no small feat. To get their support, I tried to pose hypotheticals of how such an unprecedented power might be abused by a subsequent president. To John, I had asked, "How do you think a President Hillary Clinton might use such a power?" To Erwin, I posed a different hypothetical, trying to conjure up the most terrifying specter he could imagine. I asked, "How do you think a President Dick Cheney would use such a power?" Each shuddered at the prospect.

Importantly, the Bush administration was not arguing that it was bound by treaties to take the position it did. Indeed, the Bush administration explicitly conceded that nothing in the treaties actually required it to cede to the World Court jurisdiction over our justice system. Instead, the Bush administration argued for what it admitted was an "unprecedented" authority—for the president, as a matter of sheer comity, to decide to bind the state courts anyway. Their argument boiled down to: any time the president believed it would make our allies happier, as a matter of foreign policy, the president could disregard state laws that our allies happened to disagree with.

To the conservatives joining this brief of legal scholars supporting us, I asked, "What might happen if a President Hillary Clinton decides that the marriage laws of the United States are politically inconvenient and that comity abroad would be furthered by setting them aside? Could Hillary Clinton do so? Or how about the death penalty laws we have? Most of our allies have long since abolished the death penalty, and there is no doubt a liberal president would earn hosannas for trying to do the same in America. Does the president need to try to pass a law through Congress to accomplish that, or can the president simply write a two-page memo that sets aside those state laws?"

To the liberals joining this brief of legal scholars supporting us, I asked, "If the president has this authority, what would stop a President Dick Cheney from setting aside California's environmental laws—which, after all, some of our allies find costly and inconvenient? Or perhaps setting aside states' punitive damages laws, which foreign companies certainly don't like paying if a jury verdict comes out against them?"

If the Bush administration was right that, in the exercise of foreign policy, the president could set aside inconvenient state laws, that had profound implications. And it had profound implications for everyone, no matter what someone might believe as a matter of public policy.

The Supreme Court oral argument in *Medellín v. Texas* was vigorously contested, and it featured at least one unusual twist. Now, many envision Supreme Court arguments as moments of soaring oratory—as advocates arguing passionately like Clarence Darrow or Dr. Martin Luther King Jr. But Supreme Court arguments are better thought of as active combat. One of the first things a lawyer notices before arguing before the Supreme Court is just how small the courtroom is. Although the gold-inlaid ceilings seem to extend high up into the heavens, the courtroom itself is remarkable for its intimacy. The oral advocate stands at the podium just a few feet away from the justices' bench. For decades, the bench was straight, with nine Justices sitting in a row before the advocate. Then, in January 1972, then-Chief Justice Warren Burger changed the bench so that the right and left sides of the bench are bent forward, almost encircling the advocate. When you argue before the Court, the justices are so close that you can practically reach out and shake the chief justice's hand.

Supreme Court oral arguments typically last one hour: thirty minutes for each side. Every argument begins the same way: "Mr. Chief Justice, and may it please the Court." But instead of soaring oration, an advocate is typically lucky if he or she even gets a few sentences out. In any hot or contested case, the justices will fire questions relentlessly. (In 2019, the Court changed its practice to allow advocates two minutes of uninterrupted argument at the outset, followed by twenty-eight minutes of merciless questioning.)

The justices' questions are not typically efforts to discover new information, whether factual or legal. Going into the argument in any close case, there are usually three or four justices who have made up their minds on one side, three or four justices who have made up their minds on the other side, and two or three justices who might be persuadable in the middle. The justices themselves almost never discuss a given case before oral argument. In the vast majority of cases, they haven't spoken a word to each other about the case before ascending the bench for oral argument. So the oral argument is typically the first time the justices discuss the case with each other. The questions are the vehicle by which they do so.

Typically, a justice who disagrees with your position will fire a question at you not with the purpose of discovering the answer, but with the purpose of demonstrating that your answer is so untenable or imbecilic that the swing justices couldn't possibly agree with your position. What makes arguing before the Supreme Court so invigorating is that these questions can often be among the first in a string of questions designed to lead you down a slippery slope. That slippery slope, inevitably, might lead you to an outcome that you couldn't possibly defend. And so an oral advocate has to respond immediately, and in a fraction of a second anticipate where the justice is going with the line of questioning and frame his answers in a way that he doesn't drive away the swing votes needed to win the case. It's unbelievably fast, and the adrenaline flows.

Rarely does an advocate get more than a sentence or two to respond to a question before another justice jumps in with yet another question. And the justices who agree with your position typically don't think you're arguing it the best way; they'll often ask "friendly" questions like, "Counsel, don't you really mean to say such and such?" Again, they are trying to argue through you to get to the swing justices who might be persuadable.

In the *Medellín* argument, in response to a question from Justice Stephen Breyer, I responded that there are "six separate reasons" why the decision of the World Court is not enforceable and binding upon the U.S. justice system. As I was working through the first reason, amidst a lengthy exchange primarily with Justice Breyer, Justice Kennedy interjected with a separate question. But at that point, Justice John Paul Stevens—the lion of the left, a small Midwestern man, unfailingly polite, always wearing a bow tie, with a brilliant mind and always the most dangerous of the liberals when it came to hostile questioning—interrupted. Justice Stevens stated: "It's critical to me to understand the effect of the judgment, and you said there are six reasons why it's not an ordinary judgment. I really would like to hear what those reasons are...without interruption from all of my colleagues."

Laughter engulfed the courtroom. A justice's asking to hear in full an advocate's line of argumentation, as bluntly and characteristically politely as Justice Stevens had requested it, is something that had never happened to me before at the Court, and it has not happened since. The other justices relented, for a few moments, and they allowed me the opportunity to lay out all six of the arguments I had for why the decision of the World Court was not enforceable and binding upon the U.S. justice system.

Ultimately when the decision came down, the Supreme Court agreed with us. Texas won, 6–3. The opinion was authored by Chief Justice Roberts, and it agreed with Texas across the board. It struck down the World Court's assertion of authority over the U.S. justice system, and it struck down the president's order as exceeding his authority under the Constitution.

Texas had argued that no foreign court has the authority to bind the American justice system and that no president, Republican or Democrat, has the constitutional authority to give away U.S. sovereignty. And the Supreme Court agreed.

Not only did we win the support of the more conservative members of the Court, but we also won the vote of Justice Kennedy and even Justice Stevens, the leader of the Court's liberal wing who had requested to hear my full line of argumentation during oral argument and who separately concurred with Chief Justice Roberts's majority opinion.

The stakes in that case were enormous. As legal scholar Ilya Shapiro put it at the time, "*Medellín* was a significant victory for national sovereignty and democratic legitimacy."

Medellín was decided in 2008—twelve years ago. We prevailed 6–3, but Justice Stevens has since been replaced by Justice Elena Kagan. And, although she has not yet squarely faced the question, there is little reason to believe Justice Kagan would vote differently than the three dissenters.

On August 5, 2008, José Ernesto Medellín was put to death at the Texas State Penitentiary at Huntsville. Medellín went to meet his Maker and face judgment for the unspeakable crimes he committed fifteen years earlier against two teenage girls.

On the day I argued the case, I stood on the steps of the Supreme Court consoling the parents of one of those girls. The pain was etched on their faces; they had gone through seemingly endless litigation, reliving over and over again the horror of their daughter's last night. My heart grieved for them—as a parent, I could only imagine their soul-wrenching agony. And yet, in *Medellín*, the dissenting justices were willing to extend those proceedings for many more years.

The case exposed a massive and far-reaching divide on the Court between those justices who would uphold American sovereignty and those justices willing to cede the ability to bind our justice system to the World Court and the United Nations, willing to allow the president the power to undermine our justice system and the rule of law.

On that fundamental issue, with the Court today, in all likelihood, we're just one vote away.

◆   ◆   ◆   ◆

As with virtually every other policy matter, on questions of national sovereignty and nationalism versus transnationalism, Democrats and the broader political left today have only become more radical.

The Obama administration chomped at the bit to empower the unaccountable mandarins working at transnational institutions at the expense of our own national sovereignty. Time and time again, Obama, alongside Secretaries of State Hillary Clinton and John Kerry, worked to elevate undemocratic institutions such as the United Nations. As the UN and other faceless bureaucracies from foreign nations were elevated, Obama concurrently diminished the capacity of the American people to make our own decisions about the future of our own nation through our elected officials.

One particularly galling example was the Obama Iran nuclear deal, otherwise known in Washington-speak as the Joint Comprehensive Plan of Action ("JCPOA"). At the time of the international and internal debate over this highly flawed accord, I was its most vociferous critic. From day one, the Iran nuclear deal was a foolhardy and dangerous capitulation to Tehran's jihadist regime. It was a devastating blow to America's security, to our ally Israel's security, and to the security and stability of the broader Middle East.

Iran's Islamic revolution erupted in 1979, as religious radicals overthrew the secular government and took 66 Americans hostage, eventually holding 52 of them for 444 days. While our hostages languished in captivity, President Jimmy Carter wrung his hands, unsure of what to do. He eventually approved a military rescue mission, but our helicopters crashed tragically in the desert under no opposing fire. Our hostages were finally released on January 20, 1981, the day that Ronald Reagan was sworn into office.

Against bullies and tyrants, weakness does not work. Only clarity and strength have any demonstrable record of success. History teaches repeatedly that appeasement is provocative, ironically increasing the chances of military conflict. As I have joked, there is a reason nobody studies at the Neville Chamberlain school of foreign policy.

The Ayatollah Khamenei hates America. He is a religious zealot who regularly leads mobs in chanting "Death to America." Indeed, Iran each year celebrates as a holiday "Death to America" day, commemorating their taking of our hostages in 1979. He routinely refers to Israel as "the little Satan," and the United States as "the great Satan."

Iran is the world's leading state sponsor of terrorism. Over the past four decades, they have spent tens of billions of dollars funding jihadists all over the world, in the Middle East, in Africa, in Europe, in South America, and in the United States.

The Obama Iran nuclear deal allowed over $100 billion in frozen offshore assets to flow into Iran, with the promise of hundreds of billions of dollars more in sanctions relief. Additionally $1.7 billion in cash was flown on pallets in the dark of night into Iran as ransom for hostages. Normally, laundering money on secret pallets of unmarked bills is indicative of wrongful conduct, and that was certainly true with this ill-advised deal.

As then-Secretary of State John Kerry later admitted less than a year after the nuclear deal was inked, "some" of the $150 billion in sanctions relief that the deal brought to fruition "will end up in the hands of the Iranian Revolutionary Guard Corps or other entities, some of which are labeled terrorists." Kerry admitted, that is, that the flooding of American dollars into Iran would be used to murder Americans. "I'm not going to sit here and tell you that every component of that [funding] can be prevented," Kerry continued.

If history teaches anything, it is that when people tell you they want to kill you, believe them. Or, at a minimum, don't give them hundreds of billions of dollars to help them accomplish their objective.

But, for whatever reason, Obama desperately wanted a deal with Iran. Indeed, Ben Rhodes, Obama's deputy national security advisor (and, it so happens, the brother of the head of CBS News), described their objective of completing an Iran nuclear deal as "the Obamacare of the second term" (which I think he meant as a compliment).

At the time, much of the rest of the world thought this plan was madness. I recall ambassadors from major European allies sitting in my office, asking for my help to try to stop the deal; the Obama administration was putting the full force of U.S. foreign policy behind it, and they wanted assistance pushing back.

On the face of the deal, there were numerous obvious failings: before any facilities could be inspected to determine if nuclear weapons were being developed, Iran had to receive twenty-four days advance notice (plenty of time to scrub the facility); certain "military" facilities were exempted from inspection (obviously, where Iran would base their nuclear weapon development); for one military facility where Iran had done nuclear weapons work, Iran would be trusted to "self-inspect"; and the deal gutted limitations on Iran's continuing to develop ICBMs (intercontinental ballistic missiles that would be used to carry a nuclear warhead to the United States). Nor did the deal put any constraints on Iran's continuing to fund anti-America and anti-Israel jihadists. And, by its own terms and according to even President Obama, as the deal began its "sunset" in a little over a decade, the international world would entirely allow Iran to develop everything it needed for nuclear weapons.

Any rational commander in chief should make clear and unequivocal: under no circumstances will the Ayatollah Khamenei *ever* be allowed to acquire nuclear weapons.

On March 3, 2015, Israel's prime minister Benjamin Netanyahu gave a powerful—even Churchillian—speech before a joint session of Congress, which, sadly, many Democrats boycotted. He explained: "Iran's regime is not merely a Jewish problem, any more than the Nazi regime was merely a Jewish problem. The six million Jews murdered by the Nazis were but a fraction of the 60 million people killed in World War II. So, too, Iran's regime poses a grave threat, not only to Israel, but also the peace of the entire world."

On September 9, 2015, I helped organize a rally against the Iran deal on the steps of the Capitol. Thousands came out to join us to oppose funding the world's leading state sponsor of terrorism. At the time, I was running for president, and I made the unusual decision to invite one of my opponents in the race, Donald J. Trump, to join me at the rally. Generally speaking, you don't invite your opponents to participate in your political rallies, but I cared passionately about the issue, and I knew that Trump's attendance would bring TV cameras like rats following the Pied Piper to the Capitol steps.

When Trump was elected president, I began working with him very closely, on a weekly or even a daily basis, on a number of issues, especially concerning foreign policy and national security. In the first few years of the administration, that was manifest most significantly in two interrelated policy decisions: moving our embassy in Israel to Jerusalem, and pulling out of the Iran deal.

During the 2016 presidential campaign I had pledged to make both decisions on my first day in office. And within the Trump administration, both proved hotly contested.

Both State and Defense were strongly opposed to moving our embassy in Israel. For years, Democratic and Republican presidents had promised to move our embassy to Jerusalem, and presidents of both parties had repeatedly broken that promise. For other countries, America puts our embassy in the capital city. But for Israel, our embassy was in Tel Aviv, because the Palestinians dispute Israel's right to have Jerusalem as their capital. For that reason, Secretary of State Rex Tillerson and Defense Secretary James Mattis both argued that moving our embassy would enrage the enemies of Israel and impede the Middle East peace process.

I strongly disagreed. I urged President Trump that strength and clarity were the only ways to make progress in the Middle East. And if we moved the embassy to Jerusalem, our Arab allies—in Egypt and Jordan and Saudi Arabia—even though they would feel obliged politically to publicly denounce the decision, would be secretly overjoyed. I argued those allies would reason that any president with the courage and backbone to stand up to the torrent of criticism from the world and the *New York Times* on the issue of Jerusalem, would maybe, just maybe, have the courage also to withdraw from the Obama Iran nuclear deal, which they rightly viewed as profoundly dangerous to their security and to ours.

President Trump agreed with my advice and overruled his own State Department and Defense Department. He courageously did what prior presidents had feared to do: he moved the U.S. embassy in Israel, and I was there in Jerusalem the day our embassy opened, on the seventieth anniversary of the creation of the modern state of Israel. It was a powerful, moving experience. At the opening, I visited with multiple Americans and Israelis moved to tears, including one woman who was a Holocaust survivor and simply said, "I never thought I would live to see it happen."

I do not believe it was a coincidence that within one week of opening our embassy in Jerusalem we also announced that we were withdrawing from the Obama Iran deal.

As with the embassy, both State and Defense fought hard to prevent it from happening. Tillerson and Mattis both vigorously defended the deal and pressed Trump hard to stay bound by it. Repeatedly, I made the case directly to President Trump that we should pull out of the deal, that sending billions to a religious zealot who wants to murder us was profoundly dangerous.

And, as with the embassy, Trump ended up agreeing with me and overruling both State and Defense. I believe that pulling out of the Obama Iran deal was the single most significant national security decision made by President Trump.

That decision also highlights the ongoing threat to national sovereignty we see from modern-day Democrats and from transnational institutions. In support of the deal, Secretary Mattis, both publicly and privately, kept saying "a deal is a deal" and "when America gives her word, we have to live up to it." That was wrong.

Put simply, in the Iran deal, the United States did *not* give its word. There are two ways, and two ways only, that binding law is made under our Constitution: either a statute is passed by both Houses of Congress and signed by the president, or a treaty is signed by the president and ratified by two-thirds of the Senate. Those are the only two ways the United States can make binding commitments.

President Obama deliberately circumvented the constitutional process. He knew he didn't have the votes to have Congress pass the Iran deal by statute, nor did he have the votes for the Senate to ratify it as a treaty. So he decided to ignore both.

Instead, Obama signed the Joint Comprehensive Plan of Action as an international agreement between Iran, the United States, the United Kingdom, France, Germany, Russia, and China. It was announced not from Washington, but in Vienna on July 14, 2015.

And he didn't take it to the elected branches in Congress to be adopted or ratified; instead, he took it to the United Nations Security Council.

Rather than negotiating a treaty that could earn the support of two-thirds of the Senate—admittedly no easy task—the Obama administration chose to "implement" the nuclear deal by having Ambassador to the United Nations Samantha Power cast a UN Security Council vote in favor of UN Security Council Resolution 2231, which was the UN's way of ratifying JCPOA.

But, as *Medellín* made clear, the United Nations cannot make binding law in the United States.

Not only was Obama's catastrophic deal not ratified by the U.S. Senate, it was actively opposed by the Senate. A bipartisan majority of the Senate (58–42) voted *against* the JCPOA and made unequivocally clear that we believed it to be disastrous foreign policy.

When it comes to presidential power, the seminal case laying out the parameters and limits of the president's authority is the steel seizure case (*Youngstown Sheet & Tube Co. v. Sawyer*), in which the Supreme Court struck down Harry S Truman's attempted seizure of steel plants during the Korean War. The central analysis was in Justice Robert Jackson's concurring opinion, which explained that "when the President takes measures incompatible with the expressed or implied will of Congress, his power is at its lowest ebb, for then he can rely only upon his own constitutional powers minus any constitutional powers of Congress over the matter."

Justice Jackson is universally considered one of the most brilliant justices ever to have served. He was a self-taught lawyer who never went to law school, and he became solicitor general and attorney general for Franklin Delano Roosevelt before FDR put him on the Court. After World War II, Jackson took a leave of absence from the Court to serve as the chief prosecutor at Nuremburg, brilliantly trying the Nazi leadership for war crimes. His Nuremburg opening statement was majestic. One passage I long ago committed to memory:

> That four great nations, flushed with victory and stung with injury, stay the hand of vengeance and voluntarily submit their captive enemies to the judgment of the law is one of the most significant tributes that Power have ever paid to Reason.

As a young lawyer, William Rehnquist was a law clerk to Justice Jackson, whom he admired immensely. Every Christmas, Jackson would give each of that year's law clerks a picture of the Court autographed by all nine justices. On each photograph he would write an identical inscription; as the Chief's read, "To William Rehnquist, with the friendship and esteem of Robert Jackson." When Rehnquist became a justice, he continued the tradition; on the wall of my Senate office is a picture of the Court inscribed "with the friendship and esteem of William H. Rehnquist." John Roberts, too, was a Rehnquist clerk; he has the same photograph, and he has continued the tradition, giving his own clerks pictures "with the friendship and esteem of John G. Roberts." Three generations of justices over seventy years have used word-for-word the identical inscription.

Returning to the JCPOA, President Obama's authority was at what Justice Jackson described as the nadir of presidential power—exercised in direct opposition to the will of Congress.

For that reason, Secretary Mattis was wrong. The United States did not "give its word"; instead, Obama made a political promise and tried to use the United Nations to carry out an end run around the constitutional provisions for duly ratifying a treaty.

As we litigated in *Medellín*, these provisions comprise vital checks and balances in our constitutional system. Binding law in the United States cannot be made without the concurrence of *both* elected branches: either as a statute, with a majority of both Houses and the president's signature (or, if vetoed, with the override of two-thirds of both Houses), or as a treaty, with the president's signature and two-thirds of the Senate.

Especially in matters of foreign policy and national security, those checks and balances are critical to protecting our nation's interests. No one president, of either party, has the unilateral power to make binding law. The treaty power is divided between the president and the Senate because the Framers, in their wisdom, understood that it is only healthy to commit the nation to foreign obligations and entanglements when a directly accountable institution, such as a chamber of Congress, agrees to the commitment. It is for the same reason that the Constitution gives Congress the power to declare war.

And the Senate, in particular, has historically had a central role in foreign policy. Here's how Senator Henry Cabot Lodge, legendary chairman of the Senate Foreign Relations Committee, put it: "War can be declared without the assent of the Executive, and peace can be made without the assent of the House...but neither war nor peace can be made without the assent of the Senate."

The good news about Obama's circumvention of the constitutional treaty requirements was that it permitted President Trump to pull out of the deal entirely and instantaneously. Obama famously said, in defending unilateral presidential power, "I have a pen and I have a phone." As he learned with the JCPOA, if you live by the pen, you die by the pen.

◆　　◆　　◆　　◆

Another flash point where U.S. sovereignty is being threatened concerns the International Criminal Court, which is more and more trying to intervene in the domestic affairs of Western democracies—including both the United States and Israel. The ICC, much like the World Court, is an unaccountable transnational tribunal located in The Hague, Netherlands.

The ICC ostensibly exists to prosecute international war crimes and crimes against humanity. But ever since its inception in 2002, it has had a morally perverse obsession with liberal Western democracies who act in legally and morally justifiable self-defense against radical Islamic terrorist groups.

For a number of years, the ICC has placed in its crosshairs American troops operating against terrorist enemies in Islamic nations. In fact, earlier this year, the ICC directly authorized an investigation into alleged U.S. "war crimes" in Afghanistan.

The Trump administration has pressed back hard against this threat to our sovereignty. The State Department rightly announced that it would issue a visa ban on any ICC personnel involved in the ICC investigations, which prevents them from traveling to the United States. Here's what Secretary of State Mike Pompeo said in response to the ICC "investigation" of America:

> This is a truly breathtaking action by an unaccountable political institution masquerading as a legal body....It is all the more reckless for this ruling to come just days after the United States signed a historic peace deal on Afghanistan, which is the best chance for peace in a generation. The United States is not a party to the ICC, and we will take all necessary measures to protect our citizens from this renegade, so-called court.

Like other transnational institutions such as the United Nations or the World Court, the ICC has long been plagued by anti-American animus and virulent anti-Semitism, the latter of which leads them to be obsessed with attacking Israel. When terrorists attack innocent civilians in Israel and the Israeli Defense Force strikes back at the terrorists, the ICC is wont to consider Israel's self-defense a "war crime." Of course, the two are not morally equivalent; Hamas terrorists target civilians and innocent women and children. In Gaza, they placed their terror headquarters in the basement of a hospital, using Palestinian mothers and their infants being delivered above as human shields. They were caught storing their rockets in an elementary school for the same reason. As Prime Minister Netanyahu put it—in the midst of Hamas missiles raining down—"We are using missile defense to protect our civilians, and they're using their civilians to protect their missiles."

The first time I met Prime Minister Netanyahu was in 2012, just a few weeks after I had been elected to the Senate. It was my first of four trips to Israel, and much of my discussion with Netanyahu concerned

Medellín and how I could help protect both Israel and the United States from the ICC. I've met with him many times and have gotten to know him well.

But one meeting in particular stands out. I was in Jerusalem and had a meeting scheduled for the next day with the prime minister. The American ambassador (appointed by Obama) told me that he insisted on joining us in the meeting. I told him no, he wasn't invited. He responded by threatening to pull my security.

This was obviously a bluff. It was clear that then-Secretary of State John Kerry had told him that under no circumstances should I be allowed to meet alone with Netanyahu. So I replied, "Fine, pull my security. We'll hire private security within the hour. You're still not invited to the meeting."

The confrontation had an almost comical element to it. The two of us were standing outside the Knesset (the Israeli parliament), *literally* bumping chests. Inevitably, he backed down.

The next day, I met privately with Netanyahu in his personal office. We smoked Cuban cigars—Montecristos, a personal favorite—and spent over an hour talking about Israel, America, national security, and geopolitics. It was surreal, and I felt remarkably blessed to be friends with such an extraordinary leader.

But, in my most recent meeting with Bibi (as he's called), we returned to the ICC. He was in Washington in early 2020, and the two of us had breakfast together at Blair House (the White House guest house where he was staying). At the meeting, Netanyahu suggested a strategy: try to get the UN Security Council to pass a resolution that the ICC cannot proceed against citizens of any nation that is not a party to the Rome Statute (which created the ICC).

This would benefit Israel and the United States. To get through, it would take the agreement of all five permanent members of the Security Council. Russia and China, Bibi reasoned, might well agree because they don't want to be hauled before the ICC. And France and the United Kingdom might agree if the U.S. really pressed them.

And, if the Security Council passed that resolution, it couldn't be undone without another Security Council resolution—which any of the five could veto. Essentially, it would reverse the default.

One of the things I admire most about Prime Minister Netanyahu is how strategic he is, and, at the time of writing, I'm pressing hard to carry out his plan. If we succeed, it will be a kind of jujitsu: using the rules of a transnational institution against another transnational institution to protect our sovereignty from outside assaults.

Regardless of whether this particular effort is successful, the continued onslaught against sovereignty will continue. From the United Nations, the World Court, and the ICC. From today's increasingly radicalized Democratic Party. And, when it comes to defending our sovereignty at the Supreme Court today, we're just one vote away.

CHAPTER 5

ABORTION AND
GONZALES V. CARHART

O n January 22, 1973, the Supreme Court and judicial nominations
fundamentally changed, and the character of our electoral democracy was profoundly altered.

Under our constitutional system, most public policy issues are left
to elected legislators. And for nearly 200 years, that was the case with
abortion laws, as well. For two centuries, each of the state legislatures
decided what laws would govern the practice of abortion in their
states. As a result, state laws varied as different legislatures and electorates came to different determinations about the appropriate
standard.

But in the decision of *Roe v. Wade*, the Supreme Court decreed that
the people no longer had that authority. Abortion is a deeply personal
issue on which passions run high. Many who favor a legal right to abortion are deeply committed to that proposition. And many who favor the
robust protection of unborn children are every bit as fervent.

Our constitutional system allows for differing views to play out
through the democratic process. But the Supreme Court determined that
somehow abortion was different. One will scour the Constitution in vain

trying to find any reference at all to abortion. The word is found nowhere in the Constitution, nowhere in the Bill of Rights, and yet, in the Court's opinion, authored by Justice Blackmun, this brand-new constitutional right was created out of whole cloth.

At the time *Roe* was handed down, many liberal-leaning states across America were already in the process of expanding access to abortion. A national conversation was playing out in real-time. To borrow Justice Louis Brandeis's famous formulation, the states were properly serving their constitutional roles as our "laboratories of democracy." But the Court short-circuited that profoundly important debate by fabricating this newfound constitutional right in *Roe*. Rather than dousing the flames, the Court's ruling poured gasoline on the fire. In the words of Justice Ruth Bader Ginsburg, herself a lifelong advocate of expanded access to abortion, the Court's decision in *Roe* "seemed to have stopped the momentum on the side of change."

When it comes to the right to life, I am deeply and unequivocally pro-life. I believe that every child is an incredible gift from God and should be protected in law. For many Americans, being pro-life is a reflection of their religious faith. For observant Jews or faithful Christians, there is a strong scriptural foundation for protecting the innocent lives of unborn children. For example, Jeremiah 1:5 declares: "Before I formed you in the womb I knew you, before you were born I set you apart...." And Psalms 139:13–16 tells us,

> For you created my inmost being; you knit me together in my mother's womb. I praise you because I am fearfully and wonderfully made; your works are wonderful, I know that full well. My frame was not hidden from you when I was made in the secret place, when I was woven together in the depths of the earth. Your eyes saw my unformed body; all the days ordained for me were written in your book before one of them came to be.

Likewise, in the New Testament, Luke 1:41–44 recounts, "When Elizabeth heard Mary's greeting, the baby leaped in her womb.... [And she exclaimed,] when the sound of your greeting reached my ears, the baby leaped in my womb for joy."

But one need not be a person of faith to be pro-life. Indeed, there are compelling personal, legal, constitutional, and philosophical reasons to support protecting the most vulnerable and defenseless among us. Every parent will remember that first magical moment when you looked at your child's sonogram. When you saw your daughter or son move or kick or suck their thumb. The pride, the love, the pure amazement of hearing that heartbeat and seeing that incredible, living, tiny child. We talk to our children before they are born, we play music for our children before they are born, we are deeply connected to our children long before birth.

That's one of the reasons why, tragically, among abortion's millions of victims, are so many mothers who experience grief, pain, regret, guilt, and depression for decades afterwards. In 2019, the movie *Unplanned* told the powerful true story of Abby Johnson, who spent eight years working for Planned Parenthood until the horror of what she saw and experienced drove her to leave and become a leading pro-life activist. The movie is brutally real and can be difficult to watch, but it is also personal, beautiful, and deeply moving. Abby, in making the movie, said she wanted it to be "a love letter to those working in the abortion industry," and to help provide them and so many grieving mothers a pathway out.

Turning to the legal and constitutional basis for protecting life, consider Thomas Jefferson's language from the Declaration of Independence, which committed our young nation to the proposition that "all men are created equal, that they are endowed by their Creator with certain unalienable Rights, that among these are Life, Liberty and the pursuit of Happiness."

The reader will note that "Life" is the very first "unalienable Right" listed. It is the first natural right—the very securing of which, Jefferson goes on to tell us, is why "[g]overnments are instituted among Men."

Securing the right to life was the preeminent reason that America rebelled against the British Crown and that America came into existence.

When our Constitution was adopted, and for over a century thereafter, abortion was uniformly defined as a crime, and the lives of unborn children were protected by law. For the same reason, the Hippocratic oath, taken by doctors for over 2000 years—which traces back to the Greek Hippocrates, the "Father of Medicine"—provided expressly, "I will give no deadly medicine to anyone if asked, nor suggest any such counsel; and in like manner I will not give to a woman a pessary to produce abortion."

Protecting human life is the central responsibility of the law, and yet those who are most vulnerable—the unborn—are completely unable to speak out for themselves. As Ronald Reagan once quipped, "I've noticed that everyone who is for abortion has already been born."

In the Senate, I have been proud to stand for life throughout my career. One notable instance came early in my Senate tenure, following the horrifying details that emerged surrounding late-term abortionist and now convicted murderer Kermit Gosnell. The facts of the case were gruesome. Even *The Atlantic* (hardly a conservative publication) wrote about it in 2013 and is worth quoting at length:

> The grand jury report in the case of Kermit Gosnell, 72, is among the most horrifying I've read. "This case is about a doctor who killed babies and endangered women. What we mean is that he regularly and illegally delivered live, viable babies in the third trimester of pregnancy—and then murdered these newborns by severing their spinal cords with scissors," it states. "The medical practice by which he carried out this business was a filthy fraud in which he overdosed his patients with dangerous drugs, spread venereal disease among them with infected instruments, perforated their wombs and bowels—and, on at least two occasions, caused their deaths."...

One former employee described hearing a baby screaming after it was delivered during an abortion procedure. "I can't describe it. It sounded like a little alien," she testified. Said the *Philadelphia Inquirer* in its coverage, "Prosecutors have cited the dozens of jars of severed baby feet as an example of Gosnell's idiosyncratic and illegal practice of providing abortions for cash to poor women pregnant longer than the 24-week cutoff for legal abortions in Pennsylvania."

At trial in Pennsylvania state court, the jury convicted Gosnell of three counts of homicide of three infants who were born alive during attempted abortion procedures and also of involuntary manslaughter of one woman during an abortion procedure. He was sentenced to life, plus thirty years.

In the wake of Gosnell's conviction, I joined my friend Senator Mike Lee in fighting to try to find out how many other Kermit Gosnells there might be across our nation. Together, we introduced a Senate resolution calling on Congress and state governments to both investigate and prevent abusive, unsanitary, dangerous, and illegal late-term abortion practices across America. Speaking on the Senate floor, I urged,

> Everyone in this body should be supporting an investigation to make sure there are not other Kermit Gosnells across this country. Everyone who proclaims to be a champion for women and children should enthusiastically support this resolution. Anyone who proclaims himself a champion dedicated to helping the most vulnerable should be supporting this resolution.

Sadly, the Democrats objected on the floor and blocked any congressional investigation.

But the Gosnell horror show, as utterly tragic as it was, represents one specific instance of abortion policy. From a broader legal perspective, the question facing any society is whether the rule of law should presume in favor of life.

History is filled with sad and sorry examples of legal rules presuming against life, from the *Dred Scott* Supreme Court decision that barbarically justified treating African-American slaves as "property" and not as humans, to the Nazi propaganda dehumanizing Jews that helped give rise to the genocidal murder of the Holocaust. There are countless other examples. Predictably, whenever the law has presumed against life, the results have been horrifying.

I believe the law should presume in favor of life.

Importantly, if there comes a day when a majority of the Court overrules *Roe v. Wade*, the result would not be that abortion would suddenly be made illegal across America. Instead, if *Roe* were overruled, the state of the law would return to the status quo ante—meaning that questions of abortion would be left, once again, to elected state legislatures.

Although I am strongly pro-life, it is clear that, if *Roe* were overturned, at least right now, a number of states would not choose to enact robust legislation protecting unborn life. And for those of us who aspire to arrive at the day when the law protects every human life, from conception to natural death, we will have to work hard to change the hearts and minds of a considerable number of Americans for that to occur.

Encouragingly, those changes have been occurring; although there are some issues on which our cultural mores are moving in a decidedly harmful direction, America is steadily growing more and more pro-life. Our efforts to persuade have yielded fruit, and the movement has been fueled by two additional factors: (1) on abortion, national Democrats have gotten much more extreme, and (2) scientific advancement has conclusively demonstrated that unborn children feel pain and suffer during late-term abortions, and medical science has now made it possible for infants born at earlier and earlier points to survive and thrive outside the womb.

Were the matter to be resolved through the democratic process, it would enable everyone who has strong views on the subject to have a voice in the resolution. Five unelected judges wouldn't decide the question

for all of us. Here, *what* the people decide is not the only relevant factor—*who* decides is also crucial.

Legislatures can hear evidence, can hear testimony, can weigh conflicting policy arguments, and can structure different standards to meet
different circumstances. The Court's opinion in *Roe* attempted to fulfill
precisely that legislative function, somehow divining in the Constitution
differing standards that happened to reflect the justices' flawed and
limited understanding of medical science. Putting on their legislative hats,
the Court decreed that differing constitutional standards would apply
for the first trimester of pregnancy, for the second trimester of pregnancy,
and for the third trimester of pregnancy. Needless to say, justices are not
medical doctors. Nor are they legislators. Neither is the court system
particularly well suited to resolving contested issues of science. And yet,
in *Roe*, the Court purported to do just that.

The Court acknowledged that the word "abortion" appears nowhere
in the Constitution. *Roe* purported to find this newly created constitutional right hidden in the shadows. Specifically, *Roe* relied on a prior
case, *Griswold v. Connecticut*, which had engaged in mental gymnastics
to conclude that the Court's cases "suggest that specific guarantees in
the Bill of Rights have penumbras, formed by emanations from those
guarantees that help give them life and substance."

For those who may not follow the metaphysical language, a penum-
bra is a ten-penny word for a shadow. So, the Court was saying, the rights
in the Bill of Rights have "emanations," which cast "penumbras," and
in those shadows is where this new right was supposedly discovered. All
unbeknownst to the Framers and over a century's worth of elected
legislatures.

That is not law. It is decreeing a policy outcome that the justices
happen to like.

Criticism of *Roe* as a judicial opinion has been nearly universal. In
his dissent in *Doe v. Bolton* (the companion case to *Roe*), Justice Byron
White (the lone justice appointed by President John F. Kennedy) wrote,
joined by then-Justice Rehnquist:

I find nothing in the language or history of the Constitution to support the Court's judgment. The Court simply fashions and announces a new constitutional right for pregnant mothers...and, with scarcely any reason or authority for its action, invests that right with sufficient substance to override most existing state abortion statutes. The upshot is that the people and the legislatures of the 50 states are constitutionally disentitled to weigh the relative importance of the continued existence and development of the fetus, on the one hand, against a spectrum of possible impacts on the mother, on the other hand. As an exercise of raw judicial power, the Court perhaps has authority to do what it does today; but, in my view, its judgment is an improvident and extravagant exercise of the power of judicial review that the Constitution extends to this Court.

Likewise, Professor Geoffrey Stone, the former dean of the University of Chicago Law School and a clerk for Justice Brennan (who joined the majority), conceded the year *Roe* was decided that "[e]veryone in the Supreme Court, all the justices, all the law clerks knew it was 'legislative' or 'arbitrary.'" And Justice Blackmun, *Roe*'s author, knew it as well. When Justice William O. Douglas released his papers to the public in 1988, they included internal Court memos from when *Roe* was decided. Included was a memo from Justice Blackmun to the other justices explaining why he had determined to set the first cutoff at the first trimester (the first thirteen weeks of pregnancy): "This is arbitrary, but perhaps any other selected point, such as quickening or viability (of the fetus), is equally arbitrary."

Of course, the purpose of the Supreme Court is not to draw arbitrary lines, nor to legislate public policy. As Yale Law School Professor (and later dean of Stanford Law School) John Hart Ely observed, *Roe v. Wade* "is bad because it is bad constitutional law, or rather because it is not constitutional law and gives almost no sense of an obligation to try to be."

Another liberal commentator, Edward Lazarus, himself a former clerk for Justice Blackmun, agreed: "As a matter of constitutional interpretation and judicial method, *Roe* borders on the indefensible. I say this as someone utterly committed to the right to choose, as someone who believes such a right has grounding elsewhere in the Constitution instead of where *Roe* placed it, and as someone who loved *Roe*'s author like a grandfather...."

In the nearly five decades since *Roe*, few if any issues have contributed more to polarization, anger, and division in our political process than has the arrogance of a Supreme Court majority declaring that the people had no right to decide the issue of abortion for themselves. As a result of *Roe*, Supreme Court nominations and confirmations are now gladiatorial battles. Robert Bork's and Clarence Thomas's bloody confirmation spectacles were the direct result of the justices' setting themselves up as arbiters of an issue that otherwise would have been left to the people.

Likewise, the sad carnival attached to the confirmation of Brett Kavanaugh was driven, at its heart, by the Court's usurpation of power in *Roe*. Indeed, after Justice Kavanaugh was confirmed, one of the lead lawyers who presented the uncorroborated sexual assault allegations against then-Judge Kavanaugh admitted publicly that savaging the reputation of a Supreme Court nominee thought to be skeptical of *Roe* is "part of what motivated" her client, Dr. Christine Blasey Ford. As a result, Kavanaugh "will always have an asterisk next to his name," Dr. Ford's lawyer said, so that "when he takes a scalpel to *Roe v. Wade*, we will know who he is, we know his character."

Following *Roe*, our nation convulsed and divided into two warring camps: pro-life and pro-choice, although neither uses the terminology preferred by the other. Had the issue remained in the hand of elected legislatures, those warring camps would have had a natural outlet: an avenue to express their views, to make their arguments, to marshal their scientists, to present their evidence. They would have had myriad elections in which to engage, and our country would have reflected a diversity of views. Nobody believes California would choose to enact the same abortion laws that Texas would. Or that New York would enact the same laws as Alabama. Part of the genius of our Constitution's Framers was establishing a system in which fifty states can enact fifty different standards to reflect the values and policy judgments of their respective citizens. But when nine unelected judges instead decree what is and is not acceptable on a policy as personal and far-reaching as abortion, it produces enormous social division.

Everyone thought *Roe* was going away thirty years ago. President Ronald Reagan nominated three new justices who were confirmed to the Court. Sandra Day O'Connor was Reagan's first nominee to the Court, and she became both the first woman nominated and the first woman to serve on the Court. Antonin Scalia was the second Reagan nominee to the Court, and Anthony Kennedy was third. At the same time that Reagan nominated Scalia, he elevated William Rehnquist to be chief justice of the United States. Then, President George Herbert Walker Bush had two more Justices confirmed: David Souter and Clarence Thomas.

In 1992, the case that most observers believed would return the issue of abortion to the elected state legislatures made its way to the Court. In *Planned Parenthood v. Casey*, Court-watchers, the media, the legal academy, and the political world all counted noses and assumed the votes were finally there to end the Supreme Court's dominance of abortion issues.

But sadly, when the Court issued its opinion, three of the justices expected by observers to respect the limited role of the Court—a role constrained to the constitutional text—made a different decision instead. Justices Kennedy, O'Connor, and Souter joined together in a rare joint opinion. Typically, a given opinion is authored by a particular justice, and right at the front of the opinion, it will say which justice authored that opinion. Other justices then can choose to join an opinion or not. Or, alternatively, they can write a concurrence (agreeing with the result but for different reasons) or a dissent (disagreeing with the result).

In *Casey*, the "joint opinion" has no author. Instead, each of the three justices sought to hide behind the others. One portion of *Casey* is particularly notable, and it has since been acknowledged that it was authored by Justice Kennedy. Justice Kennedy opined that "at the heart of liberty is the right to define one's own concept of existence, of meaning, of the universe, and of the mystery of human life."

Pause for a moment to reflect upon what particular expertise lawyers or judges might have about the "meaning of the universe," or about the "mystery of human life." If we are resolving existential questions, who in their right mind would choose unelected lawyers in black robes to make those decisions for us? If, on the other hand, we are choosing arbiters to apply statutes or the text of the Constitution, then relying on judges makes good sense.

Casey shocked and astonished observers on both left and right and ushered in even greater anger and division over the question of life. Although it refashioned the legal framework the Court set down in *Roe*, the core holding of an individual constitutional right to abort an unborn child was upheld.

Shortly after *Casey*, newly elected Democratic President Bill Clinton stood on the floor of the House of Representatives and expressed a desire that abortion be "safe, legal, and rare."

That is no longer the Democratic position. In the three decades since, the leadership of the Democratic Party has grown more and more extreme on the question of abortion. Nationally, opinion polls show that roughly 9 percent of Americans support unlimited abortion on-demand up until the moment of birth. And yet, increasingly, that is becoming the uniform position of the Democratic Party. Leading politicians like Bernie Sanders and Democratic National Committee Chairman Tom Perez have expressed, as they both did in 2020, that there is "no place" in the Democratic Party for pro-life Democrats.

In the aftermath of *Casey*, the views of Americans grew steadily more pro-life while Democratic Party leadership grew more extreme.

Pro-life activists began focusing on changing people's hearts and minds by adopting an incremental legislative strategy.

One common legislative strategy was to enact parental consent statutes for minors seeking to procure abortions. In fact, in *Casey* itself, the Court upheld the Commonwealth of Pennsylvania's requirement that minors must obtain the informed consent of at least one parent or guardian prior to obtaining an abortion. This was despite the fact that *Casey* also upheld *Roe*'s core holding of an individual constitutional right to abort an unborn child. The Court deemed that such parental consent requirements do not pose an "undue burden" on a woman's right to abort an unborn child.

In *Ayotte v. Planned Parenthood of Northern New England*, a case that reached the Court in 2006, I helped defend the constitutionality of the state of New Hampshire's own parental notification law. I was Texas SG, and we filed an amicus brief at the Court on behalf of Texas and seventeen other states. In our brief, we argued that New Hampshire's parental notification law was constitutional, and that forty-three out of fifty states had laws requiring either parental notification or parental consent for a minor to get an abortion. These state laws included a judicial bypass for abusive parents, but, in the ordinary case, these laws existed, in Justice Kennedy's words, so that a parent or guardian could give a "lonely or even terrified minor advice that is both compassionate and mature."

We argued, procedurally, that the court of appeals had erred in ruling broadly and striking down New Hampshire's law. The Court ended up agreeing with our narrow procedural argument, and that produced a rare unanimous abortion decision. By a vote of 9–0, the Court vacated the lower court's judgment, which in turn allowed the New Hampshire statute to stand.

In addition to parental consent requirements, the pro-life movement's incremental legislative effort to change hearts and minds on the issue of life has also included passing legal prohibitions of the gruesome practice of so-called "partial-birth abortion." As we saw with Gosnell, partial-birth abortion is a late-term procedure in which the physician partially delivers the unborn child and then, with the infant's head still in the mother's womb, uses scissors and forceps to pierce the skull and end the life of the child. Even many Americans who consider themselves pro-choice are horrified at the prospect of late-term abortions, and of partial-birth abortions in particular.

And so nearly thirty states across the country passed laws prohibiting this barbaric procedure. But because the Court had seized control of the abortion issue from state legislatures, declaring abortion to be a constitutionally protected right in *Roe* and *Casey*, activists on the left immediately brought litigation challenging those laws. And in 2000, the Court considered a challenge to Nebraska's partial-birth abortion law, in the case of *Stenberg v. Carhart*. Showing just how far the Court had gone, by a 5–4 vote the Court struck down Nebraska's law, concluding that it was unconstitutional because it lacked a sufficiently broad exception for the "health" of the mother.

To be sure, the Nebraska law did include an exception to protect the "life" of the mother. But five justices on the Supreme Court concluded that was not enough and that partial-birth abortion must be allowed whenever a physician concluded it advanced broader "health" concerns, including the avoidance of depression or other possible harm to a woman's mental health. Because an abortion doctor—whose entire revenue stream comes from performing as many abortions as possible—could diagnose depression or mental health concerns with virtually every abortion, the effect of the Supreme Court's ruling was to demand that the exception be written so broadly that it would eliminate the rule. Thus, notwithstanding the overwhelming national bipartisan consensus of voters against partial-birth abortion, the Court decreed that the states lacked the constitutional authority to effectively prohibit the practice.

Shortly thereafter, George W. Bush was elected president, and in 2003 he signed into law a federal prohibition on partial-birth abortion. Following the well-established pattern, activist groups immediately returned to the courts, challenging that law. The named plaintiff, LeRoy

Carhart, was in fact the very same abortion doctor who had challenged the Nebraska state law in *Stenberg*. And once again, the case returned to the Supreme Court in the form of *Gonzales v. Carhart*.

As Texas SG, I authored a brief on behalf of Texas and twelve other states in support of the constitutionality of the federal law. The arguments in the case mirrored the arguments in *Stenberg*. Once again, the plaintiffs urged the Court to strike down the partial-birth abortion prohibition because it lacked a broad exception for "health" that would allow the partial-birth procedure at the wide discretion of any abortion doctor. The arguments in defense of the law mirrored the arguments in *Stenberg*, as well.

In our *Gonzales* brief, we argued that the legal analysis of the "health" exception in *Stenberg* disregarded the "undue burden" formulation by the *Casey* Court. Partial-birth abortion is such a gruesome and barbaric procedure that legislatures, both at the level of the states and at the level of the U.S. Congress, must have wide leeway to regulate or ban the practice even under the constitutional test the Court fabricated in *Casey*.

As we argued in our brief, partial-birth abortion bans "promote at least four important governmental interests: they draw a bright line distinguishing abortion from infanticide; they help to preserve the integrity of the medical profession; they encourage respect for human life; and they prevent unnecessary cruelty to the aborted fetus." Indeed, in the initial decision of *Roe v. Wade* itself, the Court had held that the state has a strong interest in the preservation of life in the third trimester—the period in time when partial-birth abortions were most likely to occur.

This time, in *Gonzales*, we won: the Court ruled, 5–4, in support of the federal Partial-Birth Abortion Ban Act of 2003. What had changed? Only one thing: the composition of the justices. Specifically, Justice Sandra Day O'Connor had been replaced by Justice Samuel Alito, and suddenly, the five justices who had ruled that elected legislatures could not prohibit partial-birth abortion had become five justices who ruled that they could. Today, as we look at the Court, that five-justice majority that upheld the federal partial-birth abortion decision remains precarious.

The sharp divide on the Court continues today. In 2016, in the case of *Whole Woman's Health v. Hellerstedt*, a 5–3 Court majority (there were only eight justices because Justice Scalia had passed away only a few months before the decision) ruled that the state of Texas could not legally enact the commonsense health protection measures the state signed into law in 2013. These measures included a requirement that abortion providers have admitting privileges at a hospital within thirty miles of the abortion facility, as well as a requirement that abortion facilities meet the same regulatory standards as outpatient surgical centers. Even under *Roe*, protecting the health of mothers was recognized as an important government objective. Although rules to ensure sanitary and safe medical conditions are ubiquitous outside of the abortion context, the Court nonetheless ruled that those same safety regulations created an "undue burden" under *Casey* that violated a woman's right to procure an abortion.

This past summer, the Court had the opportunity to revisit its erroneous *Whole Woman's Health* decision, in the case of *June Medical Services v. Russo*, which considered a Louisiana statute almost identical to the Texas statute that had been struck down. By now, Justice Scalia's vacancy had been filled by Justice Gorsuch, and Justice Kennedy had been replaced by Justice Kavanaugh. The simple math meant that the previous 5–3 vote to strike down the Texas law would now presumably be a 5–4 vote to uphold the law.

But, alas, that was not to be. Chief Justice Roberts, who had voted in dissent in *Whole Woman's Health*, switched his vote and voted to strike down the Louisiana statute. Although not one iota of his legal reasoning had changed from four years earlier (and, obviously, the text of the Constitution had not changed), Roberts now joined the four liberal justices and ruled that under stare decisis (respect for previously decided precedents), both laws should be struck down. Sadly, stare decisis often seems to be a one-way ratchet; so-called conservatives (although Roberts is becoming less and less of one) willingly perpetuate lawless left-wing precedents, while liberals happily and reliably vote to overrule conservative precedents. The Court's vote in *June*? 5–4. One vote away.

◆   ◆   ◆   ◆

The growing extremism of elected Democrats on the issue of abortion seems to know no bounds. Medical science has advanced considerably in the nearly fifty years since *Roe*. We now know that unborn children feel pain in the womb as early as twenty weeks into gestation, and sonograms reveal their writhing in agony during late-term abortion procedures. Nevertheless, when Congress has voted to prohibit abortions after twenty weeks' gestation time, nearly every Senate Democrat (all but three, in 2018) has voted against that prohibition.

Even more ghastly, just this year, Congress voted on the Born-Alive Abortion Survivors Protection Act, which provided that if, in the course of an abortion, a child is born alive—as in, that child is outside the womb, breathing, crying, separate, and apart from its mother—then the physician must provide medical care to that child and cannot simply allow the child to die. Once again, all but three Senate Democrats voted against protecting the lives of infants already born alive. Reviewing the horror of Kermit Gosnell, it is wholly appropriate for the American people to ask who could possibly take such a vote.

Perhaps the most vivid illustration of the radicalization of today's Democrats on abortion can be seen with Virginia Governor Ralph Northam. Northam gained international infamy when his medical school yearbook page was discovered with a photograph of a white man dressed in blackface standing next to another man dressed in a KKK robe. When the news broke, Northam apologized for the racist picture on his page and explicitly acknowledged that he was one of the two men in costume (although he didn't say which one). The next day, he changed his mind and said he didn't think he was one of the two men in the photo. Although the media went into a frenzy because he might have appeared in blackface, very little attention was paid to Northam's initial acknowl-edgment suggesting it could have been him in the Klan robe instead.

Any elected official (or anyone else) should be able to say, unequivo-cally and without hesitation, "I have never worn a KKK robe." Yet nobody in the media seemed to care that the (still sitting) Democratic governor of Virginia—a state with a tragic record on race relations—could not make that straightforward statement.

Prior to the Klan scandal, Northam had made waves for his extrem-ism on abortion. He himself is an obstetrician, and in a 2019 radio interview he defended Virginia legislation that would allow abortion even up to and *during labor* while delivering the child. Northam then described the approach he believed a doctor should take if a child was born alive in the course of an abortion:

> If a mother is in labor, I can tell you exactly what would hap-pen. The infant would be delivered. The infant would be kept comfortable. The infant would be resuscitated if that's what the mother and the family desired, and then a discussion would ensue between the physicians and the mother.

Listening to that radio interview, what's so disconcerting is the total calmness in his voice. Like he's describing the weather outside. Hannah Arendt wrote powerfully of the "banality of evil." With that same banal-ity, utterly without emotion, Northam describes having a "discussion" about whether to sit back and let a newly born infant—fully born, out-side the womb—simply die.

Earlier this year, the Senate took up the Born-Alive Abortion Survivors Protection Act, legislation to ban what Northam had described, denying medical care to newborn infants. At a Senate Judiciary Committee hearing, I spoke in support of what should be commonsense legislation:

> The topic of this hearing, in my view, should not be the sub-ject of reasonable disagreement. That when one is discussing

an infant who has been born, who is alive, who is breathing, who is crying, who is outside the womb, the idea that it would be somehow debatable what to do with that child, that there would be another side, so to speak, politically, about whether to kill that child, whether to allow that child to live, or whether to do everything you can to protect that innocent life. It is a remarkable statement of just how extreme and radical the pro-abortion side of this debate has gotten.

Shortly thereafter, I went to the Senate floor to urge my colleagues to support the bill and to come together in defense of innocent life:

Mr. President, stop and think about this for a moment. There have been debates about abortion for a long, long time. This bill was allowing a mother in labor—in the process of delivering a child—this bill would allow a doctor to kill that child instead of delivering the child in the midst of labor. For a great many people, even Americans who identify as pro-choice, the idea of killing a child while the mother is in labor delivering the infant, is horrifying beyond words.

But Mr. President, Governor Northam didn't end there. He wasn't content simply with saying that abortion should be allowed even in the midst of birth. He went further. He said on that radio interview, and I quote, "The infant would be delivered. The infant would be kept comfortable. The infant would be resuscitated if that's what the mother and the family desired, and then a discussion would ensue between the physicians and the mother."

Mr. President, so nobody is lost on what Governor Northam was saying, he was describing something that has euphemistically been called "post-birth abortion." He was describing his view of the right way to approach delivering a child, which is a child that is delivered, that is outside the womb, that is breathing and crying and living, that is an infant—and Governor Northam calmly, with virtually no emotion whatsoever, described comforting that infant and then having a conversation about whether to deny that child the necessary care to live, or simply to callously let a newborn infant die.

On February 25, 2020, the Born Alive Abortion Survivors Protection Act came to a vote on the Senate floor. The Democrats filibustered the bill, and it tragically failed by a vote of 56–41. Every Republican voted yes, and all but three Democrats voted no. Sixty votes would have been needed to overcome the filibuster.

This is a radical Democratic party.

And, as for the Supreme Court, it still hangs in the balance. *Roe* and *Casey* are very much at stake—together, we need to restore a culture of life that protects the sanctity and dignity of every human life. But also at stake are countless important legal protections, including parental consent laws, clinic safety regulations, and bans on partial-birth abortion.

Each, potentially, survives or falls by a single vote. Four justices are already prepared to overturn them all, to allow unlimited abortions in every circumstance. They just need one more. The dramatic shift between *Stenberg* and *Gonzales*—both 5–4, decided opposite ways, just a few years apart, on nearly identical statutes—powerfully illustrates just what it means to be one vote away.

CHAPTER 6

FREE SPEECH AND *CITIZENS UNITED V. FEDERAL ELECTION COMMISSION*

Do you have the right to criticize elected officials? Do you have the right to disagree with candidates running for president of the United States? Does the Constitution protect your right to say, "Hillary is a crook," or "Donald Trump is a bully," or "Joe Biden is soft on China"? Some might think those are simple and straightforward questions—even obvious—but today that fundamental liberty is very much in jeopardy.

Those were precisely the questions at the heart of *Citizens United v. Federal Election Commission*, which was decided in 2010 by a narrow vote of 5–4. Citizens United is a nonprofit organization that made a movie critical of Hillary Clinton. Citizens United disagreed with Hillary's policies and had serious concerns about her ethical and legal failings—all of which were reflected in the movie they produced entitled, *Hillary: The Movie.*

However, because Citizens United sought to run advertisements for its movie in the period immediately preceding an election, the Federal Election Commission asserted the power to fine Citizens United under the McCain–Feingold campaign finance legislation, passed in 2002. Citizens United filed a lawsuit challenging the constitutionality of the government's asserted power to regulate core political speech. And that case proceeded to the Supreme Court. Ultimately, the Supreme Court struck down the provisions of McCain-Feingold that purported to restrict Citizens United's ability to publish and advertise its movie criticizing Hillary Clinton.

Few decisions in the past decade have engendered more political animosity on the left and confusion or outright misrepresentation from the press. You may have heard *Citizens United* being described as a case concerning whether corporations are people, or a case concerning whether money is speech. It has become commonplace for Democratic politicians to routinely answer "no" to both questions, and to characterize *Citizens United* as a decision that allowed giant corporations to "buy" political elections.

That can be effective as political rhetoric. It has the simple failing of not being true. On the question of whether corporations are people, the answer is that of course they are not. But, as a legal matter, they are an assembly of people. They are multiple people gathered together for a common purpose. And as a constitutional matter, there should be no serious dispute that American citizens, either individually or gathered together in the corporate form, have the right to free speech under the First Amendment.

And, as it so happens, the vast majority of speakers affected by *Citizens United* are not the big, bad, wealthy corporations portrayed by Democratic politicians. Citizens United itself was, and is, a small nonprofit corporation. It's not Exxon Mobil. It's not Citigroup. It's a conservative nonprofit that sought to portray its perspective on Hillary Clinton.

If anyone advocates, as almost all Democratic politicians do, that corporations have no free speech rights, pause to reflect that the Sierra Club is a corporation. Greenpeace is a corporation. Planned Parenthood is a corporation. NBC is a corporation. The *New York Times* is a corporation. Simon and Schuster, like all major book publishers, is a corporation. The NAACP is also a corporation. Is there any plausible argument that the aforementioned corporations have zero right under the First Amendment of the Constitution to advocate for their political views? The answer is, of course, no, but that doesn't stop politicians and four justices of the Supreme Court from concluding otherwise.

As for the second straw man frequently used to criticize the *Citizens United* decision (the proposition that money is not speech) that too is demonstrably false. The Framers of our Constitution did not believe that the only way you or I could speak was to stand atop a soapbox in the public square and yell loud enough for those around us to hear.

In our modern times, and even in the time of the American Founding, to speak effectively to any significant number of people almost invariably involves the expenditure of money. That's why candidates run TV ads, radio ads, Internet ads, and social media ads. That's why book publishers spend money to publish books. That's why the *New York Times* spends millions of dollars to pay reporters and run printing presses and purchase paper and ink to distribute its newspapers across New York City and across the world.

Imagine, for example, that the government passed a law saying no newspaper could spend any money to print newspapers. Or, if you wanted to target it, a law that says Fox News—or MSNBC, depending on your partisan affiliation—could not spend even a dollar to buy satellite time to broadcast their shows. Would anyone conceivably say, "Money is not speech, so that law is ok"?

Even in the days of the Framers, public speakers would routinely spend money to print pamphlets and other materials to circulate and communicate a message. Indeed, the *Federalist Papers*, the arguments of Alexander Hamilton, James Madison, and John Jay in support of the newly drafted but not yet ratified Constitution, were themselves drafted under the anonymous pseudonym "Publius," published as newspaper editorials, and then printed and circulated across New York and what would become the thirteen original states of the United States of America. If the proposition that free speech does not protect the expenditure of money were correct and spending money were restricted, then the *Federalist Papers* could at best have been whispered person to person but would not have been effective in communicating much of anything.

Likewise, at the time of the American Founding, it was readily understood that political speech was the very core of the Constitution's prohibition against Congress's "abridging the freedom of speech." Our Founding Fathers were deeply familiar with the great pamphleteer, Thomas Paine, and his seminal work *Common Sense*. Paine's essay, which advocated for America's independence from the British Crown, was tremendously influential at the time. It was widely distributed—printed, at considerable expense—and read aloud at pubs, taverns, town squares, and civic gatherings. It helped to usher in the American Revolution itself. And it was the quintessential example, the very paradigm, of political speech.

When it comes to mischaracterizing the decision in *Citizens United*, one of the most egregious examples was at the 2010 State of the Union Address, when President Barack Obama described the *Citizens United* decision, decided the week before the speech, as "revers[ing] a century of case law" and "open[ing] up the floodgates for special interests—including foreign corporations—to spend without limit in our elections." The characterization was so demonstrably false, and laughably so, that Justice Samuel Alito, typically a quiet and reserved judge, could not resist mouthing the words, "not true." The following year, in response, Justices Alito, Scalia, and Thomas all decided to skip the State of the Union Address.

Citizens United has become a bogeyman of the left. Barack Obama vowed to repeal *Citizens United*. Hillary Clinton vowed to repeal *Citizens United*. Bernie Sanders vowed to repeal *Citizens United*. And Joe Biden has vowed to repeal *Citizens United*—or, more precisely, to appoint justices who will do it for him.

On the question of free speech, today's Democratic Party has become truly radicalized. On June 18, 2013, fifteen Senate Democrats first introduced a constitutional amendment that purported to overrule *Citizens United*. In fact, it would have gone much further, repealing the free speech protections of the First Amendment altogether. The first version of the proposed constitutional amendment gave Congress plenary authority—a legal term meaning blanket, or total, authority—to regulate *any* expenditure of funds by any American to influence an election.

At the time, Illinois Senator Dick Durbin was the chairman of the Senate Judiciary Committee's Subcommittee on the Constitution, and I was the ranking Republican member on the Constitution Subcommittee (today, with a Republican majority, I am the chairman of the Constitution Subcommittee). Senator Durbin sought to pass this constitutional amendment, and I led the argument against it. This first version of the constitutional amendment was written so broadly that—literally—if a little old lady were to go to Home Depot and spend five dollars to buy a poster board and construct a yard sign on which she handwrote the words "Vote for Donald Trump" or "Vote for Joe Biden," then Congress would have had the authority to make that simple action a criminal offense punishable by jail time.

Under the Democrats' proposed constitutional amendment, Congress would be able to prohibit the NRA from distributing voter guides to let citizens know politicians' voting records on the Second Amendment. Under the Democrats' proposed constitutional amendment, Congress would be able to prohibit the Sierra Club from running political ads criticizing politicians for their environmental policies. Under the Democrats' proposed constitutional amendment, Congress would be able to penalize pro-life and pro-choice groups alike for spending money to advocate for their views on abortion. Under the Democrats' proposed constitutional amendment, Congress would be able to prohibit labor unions from organizing workers to go door-to-door urging voters to turn out. Under the Democrats' proposed constitutional amendment, Congress would be able to criminalize pastors who might print a message in their church bulletins encouraging their parishioners to vote.

Revealingly, the Democrats' proposed constitutional amendment also included an express provision stating, "Nothing in this article shall be construed to grant Congress the power to abridge the freedom of the press." What this means, in plain English, is that while Senate Democrats sought to empower Congress to restrict individual citizens' political speech rights, they did not want to apply that same treatment to giant media corporations like CNN and the *New York Times*.

I made these arguments vigorously in the debate that ensued in the Constitution Subcommittee, and the position became so untenable that Democrats retreated and introduced a revised amendment. This time, their proposed constitutional amendment no longer applied to individuals—so the little old lady with her five-dollar yard sign was no longer swept in; instead, the terms of the new proposed amendment applied to any and all expenditures designed to influence an election made by any corporation (except for favored media corporations).

At the Constitution Subcommittee mark-up on this proposed amendment, a radical rewriting of the free speech protections contained in the First Amendment, I posed three simple questions. First, should the federal government be able to ban movies? Second, should the federal government be able to ban books? And third, should the federal government be able to ban the NAACP from speaking on matters of politics?

To all three of the questions, I gave a resounding "hell no." But under the terms of the Democrats' proposed constitutional amendments, the government would have the power to do all three.

When it came to banning movies, that was not even a hypothetical. Citizens United, you will recall, was a conservative nonprofit corporation that had made a movie critical of Hillary Clinton. And Senate Democrats now wanted to give the federal government the constitutional authority to punish anyone for criticizing Hillary Clinton or any other political candidate.

As for the question of books, that was, in fact, a hypothetical posed to the Obama Justice Department during the *Citizens United* oral argument at the Supreme Court. Justice Alito asked Malcolm Stewart, the deputy solicitor general of the United States at the time, whether "the government's position is that the First Amendment allows the banning of a book if it's published by a corporation." In essence, Justice Alito wanted to know whether it was the legal position of the Obama Justice Department that the federal government has, or ought to have, the authority to fine a bookseller for publishing a book that was critical of a political candidate.

The fact that this was even a live question during a Supreme Court oral argument ought itself to be deeply troubling. The Obama Justice Department, remarkably, answered in the affirmative. As Deputy Solicitor General Stewart soon thereafter explained to Chief Justice John Roberts in the same line of questioning, it was the Obama Justice Department's legal position that the government "could prohibit the publication" of such a book by "using...corporate treasury funds."

It's not just Citizens United, of course, that is a corporation— Paramount Pictures, Sony Studios, every major movie maker in America and, likely in the world, is a corporation. And under the Democrats' proposed constitutional amendment, the federal government could regulate and punish if movies *ever* criticized politicians. Simon and Schuster, as it so happened, was the book publisher of Hillary Clinton's book that had just come out as we were debating this amendment. I pointed out that, under the Democrats' proposed constitutional amendment, the federal government could fine or perhaps even criminally prosecute Simon and Schuster for publishing the book if, in even one passage of the book, it either criticized or advocated for any federal candidate in any federal election.

And as for the NAACP, the NAACP is itself a corporation. It is a corporation that was formed to fight against bigotry and racial injustice. And when it comes to the proposition that government power might be used to attack the NAACP—to silence the NAACP, to persecute the NAACP—there are decades of history that show such government power has actively been used for precisely that objective. Indeed, elected politicians in Jim Crow states (virtually 100 percent of them elected Democrats) regularly used government power to persecute the NAACP. And the Supreme Court, in the landmark and unanimously decided 1958 case of *NAACP v. Alabama* ruled that the state government (under Democratic governor Big Jim Folsom) could not force the NAACP to hand over the names of its donors because those individuals would be unduly subject to government persecution.

Another example I pointed to was *Saturday Night Live*. For five decades, *SNL* has witheringly parodied politicians from both sides of the aisle. Chevy Chase tumbling down the stairs as Gerald Ford. Phil Hartman as a doddering (but secret mastermind) Ronald Reagan. Dana Carvey brilliantly as both George H. W. Bush ("Na ga do it!") and Ross Perot ("Giant sucking sound!"). Darrell Hammond as a lascivious Bill Clinton arguing with John Goodman as Moses over what is and isn't prohibited by the Ten Commandments. Will Ferrell as George W. Bush sharing his campaign "strategery." Kate McKinnon as a dishonest, power-hungry Hillary Clinton. Larry David embodying a grumpy, germophobic Bernie Sanders.

On the latter, I jokingly told Bernie on the elevator in the Capitol that "Larry David does a better Bernie than you do!" Characteristically, Bernie simply harrumphed.

Over the years, *SNL*'s portrayals have had tangible political impact. Chevy Chase's bumbling caused many Americans to think of Ford as a klutz, even though—as an All-American college football player at Michigan—he likely was the best athlete ever to occupy the Oval Office. Tina Fey's uncanny Sarah Palin resulted in many Americans to this day believing that Palin actually said "I can see Russia from my house!" (it was Fey, and not Palin who said that).

I've grown up on *SNL*'s portrayals. I haven't always liked them (especially when I was the brunt of them). But I believe they have a First Amendment right to produce whatever comedy they like, even if it's unfair, vicious, or partisan. (The four-year weekly screed against Trump has gotten consistently less funny and more than a little tiresome.) However, under the Democrats' proposed constitutional amendment, the federal government could punish NBC for airing political parodies. (Notably, NBC, which produces *SNL*, is separate from NBC News, which would be exempted under the Democrats' news media carve-out.)

At the time, it so happened that one of my colleagues on the Judiciary Committee was Al Franken, who had previously been a writer and actor for *SNL*. At the mark-up, I asked him if "Congress should have the constitutional authority to prohibit *Saturday Night Live* from making fun of politicians." He replied he didn't "intend to do that."

Of course, whatever his personal, subjective intentions may have been (perhaps just to grandstand politically), he had not one word of substantive response to the fact that the explicit terms of the amendment he was supporting—which would be engrafted into the Bill of Rights— would have given Congress blanket power to "*prohibit* [corporations, including NBC] from spending money to influence elections."

Regulating political speech—books, movies, comedy, satire—is very different from what Democrats and the media typically portray *Citizens United* as being all about: for-profit, greedy corporations trying to "buy" elections. In truth, polling over the past decade shows that, overall, a very small percentage of corporations of *any* form, type, or size directly engage in politics. Polls have shown that over 90 percent of companies surveyed do not have a super PAC and do not otherwise directly engage in politics at an institutional level.

And a substantial majority of the big-money donors are on the left, not the right. According to the data maintained by OpenSecrets.org, of the top twenty organizations who spent money on the 2016 election, *fourteen of them gave almost exclusively to Democrats*, and three more split their money roughly evenly between the parties. Only three out of the top twenty groups who spent money on the 2016 election gave primarily to Republicans. Of the top ten super PAC donors, only two were Republican, and in 2016 the top twenty super PAC donors contributed a total of $422 million to Democrats and $189 million to Republicans.

To its credit, the American Civil Liberties Union, a liberal group that has sadly gotten less principled and more partisan in recent years, managed to publicly oppose Senate Democrats' attempt to repeal the First

Amendment of the Bill of Rights. It wrote that Senate Democrats' proposed constitutional amendment would "severely limit the First Amendment, lead directly to government censorship of political speech and result in a host of unintended consequences that would undermine the goals the amendment has been introduced to advance."

Think about that for a second. The Democrats were seeking the power to ban books. Conjure for a moment Ray Bradbury's classic dystopian novel *Fahrenheit 451*, named for the temperature at which book paper ignites. In it, a despotic government rounds up and burns the books with which it disagrees. How can it be that today one of our two major political parties is on record in favor of precisely that unfettered government power? As we debated the issue, I dubbed the amendment's proponents the "Fahrenheit 451 Democrats." Notably, not a single Democrat presented any substantive argument whatsoever as to why their amendment wouldn't allow government-mandated book burning. They simply charged ahead with partisan, lock-step unity.

In the course of the mark-up before the full Senate Judiciary Committee, I introduced an amendment to the Democrats' proposed constitutional amendment. It deleted every word of their proposed amendment and replaced it with the following: "Congress shall make no law respecting an establishment of religion, or prohibiting the free exercise thereof; or abridging the freedom of speech, or of the press; or the right of the people peaceably to assemble, and to petition the Government for a redress of grievances." That was and is, of course, the text, word-for-word, of the First Amendment to the Constitution.

We then voted on my proposed amendment, and every single Democrat on the Judiciary Committee proceeded to vote against the verbatim text of the First Amendment. But the matter wasn't done then. Next, it came to a vote on the Senate floor. At the time, I was a fairly new senator, and I made an impassioned argument to my Democratic colleagues that, even if we disagreed on many matters of policy, we should come together when it came to protecting free speech.

There was a time when lions of the left routinely defended free speech. Indeed, one of the lawyers who argued the *Citizens United* case, on the side of defending the right of citizens to criticize elected officials, was Floyd Abrams, the famed left-wing lawyer who had championed dozens of free speech cases for many decades. A lifelong liberal, Abrams showed principle and consistency when he testified vigorously against the Democrats' proposed constitutional amendment. But as we have seen on so many other issues, this is not your father's Democratic Party.

One of the Court's landmark free speech cases was *Cohen v. California*, where, at the height of the Vietnam War, the State of California had tried to prosecute Paul Robert Cohen for disturbing the peace because he wore a jacket that read, "F### the draft." Personally, you might not agree with that sentiment; you might even find it obscene. But the Supreme Court nonetheless rightly reversed the conviction; as Justice John Marshall Harlan II wrote, "one man's vulgarity is another's lyric."

A robust commitment to free speech is not a means to merely protect favored, or popular, speech. It is not a means to elevate and single out speech that might be deemed "reasonable." It is not a means to prioritize only the speech that is deemed socially acceptable and inoffensive by an elite ruling class. Rather, a society protects free speech under the rule of law precisely to protect *unreasonable* speech. It protects free speech under the rule of law precisely to protect *offensive* speech.

Log on to Twitter on any given day; there are countless speakers on the political left who attack, vilify, and insult me. And, although I'd prefer that they exercise civility, I'll defend vigorously their constitutional right to say whatever nasty, false, dehumanizing attack they send my way. That's the price of public life. As the English writer Evelyn Beatrice Hall wrote, summarizing the beliefs of the great French Enlightenment thinker Voltaire: "I disapprove of what you say, but I will defend to the death your right to say it."

Free speech is not just an instrumental good. It is not just an expedient. It is not just a means toward an end. It is an intrinsic good—an end unto itself. For millennia, political theorists and philosophers have recognized that the dialectic, the iterative societal dialogue that has the pursuit of truth as its desired destination, is necessarily dependent upon free speech and the free airing of diverse viewpoints. As John Stuart Mill wrote in *On Liberty*,

> [T]he peculiar evil of silencing the expression of an opinion is, that it is robbing the human race; posterity as well as the existing generation; those who dissent from the opinion, still more than those who hold it. If the opinion is right, they are deprived of the opportunity of exchanging error for truth: if wrong, they lose, what is almost as great a benefit, the clearer perception and livelier impression of truth, produced by its collision with error.

Put another way, the best cure for bad speech is more speech. Over time, truth will prevail in the marketplace of ideas. And rather than silencing false or dissenting views, respond with truth and win the argument.

For that reason, the text of the First Amendment provides, "Congress shall make no law...abridging the freedom of speech." That is an unambiguous textual command. It is, or at least ought to be, clear as day. "Congress shall make no law" means, obviously, that "*no law*" that abridges the freedom of speech may rightfully be sanctioned by that august deliberative body. That's why, to have the power to ban political speech with which they disagreed, Democrats had to amend and repeal the First Amendment.

When the Senate had previously considered Democratic attempts to amend the free speech protections of the First Amendment, and to expand the government's authority to regulate political speech, such liberal warriors as Senator Ted Kennedy had vigorously opposed them. In 1997, many years before *Citizens United* was decided, when Democrats had tried to pass a campaign-finance constitutional amendment,

Kennedy thundered, "In the entire history of the Constitution, we have never amended the Bill of Rights, and now is no time to start. It would be wrong to carve an exception in the First Amendment."

At the same time Senator Kennedy issued that warning, Democratic Senator Russ Feingold, who would go on to co-sponsor the very campaign finance law the Court ultimately enjoined in *Citizens United*, said, "The Constitution of this country was not a rough draft. We must stop treating it as such." And so Feingold opposed the Democrats' constitutional amendment. Later, in 2001, when Senate Democrats again attempted a constitutional amendment similar to the ones that they proposed in 1997 and in 2014, Senator Feingold replied, "I find nothing more sacred and treasured in our nation's history than the First Amendment. I want to leave the First Amendment undisturbed."

I pleaded with my Democratic colleagues. Surely one of you, I asked, must agree with Ted Kennedy. Or Russ Feingold. Or Floyd Abrams. Or the ACLU. Surely one of you, I asked, must agree that the free speech provisions of the First Amendment deserve to be protected. I spoke passionately on the issue—an issue that embodies the American experiment and the Liberty at its heart:

> Mr. President, this proposal before the Senate is, bar none, the most radical proposal that has been considered by the United States Senate in the time I have served. If this proposal were to pass, its effects would be breathtaking. It would be the most massive intrusion on civil liberties and expansion of federal government power in modern times.

Later on in that speech, I explained that the purpose of the First Amendment is not merely to protect the speech that politicians deem reasonable, socially permissible, or otherwise acceptable. On the contrary, our First Amendment exists to protect the most unpopular and unfavored speech among us:

The First Amendment is not about reasonable speech. The First Amendment was enacted to protect *unreasonable* speech. I, for one, certainly don't want our speech limited to that speech that elected politicians in Washington think is reasonable.

There was a time when this body thought the Alien and Sedition Acts prohibiting criticizing the government were reasonable. There is a reason the Constitution doesn't say, "let's trust politicians to determine what speech is reasonable and what isn't." And I would note that the Supreme Court has long made clear that the First Amendment is all about *unreasonable* speech. For example, when the Nazis wanted to march in Skokie, Illinois. Nazi speech is the paradigmatic example of unreasonable speech. It is hateful, bigoted, ignorant speech. And the Supreme Court said the Nazis have a constitutional right to march down the street in Skokie, Illinois, with their hateful, bigoted, ignorant speech. Now, every one of us then has a moral obligation to condemn it as hateful and bigoted and ignorant, but the First Amendment is all about saying government doesn't get to decide what you say is reasonable and what you say is not.

As I concluded my speech on the Senate floor, I made sure everyone knew that this was not about politics at all. This was about doing the right thing. This was about making sure we didn't erase one of the most foundational provisions in the entire Bill of Rights:

Madam President, I assure you if it were my party proposing this egregious amendment, I would be standing on the floor of this Senate giving the very same speech, trying to hold my party to account. Because, you know, at the end of the day, when we take our oath of office, it's not to the Democratic Party or the Republican Party. It is to represent the citizens of our state—in my case, 26 million Texans—to fight for their rights, and to defend and uphold the Constitution of the United States. There is nothing the United States has done in the just under two years that I've been in this body that I find more disturbing, more dangerous, than the fact that 49 Democrats would put their name to a proposal to repeal the First Amendment.

In 1997, when Democrats had tried to pass a constitutional amendment restricting political speech, thankfully, eleven Democrats voted no (Bumpers, Durbin, Feingold, Kennedy, Kerrey, Kohl, Leahy, Moseley-Braun, Moynihan, Rockefeller, and Torricelli). In 2001, when Democrats again tried to pass a constitutional amendment repealing the political speech protections of the First Amendment, a different collection of eleven Democrats voted no (Corzine, Edwards, Feingold, Johnson of South Dakota, Kennedy, Kohl, Leahy, Nelson of Florida, Nelson of Nebraska, Torricelli, and Wellstone).

Sadly, this last time that Democrats had the majority, in 2014, when it came to a vote on the Senate floor, *every single Senate Democrat*—100 percent of them—voted to repeal the free speech provisions of the First Amendment. Each and every one of them should be embarrassed and ashamed that they did so.

◆ ◆ ◆ ◆

On Constitution Day of that year, the National Constitution Center in Philadelphia, Pennsylvania, invited me to come debate this proposed attempt to amend the Constitution. I readily accepted. They invited Dick Durbin to come debate the other side. Senator Durbin declined. They invited Chuck Schumer. Senator Schumer declined.

At the end of the day, the National Constitution Center could not find even a single elected Democrat willing to come argue the other side of the argument. They wanted to exercise brute power, engage in partisan posturing, without actually having to defend their proposals on the merits. So I decided to proceed alone. The National Constitution Center assembled a gathering of some 600 to 700 people in Independence Hall and, for over an hour, I proceeded to, in effect, debate myself. I endeavored, as much as I could, to at least lay out the arguments that Democratic senators had made in favor of their proposed amendment. And then I laid out the counterarguments. (I'll confess, I may have been more vigorous in the latter than the former.)

When it comes to campaign finance reform, a great many people who seek to do good in the world say that there is too much money in politics and, accordingly, we should prevent the spending of money on elections. They argue that elections would be better (or more pure or more truthful or more accountable) if we simply banned citizen groups from spending money on political speech. I don't doubt that many of them are sincere, but doing so would have precisely the opposite effect on our democracy.

In any given election, there are typically three major categories of speakers—three categories of those who contribute to the discourse surrounding an election. There are, of course, incumbent politicians and the candidates who may be challenging them. There are the press. And there are individual citizens.

Campaign finance reforms, inevitably, when drafted and filed in Congress, are drafted by incumbent politicians. And, almost without exception, these so-called campaign finance reforms serve to protect those same incumbent politicians. It is in the interest—at least the narrow electoral interest—of every incumbent politician to make it as difficult as possible for anyone else to criticize them. The press, likewise, is complicit in these efforts to silence the third category of speakers: individual citizens and citizens gathered collectively through various organizations.

Every day of the year, the press—whether ABC, CBS, NBC, the *New York Times*, the *Washington Post*, Fox News, or CNN—engages in spending millions of dollars to influence elections and to praise or criticize politicians. If citizens are silenced, the press will have even more of a monopoly on political speech.

Likewise, incumbent politicians have massive structural advantages in elections. In big states, like my home state of Texas, today with 29 million people, it is absurdly difficult and expensive to communicate a message that is heard by even a small percentage of the voters. Incumbent politicians have vast advantages: widespread name identification, organizations and structures, lobbyists and special interests who will fund their campaigns, and an army of bundlers who can raise money for any given campaign. A new challenger typically lacks access to any of those resources. If incumbent politicians were to be successful in prohibiting the expenditure of money on elections, it would mean that, as a practical matter, incumbents could almost never be beaten. That is, quite frankly, un-American.

I'm an incumbent now. But I didn't start off that way. And I share the overwhelming frustration the American people have with career politicians of both parties who are captured by Washington special interests and who don't do what they said they would do. If I could push a button and throw out of office every incumbent politician in D.C., myself included, I would happily push that button. In the meantime, I'm passionately opposed to incumbent-protection schemes, of which campaign finance reform proposals are the biggest example.

In 2019, media observers were shocked when I retweeted Alexandria Ocasio-Cortez and enthusiastically agreed with her suggestion to ban former members of Congress from becoming lobbyists. Although she didn't know it at the time, AOC was agreeing with me; in 2016, while campaigning for president, I had already advocated a permanent lifetime ban on former members of Congress ever becoming lobbyists.

When I first ran for Senate in Texas in 2012, I saw firsthand the challenges of taking on a powerful incumbent. At the time, I was an upstart challenger taking on an incumbent statewide officeholder with vast personal wealth. My opponent, having been in statewide office for over a decade, had universal name ID (a very expensive thing to build).

Because of the power of his office, he had practically every lobbyist in the state behind him. And he was personally worth over $200 million, which he poured into the race.

The day I entered the race, I was at 2 percent in the polls…and the margin of error was 3 percent. Those were real numbers from the first poll we did. I was pretty excited not to be starting at zero, until Heidi wryly observed, "Technically, couldn't you be at negative 1 percent?"

When I was elected to the Senate in 2012, I had never before been elected to any other office. Indeed, as I have joked, albeit accurately, the last thing I had been elected to before that was student council.

Nonetheless, we managed to raise some $14 million from a whopping 43,160 unique donors. That was enough to overcome the 3-to-1 spending differential we faced. And we ended up winning what the *Washington Post* later characterized as the single biggest upset of 2012 and "a true grassroots victory against very long odds."

That also included $1.2 million that I personally put into the campaign, which represented all of our liquid net worth. That's a lot of money, most of which we had saved from my few years in private practice at the law firm before running. Some people assume that, because I went to Princeton and Harvard, I must have family money and come from privilege. That's not the case. I was a scholarship kid. My dad was a Cuban immigrant; my mom was the first in her family to go to college. Nobody in my family had ever gone to an Ivy League school, and when I went to college my parents had just lost their small business and declared bankruptcy. We lost our home, and I worked two jobs and took out about $100,000 in loans (which I finally paid off twelve years ago) to make it through college and law school.

It was an interesting conversation—to say the least—going to Heidi, in the last week of the primary, and asking her to agree to liquidate all of our savings to put into the campaign. Not many candidates or candidates' spouses are willing to consider that. (That's one of the reasons so many candidates are massively wealthy.) And it's a testament to what an amazing person Heidi is—my best friend and partner in every aspect of life—that she said yes immediately, without hesitation.

To put that money into the campaign, we sold all the stocks and bonds we had that didn't have significant appreciation. And, rather than sell the remaining investments (which would have taken us to zero but would have unnecessarily incurred a big capital gains tax bill), I took out two loans for the equivalent amount. One was a line of credit through Citibank, which all the partners at my law firm had access to on identical terms. The other was a margin loan from Goldman Sachs, where we kept our investments. The margin loan was available on identical terms to everyone who held investments at Goldman—just like the margin loans offered by most other brokerages—and it was directly secured by those investments (you could automatically borrow up to 50 percent of their market value). Both loans were fully paid off after the primary, when the campaign paid me back much of my loan to it. (Under a particularly burdensome—and unconstitutional—federal election rule, we were prohibited from paying ourselves back all of our loan; so we had to make, in effect, a $550,000 forced "gift" from our life savings to the campaign.)

In the 2016 presidential campaign, the *New York Times* breathlessly broke the news of these 2012 bank loans as front-page news and treated it as somehow scandalous because I had not filed the correct paperwork with the FEC. The whole thing was quite silly, because I had publicly disclosed both loans at the time on my Senate Ethics financial disclosure—which was contemporaneous and fully available to the public. But, our campaign's lawyer hadn't filed the correct form (with the identical information) also with the FEC, so it was technically a violation.

In addition to all the money we raised and spent on the campaign, we also had outside help. Spending significant money in support of my Senate race was the Club for Growth, a fiscally conservative political-advocacy organization that spent several million dollars speaking out in favor of my conservative record. If the Democrats had had their way, the Club for Growth—and any other citizen-advocacy organization—would have been silenced. And it would likely have proven impossible to defeat an incumbent statewide official with a massive personal fortune and statewide name recognition.

Pause to think about how many elected officials today are multi-millionaires with personal fortunes in the hundreds of millions of dollars and the ability simply to swamp anyone on the other side. If citizens were silenced, we'd get even more billionaires trying to buy elections.

Pause also to consider just how much more the proverbial deck would be stacked in favor of incumbents if we tried to silence all of America's great civic organizations—society's intermediating institutions about which Alexis de Tocqueville famously waxed poetic—and prevented them from donating to or advocating on behalf of challengers to incumbent politicians. Such a vision of our politics would have been anathema to the Framers of our Constitution.

Our current campaign system is, frankly, stupid. It makes no sense. Because, in the wake of *Citizens United*, when Congress lacked the authority to prohibit citizen groups from speaking, the Federal Election Commission nonetheless enforced regulations that prohibited candidates from conferring with those citizen groups. And so today, in a significant number of federal elections, the biggest speakers, in terms of dollars spent, are outside groups—or "super PACs"—with whom the ostensible candidate is legally prohibited from communicating on strategy, messaging, or substance.

That makes no sense from anybody's perspective. These super PACs are now typically run by political consultants who profit obscenely and make millions of dollars precisely because no candidate is able to oversee what the consultants are doing. And the messaging is often only tangentially related to the core of what the candidate wishes to say. This serves no one's interests (other than the greedy consultants and K Street–lobbyist fat cats).

Each year that I've been in the Senate, I've introduced legislation called the "Super PAC Elimination Act." The Super PAC Elimination Act would not prohibit super PACs, or any other citizen groups, from speaking. Rather, it would make two very simple changes. One, it would allow unlimited *individual* donations directly to a political candidate's campaign. No corporate donations, and no union donations, just individuals. And two, it would require immediate, twenty-four-hour disclosure of any such donations.

Sunlight is the best disinfectant, and political speech is no different. As Chief Justice Roberts said in the campaign finance case of *McCutcheon v. Federal Election Commission,* "Disclosure of contributions minimizes the potential for abuse of the campaign finance system."

As a practical matter, passing the Super PAC Elimination Act would functionally eliminate super PACs because every candidate would much rather control his or her own message—what he or she is saying. And with immediate disclosure, if a particular donor wrote a massive check to a particular candidate—for example, the tens of millions of dollars spent every cycle by Democratic super-donors like George Soros and Mike Bloomberg and Tom Steyer—then those donations would be disclosed immediately and could be the subject of public debate, with the electorate deciding whether the acceptance of those contributions affected their votes at the ballot box.

The system I proposed is, in fact, very similar to the system that operates in the State of Texas for state elections. Candidates for state elections in Texas can accept unlimited donations from individuals but cannot accept any donations from corporations or from labor unions. And those contributions are all exposed for public scrutiny.

Although I had never been elected to office before the Senate, for about a year, I did run as a state candidate in Texas for attorney general. In 2009, then-U.S. Senator Kay Bailey Hutchison had announced she was going to resign from the Senate in order to run for governor of Texas against the incumbent, Governor Rick Perry. As a result, Texas Lieutenant Governor David Dewhurst was expected to run for Senate, and Texas Attorney General Greg Abbott was expected to run for lieutenant governor. So I decided to launch my own run to replace my old boss as Texas attorney general.

I spent most of 2009 campaigning for AG, against four other Republicans who were expected to run: two elected State Supreme Court justices (both Abbott and his predecessor as AG, John Cornyn, had previously been elected Supreme Court justices), a state representative who was supported by many of the wealthiest business owners in Dallas, and a member of Congress who was personally worth several hundred million dollars). In contrast, I'd been SG—an appointed position—but had never run for anything.

All that year, I crisscrossed the state working to earn the support of conservative leaders, Republican women, and grassroots activists across Texas. I didn't come from money and didn't have massive personal money to put in the race. But, because Texas allowed unlimited individual donations, I was able to raise much more than anyone expected. When we filed our first campaign finance disclosure, our AG campaign had raised over $1 million—a sum that sent shock waves through the political world. Unknown, non-elected, non-wealthy candidates simply weren't supposed to be able to do that.

My biggest donor for the AG race was Peter Thiel—the billionaire former CEO of PayPal who had been the first major outside investor in Facebook. Peter and I had been friends since long before he had money. We met in the mid-90s, when I was clerking for the Court and he was a young lawyer practicing corporate law. Peter is brilliant, eccentric, and one of the most innovative thinkers in the country. He's also gay and very libertarian politically.

Peter gave $250,000 to my AG campaign; without that contribution, we never would have crossed the $1 million threshold on the first filing. And raising $1 million had real significance; I joked that $1 million in politics is ten times greater than $900,000—the "-illion" just captures people's attention (think Dr. Evil in *Austin Powers* with his pinkie to his cheek, saying "one meee-lion dollars). It drives credibility and press coverage.

All of that together—the fundraising, conservative leaders uniting, the overwhelming grassroots support—convinced all four of my potential opponents not to run. Each made that announcement, and suddenly, we had gone from nothing to effectively clearing the Republican field, which at the time meant we had basically won the AG race in Texas.

And then it disappeared. In the fall of 2009, Senator Hutchison changed her mind and announced she was not going to resign her Senate seat after all. Unable to run for Senate, David Dewhurst promptly announced he was running for re-election as lieutenant governor, and that left Greg Abbott with no place to go but to announce he was running for re-election as attorney general. Within hours, I suspended my campaign for AG. I was never going to run against my friend and former boss; the plan had always been to succeed him.

At the time, I was unbelievably frustrated with Kay. When she changed her mind on resigning, it made all the work we had done for the past year disappear. But then she lost badly to Rick Perry in the gubernatorial primary and announced she was not going to run for re-election to Senate two years later.

And so we contemplated an even more audacious move. In considering whether to run for Senate, the biggest initial barrier was fundraising. To run a campaign that had even a chance to be heard statewide in Texas, I assessed that we'd need a minimum of $5 million. If we couldn't raise that, we'd lose. Period. If we could raise closer to $10 million, we would have enough to really communicate effectively, and I believed we'd win.

Here's where the federal limits come into play. At the time, the maximum a person could give to the primary was $2500. That means you need 400 people to max out to get to $1 million, and you need 4000 people to max out to get to $10 million. That, frankly, is really, really hard.

If you're an incumbent, it's not all that difficult. You have an existing infrastructure, you have "bundlers" in place (people who work to get lots of others to max out), you have name ID. "The rich get richer" is certainly how the political racket usually operates. I was trying to break that cycle.

The only reason I had a prayer of raising what we needed was that I had spent the past year running for AG. We had built at least some of the infrastructure; without it, I would have had zero chance of winning.

Texas's no-limits system is what had let an unknown candidate without personal wealth start from nothing and succeed. That's the counter-intuitive part: the campaign-finance limits help incumbents and substantially hurt unknown challengers. That's exactly what they're designed to do.

Many people misunderstand the role campaign funding typically plays. In the 1990s, Eddie Murphy starred in a light comedy called *The Distinguished Gentleman*, where he played a shady local con man who managed to get elected to Congress. He was thoroughly corrupt and simply wanted to raise as much money as possible. In the movie, Murphy has the following conversation with a leading D.C. lobbyist:

> Lobbyist: "I'd like to do more money for you. But first I've got to get your positions on a few issues. Where are you on sugar price supports?"
>
> New Congressman (looking quizzical): "Sugar price supports...where should I be, Terry?"
>
> Lobbyist: "...Makes no difference to me. If you're for 'em, I got money for you from my sugar producers in Louisiana and Hawaii; if you against 'em, I got money for you from the candy manufacturers."
>
> New Congressman (grinning): "You pick."

Although somewhat exaggerated, that comedy exchange is basically right. Most people in Congress pick their positions on a given issue and then raise money from those who already support that issue. Whether sugar subsidies (I'm against) or Second Amendment rights (I'm for), there are donors who care about those issues and support candidates who do too. But, if I were on the other side of those issues (or a thousand more), there are donors on the other side who will happily support campaigns as well.

What the Washington Swamp is biased towards is the status quo. Incumbents. Established power players (on both sides). That's why massive new spending bills are typically a bipartisan extravaganza. And strict individual limits favor—and are designed to favor—those with institutional power.

Take an issue like an Internet sales tax—something I'm passionately against. The Swamp is overwhelmingly for it because the large brick-and-mortar retailers are for it, and the large Internet retailers are as well (because it hammers their rivals). The only losers are the small online retailers, the mom-and-pop internet sellers. And they don't have lobbyists. That's why 70–80 percent of the Senate, from both parties, support creating on online sales tax—because it's an issue that unites all the D.C. lobbyists. For eight years, I've led the opposition because it's terrible policy, especially for the little guy.

Let's look more closely at my races. My AG race was viable because we raised enough to be taken seriously; Peter Thiel's $250,000 was essential for that. When I ran for Senate, the rules were more complicated. Federal candidates are not allowed to solicit more than the federal limits (then $2500). But, the rules say, you *are* allowed to introduce a donor to a super PAC, so long as you don't make any requests for money yourself and you don't discuss non-public campaign strategy.

So I introduced Peter to the Club for Growth. I followed the rules meticulously, so I didn't ask him anything, I just told him that the Club was really good and effective. Peter wanted to have an impact on the race, so he gave the Club for Growth $1 million.

Then, the Dewhurst campaign did something stupid. They planted a nasty article entitled "Cruz Mega-Donor is Gay, Pro-Pot Billionaire." The article highlighted Peter's libertarian positions and slammed Peter directly, with on-the-record quotes from Dewhurst's campaign. I was embarrassed that my friend was being made a political target. I called Peter to tell him about the article. He read it and was, understandably, pissed. So he promptly gave the Club for Growth another $1 million.

Over the years, my campaigns have received millions of individual contributions. In the presidential race alone, we had a total of 1.8 million contributions. And, with almost all of them, they've never asked me for anything. Most of our supporters have not been D.C.-lobbyist types, but individuals and small business owners. They just want someone to keep his word and defend the Constitution.

Peter, for all his generous support, has never asked me for anything. I presume from the press coverage that we disagree on gay marriage, but we've never discussed it. We may also disagree on marijuana legalization (I'd leave it to each state to decide), but I don't know because we haven't discussed that either.

When we do talk, it's mostly two old friends hanging out. Many of our conversations concern Big Tech censorship, and what can be done about it. Peter's on the board of Facebook, and he knows Silicon Valley and the tech world extremely well. And he's one of the few people in that world really concerned about tech's growing power and aggressive censorship, so his insight and advice on those issues is helpful.

He was able to support my Senate campaign, but only through the ridiculous means of a super PAC. That meant I had no input on how the money was spent, no role in selecting the messages. All told, the Club for Growth raised and spent about $6 million on my Senate campaign, which, when added to the $9.5 million we raised directly for the primary campaign, is the only way we were able to win (and win decisively, winning the primary by 14 points and then the general by 16 points). But I literally had to wait and see each week what ads the Club was going to run, whenever they actually went on air, and hope whatever they were saying was somehow related to what we wanted to say in the election.

What an asinine way to run elections. It would have been far better—simpler, fairer—if he could have contributed directly to the campaign, subject to immediate disclosure. Then, we could have spent the money to convey the message we wanted, without enriching a bunch of campaign consultants at the same time.

That's how the Texas state system works. A total of eleven states right now (Alabama, Indiana, Iowa, Mississippi, Nebraska, North Dakota, Oregon, Pennsylvania, Texas, Utah, and Virginia) have no limits on individual contributions. And that system works well.

The current federal system benefits incumbents and people with vast personal fortunes. The president is a billionaire. Two of the top Democratic contenders for president were billionaires. Right now, the Democratic governor of Illinois is a billionaire, the Republican governor of Tennessee is a billionaire, the Democratic governor of Minnesota is a billionaire, and the Republican governor of West Virginia is a billionaire. And the following current office-holders are centi-millionaires (personally worth at least $100 million): governor of Colorado (a Democrat), governor of Connecticut (a Democrat), a senator from Georgia (a Republican), a senator from Florida (a Republican), a senator from Utah (a Republican), a senator from Virginia (a Democrat), and Speaker of the House Nancy Pelosi (a Democrat).

That's no way to run a democracy.

Instead we need more freedom and more transparency. That, in turn, results in more speech. Which is a much better way for our elections to operate.

As a political matter, the assault from elected Democrats on free speech is sure to continue. An abject willingness to strip away the free speech rights of American citizens has become an explicit litmus test for judicial appointments from today's radicalized Democrats. And, as a constitutional matter, on the Supreme Court, when it comes to either protecting or destroying our fundamental protections for political speech—the very heart and soul of our representative democracy—we are, sadly, only one vote away.

CHAPTER 7

CRIME, LAW AND ORDER, CAPITAL PUNISHMENT, AND *KENNEDY V. LOUISIANA*

Few issues personalize judicial activism like crime and punishment. Indeed, with the rise of the activist Supreme Court in the 1960s, it was criminal-law issues, in particular, that cut through the noise and outraged the American populace. "Impeach Earl Warren" bumper stickers began to appear in the 1970s, as rising crime followed a string of Supreme Court decisions favoring criminal defendants and mandating, in far too many cases, the release of the guilty based on legal technicalities.

One of the most inglorious criminal-law excesses of the 1960s was the extension of the so-called "exclusionary rule." Under the exclusionary rule, evidence collected in violation of a criminal defendant's constitutional rights cannot be used in a court of law. It is a judge-made rule that has no basis in the text of the Fourth Amendment.

Moreover, it is a rule designed *only* to protect the guilty. Think about it: suppose the police illegally break down your door and search your home. If you're innocent, they won't find anything, and so the exclusionary rule does nothing to help you. But, if you're guilty of a crime—let's say they find a bloody axe with your fingerprints on it and a map of where you buried the bodies—then the exclusionary rule can spare you from being convicted.

Illegal searches are bad, and we need serious tools to prevent them— I've long helped lead the charge in the Senate for greater protection of our civil liberties and legal safeguards of the privacy rights of law-abiding citizens to be free from unreasonable searches. And we also need real remedies for those—especially the innocent—whose rights have been violated by overly aggressive law enforcement. But how is society benefitted from letting an axe murderer go free? Does it help his next victim, if the court turns a blind eye to clear evidence of guilt?

It was not until the landmark 1961 Supreme Court case of *Mapp v. Ohio* that the exclusionary rule came to apply not merely to federal courts, but also to state courts across the country. *Mapp* was an activist ruling. Nothing in the Constitution mandates that state courts must follow the exclusionary rule, and the *Mapp* Court didn't purport to say otherwise. Instead, the Court just announced the new rule because the justices thought it was good policy (never mind the rising crime rates that followed the announcement of *Mapp*).

The harmful consequences of *Mapp* were made much worse five years later when the Court decided the 1966 case of *Miranda v. Arizona*. Today, *Miranda* is famous. If you watch *Law & Order* or any other cop show, you know the *Miranda* warnings by memory: "You have the right to remain silent. Anything you say can and will be used against you. You have the right to an attorney. If you cannot afford an attorney, one will be appointed for you." What you probably don't know is that the 5–4 majority in *Miranda* just made that up.

Nowhere in the Constitution is there any reference to the *Miranda* warnings. That familiar text isn't anywhere in the Bill of Rights. It's true that you have the right to remain silent (that *is* in the Constitution, the Fifth Amendment), and the right to an attorney (the Sixth Amendment), but for two hundred years police officers didn't have to affirmatively tell you about those particular rights. Until the Court decided they should. *Miranda* was, in effect, legislation. The justices decided it would be good policy to mandate these warnings, so they wrote out the text and decreed that every police officer in America must follow their script.

Together, *Miranda* and *Mapp* have resulted in a great many violent criminals going free. Suppose officers apprehend a murderer and ask something like "Why'd you kill the girl?" And the defendant confesses, "because I wanted her dead." Well, if the officer didn't first say the *Miranda* magic words, the confession would likely be thrown out. And, if the confession led to the officer's searching the killer's apartment and finding the murder weapon, that too would be tossed out, under a doctrine known as "fruit of the poisonous tree."

Over the decades, these two judge-made rules have unquestionably cost thousands of lives. When you let violent criminals go, predictably, more people get hurt and more people die. Given the soaring crime rates that *Miranda* ushered in, Ronald Reagan's great attorney general and originalist legal scholar Ed Meese famously said that if he could overturn one case and one case only, it would be *Miranda v. Arizona*.

Such was the public outcry against *Miranda* that, just two years later, Congress overturned it. You probably didn't know that either. But, in 1968, Congress passed 18 U.S.C. 3501, which on its face overturns *Miranda*. The statute was signed into law by President Lyndon B. Johnson, hardly a right-wing figure. It says that the test for whether a confession is admissible is not whether the *Miranda* warnings were given, but rather it is the test that courts had applied for two centuries—whether the confession is voluntary. In other words, if the police tie you down and beat you with rubber hoses to get your confession, then courts will exclude that confession because forced confessions are notoriously unreliable. (Under enough duress, many people will confess to just about anything.)

Then a curious thing happened: nothing. For the next three decades, practically everyone ignored that federal statute. As a matter of practice, the Department of Justice didn't cite section 3501, federal and state courts continued to apply *Miranda,* and everyone effectively pretended that the federal statute didn't exist.

Then, finally, in the 2000 case of *Dickerson v. United States*—thirty-four years after *Miranda*—the Court was forced to address section 3501. *Dickerson* came down while I was working on the 2000 George W. Bush presidential campaign. I remember literally laughing out loud when I read the opinion. Here's why.

My former boss Chief Justice Rehnquist wrote the 7–2 majority opinion, which re-affirmed *Miranda* and struck down section 3501. That caused legal and media observers to be both amazed and bewildered, even though Rehnquist had been the leading judicial critic of *Miranda* for decades.

When the Chief passed away in 2005, the *Harvard Law Review* asked me to write a tribute to him. I did so happily, reflecting on him personally and on his incredible jurisprudential legacy. But I also decided to take the opportunity to explain what I believed was really going on in *Dickerson*. That, in turn, resulted in the author of one of the leading criminal-law textbooks quoting my remembrance of the Chief at length to help explain the decision.

For three decades, Rehnquist had been fighting to limit the harmful reach of *Miranda*. And he had enjoyed considerable success, convincing the Court over time to create a number of exceptions to that very broad rule. All of those exceptions were based on the proposition that *Miranda* was not required by the Constitution; instead, it was merely what the Court called a "prophylactic" (preventative) rule.

When *Dickerson* came to the Court, I believe the Chief took a measure of his colleagues—in particular Justice Kennedy and Justice O'Connor—and concluded that they simply were not going to vote to overturn *Miranda*. I have no doubt that, had there been four other votes to do so, the Chief would have enthusiastically provided the fifth vote to overturn *Miranda*. But the votes weren't there. And that presented real danger. Because if the Chief voted to overturn *Miranda*, he would have joined Justices Scalia and Thomas in dissent. And that would mean that the majority opinion would be assigned by the senior justice in the majority, which would have been Justice Stevens.

Justice Stevens had been Rehnquist's arch-foe for decades in the battle over *Miranda*. Over and over again, Stevens dissented from Rehnquist's decisions limiting Miranda's reach. If the Court were going to preserve *Miranda*, the only way to do so was to strike down section 3501. And the only basis to strike down a federal statute is that it's unconstitutional. Which would mean, necessarily, that *Miranda* is required by the Constitution. Had the Chief voted in dissent, Justice Stevens likely would have assigned the opinion to himself and written something like the following: "The Court has many times stated that *Miranda* is merely prophylactic. But, over the decades, it has become interwoven into our constitutional fabric. And so today we make explicit what was implicit in our prior cases: *Miranda* is required by the Constitution. And so we strike down section 3501."

That holding would likely have set the stage for unwinding every single exception to *Miranda* that Rehnquist had spent thirty years carefully crafting. It would have resulted in many more guilty criminals being released and many more lives being lost.

To avoid that threat, I believe, the Chief decided to vote with the majority and author the opinion himself. And his opinion, as I read it, simply declares the following three propositions: (1) *Miranda* is *not* mandated by the Constitution, but is merely prophylactic, meaning that all of Rehnquist's carved-out exceptions therefore remain valid; (2) the LBJ-era federal statute purporting to overrule *Miranda* is not valid and is hereby struck down; (3) do not ask me why and do not ever, ever cite this opinion for any purpose whatsoever.

That's why I laughed out loud when I read it.

◆   ◆   ◆   ◆

When it comes to criminal law, capital punishment has long been one of the most divisive questions. It's an issue about which reasonable people can, and often do, disagree. Some argue that capital punishment is unnecessary, is ineffective, is too costly, and results in too long of a delay to have a sufficient deterrent effect. Or they argue that taking a life, in any circumstance, is always unjust and that the risk of error is too great. I respect those views. Others argue that capital punishment is just, that it should be reserved for the gravest of crimes, that it can and does have a significant deterrent effect on would-be murderers, and that the biblical principle of "an eye for an eye and a tooth for a tooth" embodies a fundamental tenet of justice.

Personally, I am in the latter camp. I believe in capital punishment. I believe in carrying out justice for those who commit unspeakable crimes, retribution for those who have been horribly victimized, and strong deterrence for the community to prevent the horrific crime from happening again. But under our constitutional system, you need not agree with me. You are free to arrive at a different judgment that suits your own preferences and your own set of morals.

Indeed, when I was a law clerk for Chief Justice William Rehnquist, both of my co-clerks were vocally opposed to the death penalty: one, a Democrat who leaned center-left on most policy issues, and the other, a Catholic conservative who is now a professor at Notre Dame Law School and opposed the taking of any human life. The Chief and I both disagreed and believed that capital punishment is just—and, furthermore, that the Constitution unequivocally permits it.

Indeed, during the course of my clerkship I recall instances when each of my co-clerks fervently made the case to the Chief for why he should intervene and stop the execution of a particular murderer. Each time, the Chief would patiently listen, and then with a quizzical look reply, "Why would I want to do that?"

If you oppose capital punishment, there is a constitutional avenue for you to promote your views. Make the case to your fellow citizens, to elected legislatures, and convince them; move the hearts and minds needed to democratically change the law. And, following that path, twenty-two states, in addition to Puerto Rico and the District of Columbia, have now outlawed the death penalty. So in those states, capital punishment is no longer allowed. Other states, including my home state of Texas, have instead taken the view that capital punishment saves the lives of the innocent by punishing the very worst offenders and deterring future crimes. Such is the beauty of our Constitution's federalist structure of dual spheres of sovereignty, in which the several states can each adopt the policies their citizens prefer.

For four years, however, the Supreme Court shut it all down. In 1972, in *Furman v. Georgia*, the Court struck down all death penalty laws across the United States as inconsistent with the Eighth Amendment's prohibition on "cruel and unusual punishments." This was notwithstanding the fact that the plain text of both the Fifth and Fourteenth Amendments indisputably recognizes the authority of the government to "deprive" a citizen "of life" so long as "due process of law" is afforded. That should be no surprise, given that, at the time the Bill of Rights was drafted and adopted and at the time the Fourteenth Amendment was drafted and adopted, capital punishment was widespread for the very worst crimes. Nonetheless, despite the fact that the Constitution itself refers to capital punishment explicitly and repeatedly, in *Furman*, five activist justices declared that capital punishment was unconstitutional.

In *Furman v. Georgia*, four justices dissented, including my future boss, William Rehnquist. He had just arrived on the Court, and he strongly disagreed with the activist judges' conclusion that it was not the text of the Constitution that governed, nor the two centuries of legal practice in the United States, but rather what they declared to be their own "evolving standard of decency."

To be sure, the Eighth Amendment does prohibit "cruel and unusual punishments." So if Congress or a state legislature were, for example, to enact a law providing for the public flogging and then drawing and quartering of jaywalkers, any court in the country would rightly strike that down as both "cruel" and "unusual." But as we have already seen, the Fifth Amendment, adopted at the very same moment the Eighth Amendment was adopted, explicitly recognizes capital punishment as within the proper authority of government. So whatever one might argue the Eighth Amendment prohibits, it cannot reasonably be construed to prohibit what the Constitution explicitly allows.

Furman v. Georgia remained Supreme Court law for four years, from 1972–1976. And in those years, thirty-seven states enacted new death penalty laws in an effort to comply with the new standard set out by the Court. Then, in 1976, in *Gregg v. Georgia*, the Court reversed course and once again deemed capital punishment to be constitutionally permissible. In the intervening four years, countless murderers had had their sentences reduced from death to lesser sentences because of the Court's reckless judicial activism in *Furman*.

When it comes to the death penalty, *Furman v. Georgia* began a five-decade journey into gamesmanship by liberal judicial activists. Many of the games that are played occur just below public view. Every time across this country that a criminal defendant is to be put to death, the Supreme Court justices stand prepared for the nearly inevitable torrent of last-minute appeals. In many states, executions are carried out at 12:01 a.m., so that, if there is a judicial intervention, there are a full twenty-four hours in that day before the execution warrant expires.

As a result, when I was clerking at the Supreme Court, whenever an execution was scheduled, a law clerk from each of the nine justices' chambers would remain at the Court until the execution was carried out. For executions scheduled in states on the West Coast, that typically meant remaining at the Supreme Court until 3:00 a.m. local time. Then, typically at 10:00 p.m., or 11:00 p.m., or midnight, or 1:00 a.m., a last-minute appeal would be sent over—often, in those days, on the fax machine. The appeal would be distributed to each of the nine Justices' chambers and, if you were the clerk for the justice who had responsibility for the geographic region in which the execution was set to occur, you were charged with drafting a memo summarizing the appeal. So late at night, sitting at your computer, you would hastily write a memo considering the arguments on both sides and recommending a response. You would then call your justice, often waking him or her up after he or she had gone to sleep, and over the telephone you would explain the substantive issues contained in the appeal.

Far too many of the appeals were long and complicated and were deliberately filed at the last minute so as to try to force a delay of the execution. The strategy, in effect, was to throw so much material at the justices and their law clerks so as to force them to throw up their hands and say, "We need more time to figure this out, so let's delay the execution." These last-minute appeals were not typically driven by late-breaking news. Nor, in the vast majority of circumstances, did they contain even the slightest allegation of innocence. Instead, lawyers for capital murderers would raise all sorts of technicalities which activist judges could often be counted to seize upon because they did not personally support the death penalty.

One case that illustrates the gamesmanship that pervades the federal judiciary concerns a convicted murderer from Arizona named Luis Mata. Ironically, his name was Spanish for "he kills," which in his instance, was very much the case. In 1977, Mata was tried and convicted by a jury of his peers and sentenced to death. Following extended state court litigation, Mata filed a federal habeas corpus challenge in 1985, which the federal district court took over two years to assess. At the end of those two years, the federal district court rejected his claim in a straightforward opinion on the substantive legal merits of his case.

Mata appealed to the Ninth Circuit of Appeals, which is famously the most liberal federal court of appeals in the country. The Ninth Circuit took another four years to consider the appeal and then in July 1991 rejected it on the merits. Mata filed a petition for rehearing, asking the Ninth Circuit to revisit its ruling. The Ninth Circuit took another year and a half before rejecting the petition for rehearing in November 1992. All told, activist judges had managed to delay the execution of Mata's sentence by seven and a half years, even though he had no valid legal claims and they had no argument to the contrary. Finally, in 1996— more than nineteen years after he brutally raped and murdered twenty-one-year-old Debra Lopez—Mata was put to death. Simply by dragging their feet and engaging in deliberate delay and destruction, activist judges frustrated the faithful execution of the law.

A similar Ninth Circuit case was the tale of Robert Alton Harris, who was executed in California the night of April 21, 1992, after a long night in which the Ninth Circuit issued and the Supreme Court lifted four separate stays of execution. The *Harris* case was discussed at length by my former Harvard Law School professor Charles Fried in a 1992 law review article entitled "On Impudence." The level of cynical and wily lawyering in the *Harris* case was, quite simply, absurd. The *Harris* case highlighted the abuse of our system of habeas corpus to needlessly delay the sentence of a brutal murderer. As Professor Fried wrote about one of the final twists of this sad story, "there can be no justification in law for Ninth Circuit Judge Harry Pregerson's stay, the last in [the *Harris*] case, issued after Harris was already in the gas chamber." But far too often, liberal activist lawyers and judges will go to the most extreme lengths possible to stretch out and prolong the inevitable. That was certainly what happened in the case of Robert Alton Harris's long, slow march that finally resulted in the carrying out of justice.

Congress corrected some of these abuses in 1996 with the passage of the Antiterrorism and Effective Death Penalty Act, otherwise known as AEDPA. That statute imposed meaningful time limits to expedite judicial consideration of death penalty cases. But even with AEDPA, death penalty cases take many years and consume millions of dollars of resources—almost always without serious claims of innocence.

I remember well one case out of Virginia that came before the Fourth Circuit of Appeals when I was clerking for Judge J. Michael Luttig, and which also came before the Supreme Court the next year, when I clerked for the chief justice. Joseph Roger O'Dell III had committed a horrific crime. He had murdered a forty-four-year-old woman, Helen Schartner, in cold blood. It was a brutal rape and murder by a depraved killer, and O'Dell was ultimately indicted for capital murder, abduction, rape, and sodomy.

In his defense, O'Dell raised numerous technical issues, all of which were ultimately rejected by the federal court of appeals and then by the

Supreme Court in a 5–4 vote. One of his claims, which his lawyers tacked on at the end of his appeals, was ostensibly a claim of actual innocence. When he was convicted, the trousers he had been wearing on the night of the crime had several blood stains. Forensic scientists had tested the blood and concluded, based on the available technology at the time, that the blood on his trousers was the victim's blood. Subsequently, DNA tests were developed that were able to ascertain with far greater certainty to whom a particular blood stain belonged.

O'Dell's lawyers subjected the trousers to DNA tests, and the lab that they hired concluded that one of the blood stains on O'Dell's pants *was* conclusively from the victim. That same lab also concluded that another blood stain on his pants *was not* from the victim.

And so, remarkably, O'Dell argued to the courts that the laboratory that he had hired was credible and should be believed when talking about the second blood stain, but the very same laboratory was *not* credible and should *not* be believed when talking about the first blood stain (which DNA showed to be the victim's). This was a claim that was understandably rejected by every judge who considered it: the federal district judge, all thirteen of the federal court of appeals judges on the Fourth Circuit, and all nine justices of the Supreme Court.

Nonetheless, given the highly politicized context of death penalty cases, O'Dell's case became something of a cause célèbre, with international calls for his execution to be stopped from many luminaries, including the pope. It went so far that the Sicilian city of Palermo awarded O'Dell honorary citizenship and ordered the flags flown at half-mast when he was executed.

When the Court rejected O'Dell's legal claims, I stayed late at the Court that evening. I remember driving home that night and listening to news that reported something to the effect of, "tonight, by a 5–4 vote, the Supreme Court allowed the execution of a man whom DNA evidence had proven was innocent."

Here's the opening paragraph of how the *L.A. Times* story covered it: "The Supreme Court upheld a death sentence Thursday in the strange case of a Virginia inmate who was convicted of a brutal murder but has won international acclaim as an innocent man wrongly facing the ultimate punishment."

I remember yelling out loud at the news reports because they was so patently contrary to what the facts of the case had shown, as demonstrated by the fact that every single federal judge who had considered his "innocence" claim had rejected it. DNA evidence had not shown he was innocent; to the contrary, the DNA lab actually confirmed that the victim's blood was on O'Dell's pants. Instead, all DNA proved was that he had *also* contacted somebody else's blood—and whatever conduct may have led to that other blood stain was never explained.

In my view, claims of actual innocence are qualitatively different from any other claims in criminal justice. Our justice system exists to ensure that the guilty are punished and that the innocent are freed. And I believe the justice system should *always* consider real and credible evidence of innocence.

Indeed, when I was a lawyer in private practice, one case I was particularly proud to work on involved John Thompson, a man who had been wrongfully accused and wrongfully convicted of murder in Louisiana. My law firm had represented Mr. Thompson for years, and my firm and I represented him *pro bono*—without charge. After his conviction, it was unearthed that prosecutors in Louisiana had wrongfully suppressed blood evidence that, when analyzed, proved Mr. Thompson's innocence. The judicial process worked; Mr. Thompson was subsequently freed because he had not committed the crime with which he had been charged. And the prosecutors, in that instance, had committed serious misconduct in suppressing the evidence.

I represented Mr. Thompson before the Supreme Court in his civil case, where he sued the prosecutors who had prosecuted him and wrongfully suppressed the evidence. I joined my law partners in urging the Court to uphold the $14 million damage judgment he had won—$1 million for every year he had languished undeservedly on death row. Unfortunately, we didn't prevail in that case, and Mr. Thompson lost

5–4. He died of a heart attack in 2017, having received public compensation of only $150,000 for the fourteen years stolen from him. But he was rightly freed because there was credible and, indeed, compelling evidence that he had been wrongfully accused.

But the case of *Connick v. Thompson* is very much the exception when it comes to death penalty cases. In almost all federal death penalty cases, there is no genuine issue as to guilt and innocence.

That was certainly true with the case of *Kennedy v. Louisiana.* Patrick Kennedy committed an unspeakable crime. He savagely raped his eight-year-old stepdaughter, leaving her badly injured and bleeding in her bed. Kennedy was a recidivist child rapist, and this was the second time he had brutally raped a young girl. Louisiana law at the time provided for capital punishment for aggravated child rape—for the very worst child rapists. Kennedy was tried and convicted by a jury of his peers and sentenced to death. His case went all the way to the Supreme Court, and I argued on behalf of Texas and eight other states, supporting Louisiana. The question before the Court was whether it should strike down every law in the country providing capital punishment for the very worst child rapists.

The preceding year, Texas had enacted legislation known as Jessica's Law, a law targeting sex criminals with child victims. It was named for Jessica Lunsford, a nine-year-old girl who was kidnapped, sexually assaulted, and murdered in 2005 in Florida by a registered sex offender. The Texas Legislature joined the Legislatures of Florida, Louisiana, Montana, Oklahoma, and South Carolina in authorizing the death penalty for people who commit repeated sex crimes against children. At the time the case was argued, similar legislation was under active consideration in Alabama, Colorado, Mississippi, Missouri, and Tennessee.

Louisiana was the party to the case, but the Court granted Texas argument time to appear as an amicus—a friend of the Court. It was the first time in nearly a decade that the Court had granted argument time to a state that was not a party to the case. Kennedy argued that the "evolving standards of decency"—the same amorphous standard that the Court had invoked to strike down the death penalty in *Furman v. Georgia* in 1972—had now evolved to the point that the Court should prohibit, in all circumstances, capital punishment for child rape.

In 1977, in *Coker v. Georgia*, the Court had already struck down capital punishment for adult rape. The *Coker* plurality opinion was careful to carve out that it was addressing the rape of an "adult woman" fourteen separate times, as opposed to the rape of a child. Patrick Kennedy's lawyers argued that, in the time that had passed between 1977 and 2008, society's "standards of decency" had sufficiently "evolved" so as now to mandate extending the same legal logic not just to adult rapists, but also child rapists.

Another one of the arguments Kennedy put forward was that the Constitution forbids the imposition of capital punishment in any non-homicide crime—in all types of crime, that is, where no one's life is lost. Although it might have some intuitive appeal, that proposition directly contradicts criminal laws across the country. Indeed, at the time the case was argued, non-homicide crimes that state and federal criminal codes made eligible for the death penalty included child rape; treason; aggravated kidnapping; drug trafficking; aircraft hijacking; espionage; aggravated assault by incarcerated, persistent felons; and attempting, authorizing, or advising the killing of any officer, juror, or a witness in a case involving a continuing criminal enterprise.

Of those non-homicide crimes, treason stands out because it is the only crime defined in the text of the Constitution—in Article III, Section 3—and the Constitution explicitly confers on Congress the "Power to declare the Punishment of Treason." Under that constitutional authority, a congressional enactment authorizing the death penalty for treason has been in continuous effect since 1790. To this day, it is enacted in the U.S. Code at 18 U.S.C. § 2381.

Also central to Kennedy's argument was his contention that there was an "evolving national consensus" against the death penalty for child rape because it was no longer permitted in many states. At the oral argument, there was one particularly notable exchange. Justice John Paul

Stevens asked if, in the course of the history of criminal jurisprudence, standards of punishment had ever evolved in any direction other than greater lenience. As it so happened, I had an example to point to. In the thirteenth century, under Saxon law operating at the time in medieval England, the punishment for rape had been lessened from capital punishment to merely removing the culprit's eyes and the testicles.

At this point in oral argument, I committed the same error in judgment I had made at the *Van Orden* Fifth Circuit Court of Appeals oral argument: I attempted humor. I quipped that the reduction in punishment from death to just removing the eyes and testicles was "William the Conqueror's kinder, gentler version" of English common-law justice. Once again, the justices showed mercy and laughed heartily.

But I continued reading from famed legal scholar and English common lawyer William Blackstone, who noted that the lessened punishment didn't work: "that previous lenity being productive of the most terrible consequences, it was subsequently necessary to return to making it a capital offense."

Unfortunately, at the end of the day, the Supreme Court went the other way. By a vote of 5–4, the Court struck down Louisiana's law and every other law in the country providing for capital punishment for the very worst child rapists. Justice Kennedy agreed with the arguments of Patrick Kennedy and authored the majority opinion, in which he concluded that "evolving standards of decency" empowered the Court to strike down these laws. He further opined that there was an objective "national consensus" against capital punishment for child rape.

After the case was decided, it was discovered that not only had six state legislatures explicitly disagreed, but so had both the Congress of the United States and the president of the United States. Federal law, namely the Uniform Code of Military Justice, provided explicitly for capital punishment for child rape when such a horrendous crime was committed in a military context. The underlying legislation authorizing that Uniform Code of Military Justice article had passed Congress by an overwhelming majority.

Rape in the military context had long been punishable by death, at least since the 1863 Army Articles of War. In 2006, Congress separated the rape provision into several subsections and explicitly made child rape punishable by the death penalty. The Department of Defense had advocated that revision and specifically pointed to the Louisiana child-rape law as an example. That federal law passed the House (as part of a much larger package) by a vote of 374–71, and it passed the Senate by voice vote. President George W. Bush signed it, and he issued an executive order specifically implementing the child-rape provision.

These facts were demonstrably contrary to the conclusion of five justices that—in 2008, just two years later—there was some sort of "national consensus" against capital punishment for child rape. Unfortunately, prior to the decision, this federal law eluded everyone's research. Much to my frustration, neither I nor the lawyers in my office had uncovered it prior to argument. But Louisiana had also failed to discover it, as did all nine justices, and all ten briefs filed in the Court had failed to point it out. Critically, the U.S. solicitor general, who is expressly charged with defending the constitutionality of the laws of the United States, also did not discover it, and so chose not to participate in the case or present any argument to defend the underlying federal law.

When the federal law was uncovered—in a military-law blog post, of all places, after the opinion had been issued—I assisted Louisiana in filing a petition for rehearing and helped recruit a prominent Supreme Court advocate (and future Obama solicitor general) to file it on their behalf. Unfortunately, the Court had already made up its mind, so the fact that recently enacted federal law conclusively disproved the supposed objective "national consensus" did not change their underlying legal conclusion.

◆   ◆   ◆   ◆

At the end of the day, death-penalty cases remain highly contested and highly controversial. Within the federal courts, they are still deeply politicized, as illustrated powerfully by another claim that federal courts have entertained, called a *Lackey* claim. In that underlying 1995 case, *Lackey v. Texas*, another convicted murderer who had appealed his case over and over and over again, delaying the imposition of his sentence for seventeen years, argued that it was now unconstitutional to carry out the sentence because it was so delayed. At the time, both Justice Stevens and Justice Breyer had suggested that such a claim might have merit.

My former boss, Judge J. Michael Luttig, who served on the Fourth Circuit Court of Appeals, was perhaps the most prominent and respected conservative appellate judge in the country when I clerked for him. He had also been directly affected by violent crime. On April 19, 1994, Judge Luttig's father, John Luttig, was murdered after driving back from Dallas to his home in Tyler, Texas. John Luttig pulled into his family's garage, and three teenage boys followed him and his wife into the garage in order to steal his car. The criminals shot and killed John Luttig in cold blood while Judge Luttig's mother pretended to be dead. Then the boys leapt into the car, drove away, and abandoned it just blocks away from the home.

All of this occurred when I was still in law school. And Judge Luttig, a sitting federal judge at the time, was forced to go through five separate criminal trials for the murderers who killed his father. Judge Luttig gave, at one of the trials, a federal victim impact statement which remains one of the most powerful statements about the consequence of violent crime that I have ever seen. He described, in matter-of-fact fashion, but also incredibly poignantly, the small, mundane details of one's life after one's father is murdered. Judge Luttig allowed that victim impact statement to be published in the newspaper because he wished to speak for so many victims of violent crime who lacked the opportunity to speak for themselves. Here are some excerpts from his statement:

> Words seem trite in describing what follows when...your
> father is stripped from your life....it's being frightened out of
> your mind in the middle of the night by a frantic banging on
> your door...Your body goes limp as you see one of your best

friends standing in the doorway. No words need even be spoken. For you know that the worst in life has happened. Then, he tells you: "Your mom just called. Father was murdered in the driveway of your home."

...it's realizing that, at that very moment, the man you have worshipped all your life is lying on his back in your driveway with two bullets through his head.

...it's going down to the store where your dad had always shopped for clothes, to buy a shirt, a tie that will match his suit, and a package of three sets of underwear (you can only buy them in sets of three) so your dad will look nice when he is buried.

...it's sitting beside your father's grave into the night in 30-degree weather, so that he won't be alone on the first Christmas.

...If I had any wish, any wish in the world, it would be that no one ever again would have to go through what my mother and my father experienced on the night of April 19, [1994,] what my family has endured since and must carry with us the rest of our lives.

For Judge Luttig, violent crime was real and personal. And as his law clerk, I still recall standing by the judge at his father's gravesite in Charlottesville, Virginia, as the judge wept, remembering his dad. Judge Luttig was deeply committed to the Constitution and the rule of law, and I am confident that his own personal tragedy did not influence how he ruled in cases. He had been Justice Scalia's very first law clerk in Scalia's first year as a judge on the D.C. Circuit Court of Appeals. And he and Scalia remained incredibly close until Justice Scalia passed away. Indeed, when Judge Luttig's father was murdered, it was Justice Scalia who came to Judge Luttig's home late at night to beat on the door, awaken Judge Luttig and his wife, and inform them that the judge's father had just been murdered in East Texas.

I have said previously—indeed, I said it in the course of the South Carolina presidential debate in 2016—that, had I been president, I would have appointed Judge Luttig instead of John Roberts to be chief justice of the United States. Once upon a time, both men were the two finalists to replace Chief Justice William Rehnquist, and had Luttig been nominated instead of Roberts, I have complete confidence that Judge Luttig would have remained faithful to his oath to support the Constitution.

In the 1995 Fourth Circuit Court of Appeals case of *Turner v. Jabe*, a capital murderer raised a *Lackey* claim. The panel considering the appeal rejected the claim, carefully weighing the pros and cons before rejecting the case on its merits. Judge Luttig wrote a short concurrence that he typed out on his own keyboard using two fingers to type furiously, as he always did. It was extraordinarily powerful. Judge Luttig criticized the claim as "a mockery of our system of justice, and an affront to law-abiding citizens who are already rightly disillusioned with that system."

The short concurrence cut to the heart of the gamesmanship that pervades and characterizes so much capital litigation. When I was a law clerk at the Supreme Court, Justice Clarence Thomas, who is also close friends with Judge Luttig, kept a copy of Judge Luttig's opinion in this case under the glass on his desk in his chambers.

As *Kennedy v. Louisiana* demonstrated, five justices far too often have believed that they have the arbitrary power to resolve contested policy issues concerning criminal law and the death penalty. But that is not the role of judges under the Constitution. For those who wish to change the substantive standards, that responsibility is left to elected legislatures. And yet, in case after case, involving the very worst criminals committing the most unspeakable crimes, a host of lawyers, advocates, and activist judges continue to frustrate the carrying out of the laws.

When it comes to capital punishment, activist judges try to subvert the law rather than apply it. They do the same thing when they argue against particular cocktails of drugs used in lethal injection cases. This litigation strategy is an unabashed abolition strategy, trying to get the

Court to revisit the four-year period, from 1972 to 1976, when every death penalty law in America was struck down.

In 2008, the Supreme Court decided *Baze v. Rees*, a challenge to Kentucky's method of lethal injection, which was then the primary or only method of execution by the federal government and in thirty-seven states. I authored an amicus brief on behalf of Texas and nineteen other states defending the constitutionality of lethal injection. At the time, our position prevailed 7–2.

But after *Baze*, private pharmaceutical companies were all too eager to assist the activist lawyers and judges by limiting or ending production of various lethal injection drug cocktails—thereby forcing states to experiment with more novel and potentially more dangerous drugs in order to carry out the executions required by the law.

By making the injections used in capital punishment cases more risky, pharmaceutical companies gave the activists exactly what they wanted: a new avenue to ban the death penalty. In the 2015 Supreme Court case of *Glossip v. Gross*, a bare 5–4 Court majority held that lethal injection using the drug cocktail known as midazolam did not violate the Cruel and Unusual Punishments Clause. In *Glossip*, Clayton Lockett was executed in Oklahoma using midazolam, dying forty-three minutes after the lethal injection after groaning about the drug cocktail allegedly not working properly. Though the majority prevailed, liberal justices in dissent again used the case as a lever to try to enact a total ban on capital punishment.

Justice Breyer wrote that circumstances had so changed since *Gregg v. Georgia* that the death penalty itself, in all forms and instances, is once again violative of the Cruel and Unusual Punishments Clause. In other words, Justice Breyer wrote that he believes *Furman v. Georgia* should be restored. He pointed to what he saw as four separate policy reasons for this: serious unreliability of the death penalty, arbitrariness in application of the death penalty, excessive delays of the death penalty, and the fact that many places in the United States have largely abandoned use of the death penalty. Justice Breyer's dissent in *Glossip* was joined by his fellow long-standing Court liberal, Justice Ruth Bader Ginsburg. The separate dissenting opinion, written by Justice Sonia Sotomayor and also joined by Breyer, Ginsburg, and Justice Elena Kagan, reached the same outcome, albeit in the specific factual circumstances of that case.

Justice Scalia, joined by Justice Thomas, wrote a characteristically powerful concurrence, concluding with a stinging rebuke of Justice Breyer and the dissenting justices:

> Capital punishment presents moral questions that philosophers, theologians, and statesmen have grappled with for millennia. The Framers of our Constitution disagreed bitterly on the matter. For that reason, they handled it the same way they handled many other controversial issues: they left it to the People to decide. By arrogating to himself the power to overturn that decision, Justice Breyer does not just reject the death penalty, he rejects the Enlightenment.

Recent capital punishment cases at the Supreme Court suggest that now there may be four votes on the current Court to bring us back to the days of *Furman v. Georgia*. In other words, it now seems likely that there are four sitting justices who would ignore the unmistakably plain language of both the Fifth and Fourteenth Amendments and conclude that the Eighth Amendment's Cruel and Unusual Punishments Clause prohibits any and all forms and methods of execution.

If that is correct, on this issue, as with so many, we're once again just one vote away from a remaking of our constitutional order.

◆   ◆   ◆   ◆

There is a place to deal with the highly contested issues of criminal punishment, and it's not the federal bench. Violent crime has the potential to touch any family, and the question of how society should deal with those who commit the most grievous of crimes is a question with which elected legislatures always have, and always will, wrestle. Violent crime is, I believe, qualitatively different from non-violent criminal offenses.

In the Senate, I have taken up criminal justice issues in my role as a legislator. I was proud to co-sponsor the 2018 First Step Act, criminal-justice reform legislation that lessened penalties for non-violent drug offenses. In criminal sentencing, our statutory systems have vacillated between widespread judicial discretion, which produced widely varying sentences for comparable crimes, and strict mandatory minimums and sentencing guidelines, which produced more uniformity but at the same time could result in unjustly harsh sentences in at least some of the applications.

I supported the First Step Act, the most far-reaching criminal-justice reform in decades, because I believed mandatory sentences for non-violent drug offenses had gotten too strict and that our scarce law enforcement resources were better spent combating violent crime. But the price of my support for that legislation was drawing a very clear distinction between violent crime and non-violent crime.

The Senate Judiciary Committee had previously taken up criminal justice reform twice in recent years, with the effort spearheaded by my close friend Senator Mike Lee of Utah, as well as Democratic senator Dick Durbin of Illinois. Although I supported the objective, I felt compelled to offer amendments that clearly carved out violent criminals from the reform efforts, ensuring that relief only flowed to non-violent offenders and that we did not give clemency to those who had committed the crimes of murder, rape, or other violent assaults.

Twice, the Senate Judiciary Committee rejected my proposed amendments to the legislation. In each instance, there were sufficient votes on the Committee to pass the bill out of Committee and to the Senate floor: all of the Democrats and several of the Republicans. But in both instances, I argued to the Committee that although they could move the legislation out of Committee, it would never pass on the Senate floor unless and until they accepted my amendments excluding violent criminals.

Senate Republican leadership had made it clear that the bill would not be brought forward for a vote unless there was greater consensus. And numerous Republican senators indicated both privately and publicly that they shared my already-expressed concerns about releasing violent offenders from prison. Several Republican senators expressed the view in particular that, if my amendment were adopted, they would be willing to support the legislation.

When Donald Trump was elected president, he made criminal-justice reform a signature issue, tasking his son-in-law, Jared Kushner, with driving the White House's legislative effort. Despite saying he supported reform, over eight years President Obama had never been able to get it done (and, to be honest, didn't devote much effort to trying to do so). There was strong bipartisan support behind criminal-justice reform, and yet, a number of law-and-order Republicans understandably had serious concerns.

Once again, I offered my amendment excluding violent criminals from the bill's coverage. I spent hours in person and on the phone negotiating with fellow senators and with Jared and the White House legislative team. After considerable resistance, both Kushner and Senator Durbin agreed to my amendment. Within hours of my amendment's incorporation into the draft legislation, I announced my support for the bill and, the very next business day, Senate leadership announced that it would finally be brought to the Senate floor for a vote. As I said at the time, "With these changes, this bill gives non-violent offenders a better chance at rejoining society while keeping violent offenders behind bars."

The First Step Act, with my amendment, came to a vote on the floor of the Senate and passed overwhelmingly by a bipartisan majority of 87–12. Of the eighty-seven votes in favor of the legislation, thirty-eight were Republicans, and forty-nine were Democrats.

The First Step Act mirrored, in significant respects, similar legislation that the Texas Legislature had passed, reducing punishments for non-violent drug offenders and shifting law-enforcement focus to violent criminals instead. And in Texas, the results had been strongly positive.

I was proud to play an integral role in the passage of such crucial bipartisan legislation at the federal level. As I said at the time, "Too many young men, particularly young black men, face long mandatory prison sentences for nonviolent drug offenses; this bipartisan legislation corrects that injustice. And it will focus our law enforcement resources where they are most needed: preventing violent crime."

In my view, there is a profound and crucial distinction between violent and non-violent crime. Far too many young men, and young African-American and Hispanic men in particular, historically have faced long prison terms for the non-violent possession of drugs. For those struggling with addiction, there are better, more effective strategies, often dealing with treatment and rehabilitation, that can produce real results.

Violent crime is different. With violent crime, I have comforted too many grieving families mourning the loss of a child or loved one who was brutalized at the hands of a depraved rapist or killer. And I, for one, was not willing to look a mother in the eyes and tell her that I had any part in releasing early the murderer who took her child's life.

President Trump signed the First Step Act into law, and I joined him in the Oval Office with an amazing coalition of criminal-justice reform advocates, evangelical and faith-based leaders, conservative and libertarian think-tank leaders, and law-enforcement leaders. At the White House signing ceremony, I praised the spirit of compromise that governed the bill's drafting process. Because we were willing to compromise, we were able to write good legislation that keeps Americans safe while making sure that justice is properly served. That kind of compromise is what the legislative process is designed to accomplish. It's picture proof of why lawmaking should be left in the hands of legislators rather than judges.

The way the First Step Act passed, through policy, legal and constitutional arguments about what is right, appropriate, and just, through a consideration of facts and data and evidence about what is most effective in deterring crime and preventing recidivism—all of it was done through the legislative process. That is how our system is supposed to work. Elected legislatures exist to consider and to weigh policy arguments and to reflect the wishes and values of the voters who elected them. When unelected judges seize issues of the criminal law and mandate that violent criminals receive lesser punishments, they are going against both the constitutional structure and their responsibility as judges.

CHAPTER 8

DEMOCRACY AND THE ELECTORAL PROCESS

D ressed in a white pantsuit, Bo Derek bowled barefoot and with both hands. She was with us in an Austin bowling alley on Election Day 2000, lending a surreal quality to an otherwise extraordinary day.

I had just spent the last year and a half on the George W. Bush presidential campaign, where I had been part of the policy team. And, most importantly (for me at least), I had met Heidi on the campaign, my then-girlfriend and soon-to-be wife. Our boss, Joshua Bolten, was the campaign's policy director. He would later go on to become President Bush's head of the Office of Management and Budget and then chief of staff. Josh, it so happened, was dating Bo Derek, the legendary beauty who had starred in the movie *10*. Decades later, she retained her movie-star radiance.

Josh was a bowling enthusiast. Although we had worked around the clock for the entirety of the campaign, on election day, nobody wants or needs a policy team, and so Josh took us out bowling with his girl-friend. The women didn't get what the big deal was, but every man on the team, all of us in our twenties, was rendered speechless. And it would've been better if I had remained speechless because as that day and evening proceeded, we began an election-night party that kept us out until the not-so-wee hours of the morning.

By 4:00 a.m., we all stood out in the street on Congress Avenue in downtown Austin in a light drizzling rain, and Don Evans, the chairman of the campaign, came out to tell the assembled crowd that there would be no election result that evening. As we were walking home, Heidi asked me, "So, do you think Bo Derek is good looking?" Sober, I can answer that question, but at 4:00 in the morning after many hours of election-night revelry, I responded with a bit too much enthusiasm and candor. To this day, Heidi rightfully gives me grief over my foolish answer to her that evening.

As election night began, the networks called the election for Al Gore early on. At 7:50 p.m., they declared that Florida, with its pivotal twenty-five electoral votes, had voted for Gore—even before the polls had closed in the entire state of Florida. The western panhandle (the most reliably conservative part of the state), in a later time zone, still had people going to the polls when the networks declared it all over.

All of us were despondent; it seemed our efforts had been in vain, until suddenly the networks revisited their call. As more results came in, one network after the other changed the call from Florida going for Vice President Gore to being too close to call. Then, later in the evening, the networks were ready to make a call again. This time, they declared the state won by George W. Bush, and shortly thereafter, the presidency won by George W. Bush.

Al Gore called to concede, and we began the celebrations. But then, not long after, Gore called back to retract his concession. The margin had grown narrower—with Bush's lead dropping from some 50,000 votes down to just 1784 votes—and, at the end of the night, the results remained uncertain.

Two days later, Josh called me into his office and asked me to get on a plane and fly to Florida. The Gore campaign was contesting the election, and lawyers from across the country were descending on the Sunshine State like proverbial locusts. I packed a bag and headed straight to the airport. When I arrived in Tallahassee, we set up headquarters in the State Republican Party building, coincidentally named the George Herbert Walker Bush Building. Initially, there were just a handful of Republican lawyers on the ground. Our team was led by Ben Ginsburg, the campaign's outside counsel and an experienced election lawyer. Ben was a friend, and he knew well the complex world of the Federal Election Commission (FEC).

Many lawyers in Ben's position would have seen this litigation as an opportunity for them to be the stars, but Ben demonstrated a remarkable humility by recognizing early on that his primary expertise was not as a litigator, but rather as an advisor—a quarterback—on FEC matters. Accordingly, Ben and I sat down, just the two of us, in a conference room in Tallahassee with a yellow notepad and asked ourselves, "Who are the best lawyers in the country to defend Governor Bush, to try our case?"

My being in that room was a happy accident. At the time, I was just twenty-nine years old. Just a few years out of law school, I had clerked for Judge Luttig and the Chief and had spent two years in private practice. And as it so happened, I was the only practicing litigator on the full-time campaign staff in Austin. What I had practiced, albeit briefly, was constitutional litigation.

As we sat looking at the empty notepad, it was a *Field of Dreams*-type scenario: "If you call them, they will come." The first lawyer I suggested was my former boss, Mike Carvin. Mike, a brilliant Supreme Court litigator, is the best lawyer I have ever seen at anticipating unexpected questions and seeing around corners in unpredictable litigation. Ben readily agreed, so I called Mike on his cellphone. Mike was, at the time, at a wedding in Seattle. He flew from Seattle to D.C., where his wife met him at the airport with a suitcase of fresh clothing, and, hours later, he arrived on the ground in Tallahassee.

Another lawyer I suggested calling was John Roberts. John was then the head of the Supreme Court practice at Hogan & Hartson and universally considered one of the finest Supreme Court advocates in the country. I called John and asked him to come down. He dropped everything and flew to Florida.

Ted Olson, another highly respected Supreme Court advocate and the former head of the Office of Legal Counsel under Ronald Reagan, had already been tapped to lead the Supreme Court team.

And George W. Bush had brought in his father's right-hand man, Jim Baker, to lead the team overall. Baker was legendary. He had served as White House chief of staff, as secretary of the treasury, and as secretary of state. He had managed *five* presidential campaigns. He was George Herbert Walker Bush's best friend and closest confidant, but he was not particularly conservative. During the Bush 41 administration and the Reagan administration before that, Baker far too often had run circles around conservatives in those administrations.

When George W. Bush launched his 2000 presidential campaign, he notably excluded Baker and the other more moderate greybeards that had surrounded his father's administration. But, for this unpredictable mayhem, George W. Bush wisely turned to Baker because nobody alive better combined legal knowledge with cunning, ruthless savvy, a nuanced understanding of the press, and a statesman-like gravitas. Baker came to direct the entire team.

Also early on, we realized we needed trial lawyers—that we couldn't have all pointy-headed Supreme Court clerks who do appellate law. Rather, we needed courtroom lawyers who wouldn't run scared if they saw a jury. I suggested Fred Bartlit, a legendary trial lawyer who spent decades with the Chicago-based law firm Kirkland & Ellis and then started his own firm, Bartlit Beck in both Chicago and Denver. When I had finished my clerkship with the chief, I had interviewed at Bartlit Beck.

One of my closest friends clerking at the Court was Glen Summers, a Scalia clerk who was among the most conservative clerks at the Court. (Glen would later be a groomsman at Heidi and my wedding.) Glen and I both interviewed together at Bartlit Beck and at Cooper Carvin. I seriously considered going to Bartlit Beck but ultimately chose a different path. I had gotten to know Fred in the course of the interviews and recognized that we needed the skills of a seasoned trial lawyer. Ben gave the green light for me to call Glen and ask both him and Fred to come to Florida. Fred then asked if he could bring his lead partner, Phil Beck. I didn't know Phil at the time, but Fred promised that Phil was as talented a trial lawyer as there was practicing, and we needed him. I said we'd be glad to have him.

We set up the Bartlit Beck team in a different building. We told them that, at some point relatively soon, there's going to be a trial, so don't get drawn into the media circus, don't get drawn into the appellate battle, but get ready for trial. And they did.

Early in the proceedings, there were a total of seven different cases pending in different courts, all challenging the outcome of the election. The first time the votes were counted, George W. Bush won. He had the most votes, but Democrats wanted a recount—and it quickly became clear that they wanted to keep counting over and over and over again until Al Gore was finally declared the winner. That's not surprising in any election. Whoever has the fewest votes has all the incentive to want endless recounts because otherwise, they lose.

In the first few days in Florida, Secretary Baker asked me to serve on all seven of the different legal teams to ensure consistency between what we were saying in different courtrooms. And my first six days down there, I slept a total of seven hours. It was chaos. We had charts on the wall, mapping out each of the different cases, any one of which, if it went wrong, could cost the presidency of the United States.

Our trial team was led by Bartlit Beck and Houston-based Baker Botts (where I had spent two summers working in law school). They spent two weeks separated from everyone else getting ready for trial.

Of course, the Democrats had their own array of trial lawyers. But their entire team was led by, and much of the work was done by, one person, David Boies. David Boies is an amazingly talented litigator. He's brilliant, and he has a photographic memory. He seemed equally adept at questions of law and questions of fact and was as quick on his feet responding to unexpected changes as any lawyer I have seen in a courtroom.

But Boies was simply doing too much. He led the State Supreme Court effort, which for us had been led by Mike Carvin. He led the U.S. Supreme Court effort, which for us was led by Ted Olson. He led the state trial team, which for us was led by Fred Bartlit and Phil Beck. He became the chief press spokesperson for Vice President Gore, which for us was led by Jim Baker and former deputy AG George Terwilliger. In any one of these endeavors, Boies was excellent. At all of them, simultaneously, there simply were not enough hours in the day for one man.

For elections, many counties in Florida used a punch-card system of voting where the voter pushes a stylus through a punch card and pushes out what's called a "chad"—the little rectangle that the stylus pokes out. One of the arguments presented by the Democrats was that the voting machine used in Florida's punch card systems had a problem that led to systematic undercounts of the votes. The theory went that the first column of a punch card was always used in every election, whereas the second and third columns were used less frequently. Therefore, they claimed, the first column would get more chads built up under it, and, as they piled up, it would become more difficult to push the stylus through and vote for the candidate you wanted—which they presumed to be Al Gore.

This was a curious theory, on many fronts. And we knew we had significant evidence to counter it. One of the younger lawyers working on the team was preparing to take the deposition of the Democrats' trial expert, and he was eager to rip the expert apart. Fred and Phil jumped in and stopped him and said, "You will do no such thing. We are going to use this at trial. And we have zero interest in telegraphing our trial strategy at pre-trial deposition." Instead, the deposition focused primarily on questioning the expert's academic qualifications, which presumably led the Gore team to believe that, at trial, we were going to dispute whether this expert were sufficiently qualified.

The expert at issue was a Yale statistician who had prepared a report that examined prior Florida elections. He argued that in Florida, the 1998 race for U.S. Senate had been in column one, the race for governor in column two, and there were significantly more undervotes in the Senate race than in the governor's race. Specifically, 1.6 percent more votes were cast statewide in the governor's race than were cast in the Senate race. That, the Democrats argued, supported their theory that the chads would build up under the first column, and the rubber in the voting machine would get stiffer under column one, and as a result it would make it harder to push the stylus through and vote.

I remember the night before trial commenced. All of us on the trial team were in a large conference room seated around the table. Phil Beck had a baseball cap on and was wearing it backwards. He had a yellow pad in front of him. In a corner of the room, the television set was on, and David Boies was being interviewed by Larry King. Phil looked up and said, "What in the hell is he doing on *Larry King*?" He said, "We're going to trial tomorrow, and I'm going to destroy his lead witness, and he doesn't know it because he's on #@#$! *Larry King*!"

The next day, things played out just as Phil had predicted. The Yale statistician laid out his theory that prior elections showed it was harder to vote for races in column one than races in column two. Then Phil stood up for his cross-examination. Phil began gently enough, but then moved in for the kill:

"In your sworn affidavit, sir,...you said 'a closer inspection of the Palm Beach ballot reveals that the senatorial race was recorded in the first column and the gubernatorial race in the second,' right?"

"Right."

"Now, professor, you've never inspected the ballot that was used in 1998 in Palm Beach County, closely or otherwise, have you?"

[six full seconds of silence, with the professor looking deeply anxious]

"I have not seen the ballot."

"Well, I got one this morning. [showing the witness the ballot]...Now you understand, sir, that this thing I'm pointing to on the left, that's page one of the ballot....We got page one of the ballot...and then page two of the ballot....Now do you understand, sir, that the way these ballots work, on page one, everything that's on page one you vote for in the first column...."

"Yes, I understand, sir."

"Now you read please for the court...what is the race here at the top of column one?"

"...It's the...United States senator."

"And what's right underneath the United States Senate, *in column one?*"

"State governor, lieutenant governor."

"So, so what you said in your sworn affidavit, was in column two was actually in column one, right?"

"...it should have been in column one. My mistake; it was the second race, and that's what I put...."

"Well, in your affidavit, you didn't say that the fact that it was the second race was what's important, you said that the fact that the Senate was in column one and the governor was in column two, why that 'seemed to suggest' that the voting machine wasn't recording all the votes in column one...."

"I said that this was possible, yes."

"And you can see here that that sworn affidavit...that just wasn't true, was it, sir?

"It contained a mistake."

"...and when you signed that sworn statement, you were relying on the Gore legal team to give you the straight facts, weren't you?"

"I relied on the facts that I received. Yes."

"That's all I have, Judge."

It was the most stunning cross-examination I'd ever seen. Television dramas notwithstanding, "Perry Mason" moments are rare in court, and yet because our team was fully prepared—we had examined the actual ballots, we had physically tested the voting machines used in Florida elections—we utterly destroyed the Gore team's expert witness. Afterwards, that Yale statistician was seen weeping, cradling his head in his hands in the courtroom hallway.

◆   ◆   ◆   ◆

During one of the early days of the litigation, as we walked into one of the many trial court proceedings, Warren Christopher, who had been Bill Clinton's secretary of state and was helping lead Al Gore's team, turned to Jim Baker and said, "Boy, it's something else trying to manage the egos of all these lawyers." Baker responded, "Really? We haven't had that problem." Now, that was unquestionably the right political answer to give. It projected strength and calm, but as it so happens, it was also truthful.

The legal team that the George W. Bush campaign brought together in *Bush v. Gore* is the finest legal team I'm aware of that has ever been assembled in any case. It was a dream team of the top Republican lawyers across the country. Ordinarily, you could never assemble a team like that on any case and have it work. The egos would inevitably clash. Too many 800-pound gorillas on the same litigation team is not a recipe for success. *Bush v. Gore* was different, however. The Republican lawyers across the country watched what was happening, and they were horrified by it.

For example, as I mentioned, John Roberts was widely considered one of the finest, if not the finest, Supreme Court advocate alive. Prior to John's being retained, the Bush campaign had already tasked Ted Olson with leading the Supreme Court argument. Remarkably, John was content merely to help with the briefs, to draft and edit portions of them, and to help prepare Ted for oral argument at multiple moots.

One day, however, in the midst of the recount, I saw John carrying a suitcase walking out of the Tallahassee headquarters. I stopped him and said, "John, where are you going?" He said, "Back to D.C." I responded, "John, you can't leave. We're in the middle of a battle for the whole country." He somewhat sheepishly replied, "Well, I've got a U.S. Supreme Court argument tomorrow morning." John went, got on a plane, flew to D.C., and argued a complicated intellectual property case the next morning, which he ended up winning 9–0. Then he immediately returned to working to help us litigate the case. John was a truly gifted lawyer.

Our team was united by the shared conviction that the facts were clear: Bush had won. The voters had voted. The election was done. Yet in election recounts, Democrats tend to win recounts far more frequently than do Republicans. Republicans, in recounts, are often too ready to throw in the towel. Democratic activists and lawyers, in contrast, are often heavily driven by the ends justifying the means.

I recall our team discussing what to do when the Democrats initially asked for limited recounts, in just four heavily Democratic counties in Florida. We had a debate: Should we counter by asking for reciprocal recounts in four overwhelmingly Republican counties? I still remember Mike Carvin energetically arguing "no" because, he said, that in the Democratic recounts, "their guys will cheat, and they will steal. Their guys are going to be poking the chads out with their fingernails as they're counting." And every time they count, they will have more Democratic votes. "Our guys won't cheat," Mike continued "They'll actually just count it, and so it doesn't advantage us to count again in a Republican county because if our guys aren't stealing votes, counting again doesn't help us."

Now, some observers would surely dispute whether Mike's characterization was accurate or not, but I can tell you the Bush trial team believed it was true. And that is why we didn't seek targeted recounts in selected Republican counties.

I remember in those early days, sitting and helping draft the initial pleading in which we laid out a Fourteenth Amendment Equal Protection Clause claim—namely, that counting ballots under multiple different legal standards in multiple different circumstances all simultaneously violated the Constitution's guarantee for equal protection under the laws.

When we first drafted it, all of us agreed the claim was weak. At the time, it was a truly novel claim—but over the course of the thirty-six days that the recount ensued, a remarkable thing happened: each day, that claim got stronger and stronger.

The first major appeal in *Bush v. Gore* ended up in front of the Florida Supreme Court. The Florida Supreme Court, at the time, was dominated by partisan Democrats, many of whom had been appointed by Democratic governors. My old boss, Mike Carvin, was arguing the appeal for us, and the central legal question was whether the Florida election statute, which provided a strict two-week time frame to certify the election, permitted the courts to keep the election open beyond that deadline.

I remember our team got together to moot Mike as he prepared for that argument. He argued, rightly, that under the law there was no discretion to disregard the statutory two-week time frame. At the moot, several of us asked him, what if we, the imaginary, judges want to change that time frame? Mike responded adamantly, "You can't." "But what if we do?" we replied. Again, Mike responded, "You can't." At which point I interjected, "Mike, suppose they just say they're going to make up a new deadline?" Mike exploded, "Then they're barbarians!"

And so it was. The court disregarded the statute and invented a whole new deadline (extending via judicial fiat the certification date from November 14 to November 26).

That decision prompted the first time the case went to the U.S. Supreme Court. When we filed for certiorari, the lawyers working on the case disagreed about whether the Court would take it. Many thought the Court would avoid the case because it was a political hot potato. I was of the view—as were many of the other Supreme Court clerks working on the team—that the Court would choose to take the case even though it was risky, and even though it would potentially pull the Court into political controversy. I believed Chief Justice Rehnquist and the other justices would feel an obligation to the country to take the case. That proved correct, and the Court agreed to hear the appeal.

The lede in Linda Greenhouse's *New York Times* story that day reflected the conventional astonishment that the Court would hear the case: "The Supreme Court today unexpectedly placed itself in the middle of Florida's presidential vote-counting imbroglio...."

As we were preparing our Supreme Court brief, I worried that the legal argument being put forward—that federal law categorically prohibited Florida from changing its election law on certification—was too aggressive, that it tried for a complete victory, and that the justices might not be prepared to go that far. And so I suggested that we needed a fallback position in the litigation. In the years since then, I have often tried to give courts fallback positions that could still amount to meaningful victories. As a litigator seeking to represent your clients, you should never let the perfect be the enemy of the good. And a good litigator is able to pivot and find multiple ways to win for his or her clients. For that reason, I suggested that perhaps there was a result the Court could arrive at short of total victory that would nonetheless be consequential.

As a fallback, I suggested we urge the Court simply to clarify federal law and remand for reconsideration, and then I teamed up with my good friends Noel Francisco and Timothy Flanigan to draft an insert for our brief making that argument. Noel (who later was a groomsman at Heidi and my wedding) had been a clerk for Judge Luttig and Justice Scalia. I had helped recruit Noel as a young lawyer to join me at Cooper Carvin. Today, Noel just finished serving as the U.S. solicitor general under President Trump for the past three years. In the midst of the Florida recount, I recall Noel and me musing late at night about—if somehow Gore were to prevail—maybe starting our own law firm together and perhaps even trying to convince Judge Luttig to leave the bench and join us. But fate would take us on a different path.

Tim had clerked for Chief Justice Burger along with Judge Luttig, he had succeeded Luttig as the head of the Office of Legal Counsel under Bush 41, and he would later become the deputy White House counsel under George W. Bush. Tim and his wife have a total of fourteen kids, including three sets of twins. He's the only person I know who could (and did) give Justice Scalia grief on the family front, saying, "nine kids, Justice, that's a nice starter family...." When Tim went home briefly from Florida to D.C. for Thanksgiving, he jokingly referred to it as a "conjugal visit." I replied, "Tim, you do know what happens when you do that? Have you considered maybe a nice game of Parcheesi?"

Noel and Tim and I worked side-by-side. Indeed, one of my favorite memories of the entire recount is the three of us, arm-in-arm, at two in the morning reading Shakespeare's St. Crispin's Day speech aloud, "we few, we happy few, we band of brothers...."

In the late hours of the evening, the three of us drafted an insert for our Supreme Court brief, roughly a page long, that suggested the intermediate fallback. And, as it so happens, that fallback is the path the Court ended up taking. By a unanimous 9–0 vote, the Supreme Court vacated the decision of the Florida Supreme Court and, rather than ruling for us on the merits, the Court instead clarified federal law and remanded it to the Florida Supreme Court to reconsider its judgments in light of that clarified federal law. That was precisely the course we had suggested.

On remand, the Florida Supreme Court stuck to its previous position. They stubbornly issued a very similar opinion, amazingly, without even *acknowledging* the unanimous Supreme Court decision that had just vacated their prior opinion. And shortly thereafter, the recount litigation once again went up to the U.S. Supreme Court.

Over the course of the thirty-six-day legal challenge, the ballots had been counted four times. They were counted on election day, which George W. Bush won, and there was an automatic statewide recount triggered because the margin was close. And after a second counting, George W. Bush once again prevailed. The Democrats challenged the outcomes in several overwhelmingly Democratic counties, seeking to gain more Democratic votes through more recounts.

With each recount, in some instances directed by laughably partisan Democrats leading the county recount processes, Al Gore's numbers grew—though he continued to trail behind. The Florida Supreme Court ordered yet one more statewide round of recounts.

So, while the second Supreme Court appeal was pending, we found ourselves once again in Florida state trial court. Our lawyers were seeking some minimum standards that should be applied for the latest round of recounts. Some of the "chads" on punch cards were not completely removed. Some were what were called "hanging chads," where they were hanging by one corner but were not entirely separated from the punch card. Others were dubbed "swinging chads," where they hung by two corners. Others were called "pregnant chads," attached at all four corners but indented in the middle in a way that suggests a voter might have pressed the stylus into them.

We asked the state trial court to set some uniform standard for how any recount should occur. The district judge rejected every single one of our arguments, ruling that each county could conduct the recount any way it liked and use whichever standards it wanted—counting "hanging chads" or "pregnant chads" as it so desired, counting over-votes and under-votes as it so desired. Then, all of these outcomes would be tallied to achieve a different statewide vote total.

The result was so egregious that I believed it set the stage for us to win. Two of the senior lawyers in Florida were George Terwilliger, who had been deputy attorney general under Bush 41, and Kenneth Juster, who had served in the Commerce Department under Bush 41 and who is today the U.S. ambassador to India under President Trump. The three of us were sitting next to each other in the courtroom and, when the judge ruled against us across-the-board, I wrote the letters "T F V"on a slip of paper and showed it to Ken and George. The "T" stood for total, and the "V" for victory.

Ken and I went back to the office, and we typed out a supplemental filing to the Supreme Court describing just how egregiously the trial court had refused to set anything resembling uniform standards for the next recount that was about to commence. (Since Ken is a bit of a Luddite, he doesn't know how to type; I manned the keyboard for us both.) As I mentioned, when we first drafted the Equal Protection Clause claim, it was weak. But as the Florida state courts decreed utter chaos and permitted standardless and arbitrary counting of votes in each of the sixty-seven counties across Florida, and as the results of the presidential election came to hinge on the vicissitudes of the local officials in each of those counties, our constitutional argument became substantially stronger over time.

The Equal Protection claim that we had drafted in the late hours of the night and the early hours of the morning had suddenly come to fruition. Before the Supreme Court, Ted Olson presented oral argument, as he had the first time. I was sitting in the courtroom for both arguments. In the second argument, Ted made a point to emphasize that the Florida Supreme Court had not so much as even *cited* the unanimous Supreme Court decision vacating their prior ruling. That really enraged the justices, especially Justices Anthony Kennedy and Sandra Day O'Connor, both of whom seemed flabbergasted that the Florida judges would have the audacity to ignore a unanimous Supreme Court ruling and, in effect, to thumb their noses at the Supreme Court. Pissing off Kennedy and O'Connor was always a mistake, and here, especially so. Ultimately I believe that was pivotal in the fight for a winning decision.

In the end the Court agreed by a vote of 7–2 that the standardless, arbitrary chaos playing out in Florida violated the Equal Protection Clause. Today, the press rarely remembers that that vote was *seven to two*—the five "conservatives" plus Souter and Breyer.

The remedy, however, divided along more familiar lines, 5–4. There were four justices who wanted to remand the case yet again, to allow the Florida state courts yet another bite at the apple to try again to set uniform standards (the absence of which we had highlighted in our supplemental brief) and to continue the craziness that had—for over a month—consumed a nation and a world eager for electoral finality.

The final decision came down about 10:00 at night. I got a call on my cell phone from the clerk's office of the Supreme Court telling me, "We have a decision." They offered to fax the decision to me. I pulled the opinion off the fax machine and walked into Jim Baker's office late that evening.

The opinion was dense, about twenty-five pages long, and Baker quietly asked me, "What does it say?" I proceeded to read the opinion rapidly in a small room, with Jim Baker standing across from me and looking over my shoulder. I read as quickly as I could, trying not to be rattled, and then looked up and said, "It means it's over, we've won."

Baker nodded, picked up the phone, and called George W. Bush, who was at his ranch in Crawford, Texas. Bush answered the phone, and Baker's first words were, "Well, Mr. President, how does it feel?" Chills went down my spine.

It's worth remembering that, at that very same instant, reporters were standing on the steps of the Supreme Court holding the opinion and frantically trying to figure out what on earth it meant. It didn't contain one simple clear sentence, "George W. Bush wins—the election is over." Instead, it was more complicated than that.

Afterwards, Heidi couldn't help but rib me when I told her that story: "Well, it's a good thing you were right!" she replied, snorting. I laughed, relieved at the same time. I was very glad there hadn't been some footnote buried in the opinion that I had missed—one that somehow gave a window for the Gore legal team to continue the battle. As it so happened, however, the case was truly over—even though we were yet again only one vote away.

Although Bush had won the initial count by 1784 votes and he led every subsequent tally, the vote differential had varied throughout the recounts, dropping to a low of 300 on November 14, then rising to 930 on November 18 (when overseas absentee ballots were counted), and finally being certified at 537 votes on December 8 (the margin by which Bush ultimately won the presidency).

◆　　◆　　◆　　◆

In my life, a bit of personal drama loomed in the background of the entire recount. I'd met Heidi Suzanne Nelson on January 3, 2000. At the time, she was in her second year at Harvard Business School, and she came to volunteer for a month on the Bush campaign. I was doing domestic policy, and she was there to do economic policy.

Blonde, beautiful, brilliant, she runs marathons and is in ridiculous shape. Her parents were missionaries in Africa, and she is deeply committed to her faith. She's more driven than any person I've ever met, before or since. For a wife, I wanted a life partner, someone who wouldn't fight against this political journey I hoped to travel, but instead who would be a soulmate and an enthusiastic force multiplier in life. If anything, I underestimated what I was getting into.

I was smitten from the moment I first cast my eyes upon her, and the two of us began dating two days later, on January 5. It was a whirlwind romance, and things got serious almost as soon as they started. When she returned to Harvard for her final semester at the end of January, I drove her to the airport. I asked her, "What now?" She said, without hesitating, "Call me every single night." She knew that I was getting home each night at 2:00 or 3:00 in the morning…so I'd call her—every single night—at 3:00 or 4:00 in the morning East Coast time. We'd talk a good hour or so, typically until one or the other of us fell asleep while still on the phone.

A week before the election, it so happened that Heidi's parents were coming to Texas. They're Californians from San Luis Obispo, along California's central coast, but through a weird coincidence they came to Texas because a cousin of hers was getting married in Fort Worth. After the wedding party, we all went to Billy Bob's, the famed country-Western bar in Fort Worth. Willie Nelson was playing in concert that evening.

Heidi's father is an intimidating man. A dentist by profession, he and Suzanne served as missionaries in Africa, where Heidi lived several months as a young girl. An avid outdoorsman, Peter climbed Mount Everest in 1990. He nearly died just a few hours from the summit, getting pulmonary edema on the mountain, and to this day he is an extremely talented athlete and a very driven man. To put it mildly, he was more than a little daunting as the father of the love of my life.

Peter and I didn't know each other well, but I wanted to marry his daughter, and I wanted to ask Peter for her hand. Sitting at Billy Bob's with his family all around, it was difficult to get him alone, to pull him away from the herd. I spied some pool tables not too far away, and I asked Peter, "So, do you play much pool?" "No," he answered monosyllabically, looking away and adding nothing more.

I sat there in silence for a couple of minutes and then tried it again. "Would you care to play me in a game of pool?" Eyebrow raised, Peter reluctantly agreed. While we were playing pool, I told him I was madly in love with his daughter, and I asked his permission to ask her to marry me. Peter was surprised. Even for him, he seemed a bit shaken. He was quiet for a moment, and then he said, "Well, I'll have to think about it. Let me talk to Suzanne, and I'll tell you tomorrow."

The next day, Sunday, Heidi and I had arranged a brunch with her family and my family, many of whom lived in Dallas. At that brunch, Peter pulled me aside and said ominously, "Suzanne and I talked about it, and we decided we're not ready to give up our daughter."

Four long seconds of silence ensued, at which point he added, "...but we are ready to gain a son."

In the movies, when you're falling off a cliff, your life flashes before your eyes. I have to admit, those four seconds seemed like an eternity for me, as I stood there thinking, "this isn't really happening." I recall thinking, "I'm conservative, but I'm not *that* conservative. You don't actually have a veto on this marriage. I am asking you out of respect, but I guess Heidi and I are getting married by Elvis in Vegas instead!"

After relieving my crashing fears, Peter then asked me, "Have you talked to Heidi yet?" I said, "No." He asked, "When do you intend to?" I replied, "Well, the election is the day after tomorrow, Tuesday, and so I intend to ask her on Friday of this week after the election." Peter said, "You better hurry because Heidi and Suzanne talk every single day, and I don't know that she's going to be able to keep it a secret." I answered, "Well, she's going to have to."

Tuesday occurred, and, as we've already discussed, it ended in a way none of us had anticipated. By Thursday, I was headed to Tallahassee. I called Heidi on the way to the airport and told her, "Sweetheart, tell your father I had to go to Tallahassee." Heidi, I'm sure, was puzzled by the urgency with which I wanted her father to know this. I think she probably believed I was trying to brag to him about my being involved in the recount. She said something like, "Yes, yes, I'm sure he'll be impressed," but for me, there was a much greater urgency: I had told him I was going to ask Heidi on Friday, but I wasn't going to be with her on Friday.

When I flew to Tallahassee, I assumed the recount would last just a couple of days and that I would return to Austin and then ask Heidi when I got back. Nobody anticipated it would drag on for over a month. A few days later, Heidi flew to Tallahassee to join the team. She's not a lawyer, but she worked tenaciously assisting the quantitative analysis of the vote totals county by county. As time went on, I figured I'd just ask her to marry me there, but I realized I had left the engagement ring in my closet in Austin. (I knew—and still know—nothing about diamonds, but I knew that Heidi liked Tiffany's, so I had gone to the store, handed them my credit card, and told them to get me the biggest diamond they had that would fit under my credit limit; it took many months for me to pay it off, but the ring, hopefully, was for a lifetime.)

I called my roommate from the campaign to see if he could maybe FedEx the ring to me in Florida, but my roommate, unbeknownst to me, had also arrived in Florida a couple of days earlier. So I was stymied trying to get the ring to Florida.

Heidi's parents are not terribly political. I don't know that they cared deeply about who prevailed in that presidential election, but for the entire thirty-six days of the recount, her entire family knew that I was going to ask her to marry me. My entire family knew that I was going to ask her to marry me. And, as a result, her mother desperately wanted Al Gore to hurry up and concede the damn race, so that her daughter could get engaged.

The Supreme Court's decision came down on December 12. The next day, Heidi and I flew back to Austin and, on December 14, a chilly winter's day, I took her to an Austin watering hole called "The Oasis" high on the cliffs overlooking Lake Travis. At sunset, about 5:00 p.m., with the sun's rays cascading off the clear blue water hundreds of feet below us, I dropped to one knee and proposed.

Heidi's initial reaction was to laugh. She began laughing uncontrollably. I was down on one knee feeling a little uncertain, and stammered, "Usually there's an answer at this point." At which point, still laughing she said, "Yes. Yes. Yes. Now, get up off your knee. Yes."

◆   ◆   ◆   ◆

Although I was one of the most junior members of the Bush campaign's Florida-recount legal team, I was blessed to work alongside some of the most extraordinary litigators on the face of the planet, to learn from them, to see their skills and expertise in action. My tasks varied widely. I wrote portions of briefs. I edited portions of briefs. I tried to ensure that what we said in one court was consistent with what we said in each of the other courts. Often that played out in a chaotic manner. Indeed, I remember tearing pages out of briefs hours before they had to be filed because what was written there contradicted what we had said in a different proceeding while listening to the lawyer who had written that particular pleading invariably yelling at me.

At other times, my roles were more mundane. One day, shortly before Thanksgiving, most of the lawyers had gone home for the holiday, and I was tasked with filing a pleading in court. Bob Zoellick, who would later become a cabinet member and then president of the World Bank, was essentially functioning as Jim Baker's chief of staff. Zoellick grabbed me by the front of the shirt, pulling my face within inches of his protruding red mustache and unruly red eyebrows, and growled, "Ted, don't f— this up." I tried to respond calmly, "Bob, it entails walking across the street and handing a stack of papers to the clerk. I believe I can adequately perform that task."

Another job I was given was helping prepare some of our senior surrogates to make the case for Governor Bush to the press. One such surrogate was then-Senator Arlen Specter from Pennsylvania. Josh Bolten asked me to fly up to Pennsylvania, pick him up, fly back, and brief him on what was happening in the case so that he could talk to the media. That evening, I flew up to Pennsylvania in a beautiful, private jet. It was the second time in my life I'd been on a private jet—the first being the flight from Austin to Tallahassee. The next morning, I flew back with Senator Specter at 6:00 a.m. to brief him on the latest in the litigation.

Heading up to Philadelphia, I was joined on the flight by Barbara Olson. Barbara was Ted Olson's wife. She was a friend and a fiery, beautiful, tenacious conservative. She was a veteran of Capitol Hill, a Houston native, and someone who never shied away from a fight. When I was clerking for Judge Luttig, he had performed Ted and Barbara's wedding, and (unbeknownst to her) he had asked me to help him with his remarks for the ceremony.

Barbara had seen Heidi and me together in Tallahassee quite a bit. She thought we were quite the pair, and she was catching a ride on the plane to get back to their home in D.C. Barbara, for much of the trip, was chiding me aggressively, saying, "Ted, you have got to ask Heidi to marry you." As was her wont, she did not do so timidly. There was no middle ground. She asked me, didn't I have the courage to man up and ask her to marry me? What was I afraid of? Did I want to be a bachelor forever?

What Barbara didn't know, which I told her subsequently, is that I had already asked Heidi's father, that I had already purchased the ring, and that I was just waiting for the recount to end so that I could pop the question. But I kept all of that to myself, not wanting to blow the surprise to Heidi.

Barbara, tragically, was killed on September 11, 2001. She was on the plane that flew into the Pentagon. Her husband, Ted, was then serving as the U.S. solicitor general. As the plane was in the air, she called him from her cellphone and, remarkably, connected with him twice for two one-minute calls. Barbara had been supposed to fly out the day before, but she delayed her departure by a day so she could remain with Ted for his birthday dinner the previous evening. Ted's birthday was that day, September 11.

As he spoke with her, Ted knew that two other planes had already struck the towers at the World Trade Center. He knew that the terrorists who had seized the plane Barbara was on weren't seeking the land in a safe harbor, but that their objective was likely to crash the plane. Characteristically, the last words Barbara said to Ted on the phone were, "What do we do?"

Always the fighter, Barbara was no doubt preparing to lead the passengers in an assault to try to stop the terrorists. The plane flew into the Pentagon, and Heidi and I lost a friend that day. Ted lost his beloved wife. And the world lost an extraordinary woman, as our country grieved the murder of over 3000 people.

◆   ◆   ◆   ◆

Three years later, and just a few months into my tenure as Texas solicitor general, the phone rang, and Attorney General Abbott asked a curious question, "Can the speaker of the House in the Texas Legislature order the arrest of House members fleeing the state?" He had just received a call from Speaker Tom Craddick, who had posed that question to him, and Abbott, in turn, asked me.

"I have no idea," I told my boss, "but I'll research the question immediately and get you an answer." It turns out the answer is clear and straightforward: Yes. The Texas Constitution explicitly gives authority to the Speaker to arrest legislators fleeing in an attempt to deny a quorum. To wit, Article III, Section 10 of the Texas Constitution provides, "Two-thirds of each House shall constitute a quorum to do business, but a smaller number may adjourn from day to day, and compel the attendance of absent members, in such manner and under such penalties as each House may provide." That verbiage, in turn, was taken word-for-word from Article I, Section 5 of the U.S. Constitution, which likewise authorizes congressmen to compel their colleagues to attend debate.

Then-Speaker Craddick asked me these arcane legal questions because the Texas Legislature, in the Spring of 2003, had just taken up the always-contentious issue of congressional redistricting. House Democrats adamantly opposed any redistricting plan because the existing plan overwhelmingly favored the Democratic Party.

As the three-judge federal district court would later describe it, Texas's recent political history was the "story of the dominance, decline, and eventual eclipse of the Democratic Party as the state's majority party." For over a century, from Reconstruction until the 1960s, the Democratic Party dominated the political landscape in Texas. By 1978, Texas was beginning to change. William Clements Jr. was elected the first Republican governor since 1874. Throughout the 1980s and 1990s, under Presidents Reagan and George H. W. Bush, Texas grew steadily more Republican. By 1990, Republicans were earning roughly 47 percent of the statewide vote, while Democrats retained just 51 percent.

Even though statewide voting was nearly even, Democrats maintained a massive majority of congressional representation, winning nineteen of the twenty-seven seats in the 1990 election. Then, in 1991, following the 1990 decennial census, Texas was awarded three additional seats in the U.S. House of Representatives. Democrats controlled both houses of the Texas Legislature, as well as the governorship, and the 1990 congressional redistricting plan—designed in large part by Democratic congressman Martin Frost—has been described as the "shrewdest Democratic gerrymander of the 1990s."

Southern Democrats have an ugly history when it comes to gerrymandering. For a long time, the path to electing white Democratic members of Congress was clear to map drawers. To do so—for white candidates to dominate the Democratic primary—one must draw districts that have a sufficient (but not too high) number of African-American voters and a sufficient (but not too high) number of Hispanic voters. Voting patterns nationally and in Texas demonstrated that Democratic African-American primary voters were likely to vote for a white Democrat over an Hispanic Democrat. And Hispanic Democratic primary voters would likewise likely vote for a white Democrat over an African-American Democrat. However, once it came to the general election, Hispanic and African-American Democratic primary voters would reliably come together to elect that white Democrat over a Republican opponent. As African-American Democratic Congresswoman Eddie Bernice Johnson testified at trial, Martin Frost's district "was drawn for an Anglo Democrat." And, using that cynical strategy, the 1991 redistricting plan locked in Democrats' temporary statewide advantage for more than a decade.

By 1994, the tide had turned, and in that election Republicans won every statewide race in Texas. Since that time, every election for every one of Texas's statewide offices has been won by a Republican. By 1998, the Republican advantage in congressional voting statewide was 56 percent to 44 percent, but the Frost gerrymander ensured that Democrats retained the majority of the congressional delegation, seventeen to thirteen, anyway. By 2000, Texas Republicans were winning statewide elections by a margin of 59 percent to 40 percent, but the congressional delegation stubbornly remained seventeen Democrats to thirteen Republicans.

In 2001, thanks to our growing population, Texas received two more congressional seats. The Texas Legislature, charged by the Constitution with the responsibility of drawing the new congressional maps, was deadlocked. Republicans controlled the state Senate, but Democrats still controlled the state House. Because the Legislature could not agree, a federal court redrew the maps in 2001, largely staying consistent with the political determinations that had been made in the 1991 gerrymander. Thus, even though Republicans held all twenty-nine statewide elected offices in Texas, and even though the voters of Texas voted 53 percent to 44 percent in favor of Republicans in the 2002 congressional election, Democrats retained a seventeen to fifteen advantage in the congressional delegation.

Then in 2003, Republicans won the Texas state House. So the Legislature endeavored to take up the task upon which it had deadlocked two years earlier. Their objective was simple: to draw lines that would allow a substantial majority of Texas voters to elect a substantial majority of their congressional delegation. Texas Democratic House members did not want their gerrymander undone, so they fled the state to avoid taking a vote, heading to the small town of Ardmore, Oklahoma. In the press, the fleeing Democrats were dubbed the "killer Ds," in homage to the "killer bees," twelve liberal Democratic Texas senators who had busted a quorum in 1979 to prevent a vote on a presidential primary bill that was favorable to then-Republican candidate John Connally.

Their quorum busting worked, and the regular legislative session expired. But Texas Governor Rick Perry would proceed to call three consecutive special sessions to complete the task of redistricting. In the second special session, it was the Senate's turn to flee, with twelve Democrats absconding to a luxury hotel in Albuquerque, New Mexico (reflecting the differences in the chambers, their accommodations were much fancier than the House members' more mundane Holiday Inn in Ardmore).

Although arrest warrants were issued for the fleeing legislators, because they had crossed state lines to escape Texas jurisdiction, nobody was arrested. Finally, however, Democratic resistance was worn down, and by the third special session, both houses of the Legislature were able to pass a congressional redistricting bill.

Doing so was a complicated endeavor. My job as solicitor general typically entailed representing the state in court, but part of the job also required me to advise the Legislature on complicated questions of law. Here, Attorney General Abbott asked me to provide the Legislature the best legal advice as to how they could draw the map consistent with federal law.

There are numerous federal constraints on map drawing, the two most significant of which are the Voting Rights Act and the Fifteenth Amendment to the Constitution. Supreme Court case law concerning both is complicated and often contradictory. In ordinary parlance, in an ordinary life, most of us don't typically divide people into racial categories. In redistricting law, doing so is unfortunately required.

The Supreme Court has interpreted the Voting Rights Act to mandate an almost obsessive focus on race, concentrating African-American voters in districts where they are more likely to elect African-American representatives and concentrating Hispanic voters in districts where they are more likely to elect Hispanic representatives. To comply with the Voting Rights Act, legislatures are required to look precisely at the ethnic breakdown of every district. Sophisticated mapping technology enables lines to be drawn block-by-block and house-by-house, with the racial, ethnic, and partisan breakdown of each displayed.

I don't enjoy redistricting litigation because it is so obsessively focused on racial distinctions, something I find quite distasteful. And to make matters worse, the Supreme Court's requirements that a legislature must focus on race are contradicted by its constitutional rulings that a legislature can't focus *too much* on race. Interpreting the conflicting requirements is no easy task. Moreover, redistricting by its nature entails myriad political determinations. For example, more than a few Texas Republican state representatives wanted to "take out Martin Frost," because of his role in the previous Democratic gerrymander.

My instructions from General Abbott were to provide legal advice and stay out of the politics. Accordingly, I would do my best to advise whether a particular decision was consistent or inconsistent with federal law or the Constitution. But when decision-making got overtly political, I would get up, excuse myself, and leave the room, telling the representatives, "You're entitled under the law to make political determinations. I'll be outside if you have any legal questions for which you might need me."

Ultimately, the Legislature adopted a map that went from two congressional districts where African-Americans were likely to elect an African-American representative up to three congressional districts where African-Americans were likely to prevail. The map, likewise, went from seven majority-Hispanic districts to eight. The losers in the map were white Democrats, whose districts were redrawn to make their defeat more likely. The result was passionate Democratic opposition to the plan.

When the bill passed, just two Democratic representatives, Ron Wilson and Vilma Luna, voted for the redistricting plan. Representative Wilson was an African-American Democrat from inner-city Houston, and Representative Luna was an Hispanic Democrat from the South Texas town of Alice.

As soon as the map was signed into law, an array of litigants immediately sued, challenging its legality. I spent the next year in and out of trial court, helping lead our trial team and defending the multiple challenges to the map. The principal case was tried before a three-judge federal district court, which consisted of one court of appeals judge and two trial court judges. A three-judge district court is an unusual forum that exists for certain types of redistricting challenges. Two moments from the trial stood out, in particular.

First was when Representative Ron Wilson was testifying at trial, and he explained why he voted in favor of the plan. "It was never a question of if the redistricting bill would pass." Instead, he said, the question was, "Do you stand on the railroad track and try to stop the train? Or do you try to get some of your people on the train and not get run over?" As Wilson explained, he supported the plan because it was likely to elect three black Democrats to Congress from Texas, instead of merely two.

Wilson's position enraged many of his Democratic colleagues. And Lee Godfrey, one of the most accomplished trial lawyers in the country, cross-examined him. Godfrey sarcastically noted that Wilson comprised "100 percent of the African American legislators" who had voted in support of the new map. Wilson defiantly explained why he believed that that was the case. "I am the only one who had the 'things' big enough to do it," and he gestured accordingly.

It was a remarkable moment—to see a witness in a federal trial court directly referencing his own genitalia. Even more remarkably, Godfrey took the bait. "I presume the 'things' you refer to are not visible?"

Wilson retorted, "You want to see them?"

Godfrey seemed ready to demand production. But the presiding judge wisely directed, "Move on. Move on."

A second notable moment concerned our expert witness. We had retained a statistician from Oklahoma to analyze the likely effects of the map the Texas Legislature had adopted. The statistician was a nice, affable man, and he wrote a good report. As we were preparing him for trial, I had brought in my old boss, Mike Carvin, to assist with trial preparation. Mike proceeded with a mock cross-examination. Our expert, much to our dismay, on a vigorous cross-exam, seemed perfectly willing to agree to just about anything. Even though his report was carefully reasoned, the statistician's temperament was such that he just didn't like to tell a questioner no. Over and over again, Mike and I and other lawyers on the trial team would pose difficult questions to our expert, and over and over again, he seemed to want to please the questioner more than he wanted to answer the question accurately.

We quickly realized that putting our witness on the stand could end very badly. We therefore made a decision to put him on a plane and fly him back to Oklahoma. The next day, we were expected to call our expert witness. The plaintiffs had already concluded their case, and we had begun to present ours. The lead opposing lawyer, Paul Smith, was a veteran Supreme Court advocate, and I could tell he was salivating to cross-examine our expert. However, when the time came to call him, our lead trial lawyer stood and said, "Your honor, the State rests."

Virtually every Democratic lawyer leapt to his feet, crying out his objection. The bemused presiding judge, Patrick Higginbotham, a long-time veteran of the Fifth Circuit Court of Appeals, looked down, his spectacles perched on the tip of his nose. With a smile, he asked, "You object to the State resting?" Exhaling heavily, the Democratic lawyers took their seats, realizing they could not force us to call to the stand a witness we did not wish to call. Their hopes of making their case through cross-examining our witness were extinguished at that moment.

The three-judge federal district court ultimately upheld the map, and the plaintiffs appealed directly to the U.S. Supreme Court. Unlike ordinary appeals to the Court that go through the process of certiorari, or discretionary review, redistricting cases go on automatic direct appeal to the Court. And the Court, following some procedural delays, set the case for oral argument.

The multiple plaintiffs filed four separate fifty-page briefs at the Supreme Court, raising together eleven different questions presented. In our response brief, a single consolidated brief that ran 123 pages in length (more than double a typical Supreme Court brief), we took all eleven questions presented and reformulated them into five overarching questions. This was an unusual approach, but one that I had begun adopting years earlier as a college debater.

While at Princeton, I spent all four years of college debating on the intercollegiate circuit. The style of debate was parliamentary debate, which is modeled after British Parliament. Each debate was extemporaneous. You found out the topic ten minutes before the round, and a debate round extended for forty minutes.

Judges were ordinary college students, but those who were experienced debaters were taught to record the arguments in a debate on what is called a "flow." Typically, the debate judge would take a legal-size yellow pad, turn it lengthwise, and divide the pad into six columns. The first speaker in a parliamentary debate, dubbed the prime minister, would lay out the case and present a series of arguments for the position he or she was advancing. Typically, the arguments numbered three, four, or five. In an ordinary debate, the next speaker would then respond to each of those arguments, and the debate judge would draw an arrow from argument one to response one, and likewise for each of the other arguments. The next speaker would then respond to those counter-arguments, and so the arrows would continue across the columns so that the judge could flow how the debate proceeded.

By about my sophomore year, I decided to oppose cases differently. Instead of responding to the arguments presented by the prime minister, when I was in opposition I viewed my task as presenting an affirmative argument as to why the other team was wrong. As a result, flows from our debates looked very different from a typical flow. The judge would have three, four, or five arguments from the first speaker, and then I would present three or four or five totally different arguments as to why their case was wrong. Not sure where to put them, most judges would simply put them on the lower half of the page—not connected by any arrows to the initial argument, but instead as freestanding arguments.

Inevitably, the second speaker for the other team would get up and respond to each of the arguments I'd laid out, with arrows connecting those arguments. And then my debate partner, roommate, and best friend, David Panton, would continue the argument, extending the arguments I had made, and also making sure to mention a word or two about the initial long-forgotten arguments presented by the first speaker. The effect, in a debate round, is that we would subsume the flow. The prime minister's speech would be orphaned; we would totally reframe the debate, and thirty-two of the forty minutes in the round would occur on the terrain we wanted.

This was much the same approach that we took in our Supreme Court brief, posing five brand-new questions that encompassed all of the complicated noise of the plaintiffs' many, many questions, but boiling the case down to its essence so the justices could best understand it. Intricate in detail, this brief remains the most complicated brief, factually and legally, on which I have ever worked.

Typically, Supreme Court arguments began at 10:00 or 11:00 a.m., and they usually extend for an hour. Given the complexity of this case, the Court set the argument for 1:00 p.m. and scheduled it for two hours. Rather than the typical thirty minutes to present our side, I was allocated a full hour, although I ceded ten minutes to the U.S. Department of Justice, which supported the State of Texas. The central claim that the plaintiffs presented was that the U.S. Constitution prohibits an overly partisan gerrymander. There was more than a little irony in the Texas Democratic Party's presenting this argument after perpetuating for decades some of the most egregious partisan gerrymanders in the country.

In defending the State of Texas, I could have chosen to dispute the premise: to argue, no, the plan wasn't really that political. To be sure, there were other causes or purposes for the lines that were drawn. But making that argument would not have been credible, and I have long believed the greatest asset any advocate has is his or her credibility. Accordingly, I conceded flat-out: of course, this map is political. It was drawn by elected politicians.

Much as in Humphrey Bogart's *Casablanca*, "I'm shocked, shocked to find that gambling is going on in here!"—it should come as no surprise that elected politicians are, well, political. So I argued that to the Court. Of course elected officials are political, and the Framers of the Constitution knew precisely what they were doing when the Constitution gave the responsibility of redistricting to state legislatures. Though this might astonish some modern reporters, politics was not invented in the age of Trump. As long as there have been elections, politicians have been political.

Redistricting is not some novel phenomenon. Indeed, the very word "gerrymander" comes from Elbridge Gerry, a signer of the Declaration of Independence and a delegate to the 1787 Constitutional Convention, whose Massachusetts congressional district was so convoluted that it resembled a salamander.

The Framers knew well that elected politicians would be political, but they also knew that leaving redistricting decisions to elected legislators ensured that the People would ultimately decide. The leading alternative to the state legislatures' drawing maps is to have federal judges draw the maps. But if a judge draws a map inconsistent with the will of the voters, there is no remedy. The voters have no avenue of accountability over the federal judiciary. That's why the Framers allocated the decision to elected legislators instead.

Two moments from the oral argument were particularly noteworthy. One in a positive way; the other, not so much. During my argument, Justice Stevens, who was quite critical of my position, began a question to me by commenting that I made a "very persuasive argument in your brief, which I found to be very helpful...." The visual completed it: as he was saying this, he held up our brief, smiled, and shook his head ruefully, because it was clear he was trying to articulate arguments as to why we were wrong. It was kind of him to say (even though he voted against us), and it remains the only Supreme Court argument I've seen where a justice has directly complimented one of the briefs before the Court. It was a generous sentiment for which I was grateful.

The other notable moment concerned Justice Ruth Bader Ginsburg. Midway through my argument, she put her head down on the bench and fell asleep. For roughly ten minutes, Justice Ginsburg slept. Her doing so made national news at the time. When I returned to Austin the next week, I went to teach my weekly class at the University of Texas School of Law on Supreme Court litigation. My students had seen the news about Justice Ginsburg's falling asleep at the argument. Laughing, I admitted to them that I had been the counsel at the podium when she did so. I went on to tell them, "That's the objective to which every advocate aspires, to render your adjudicator unconscious." "And," I joked, "there is a method to accomplish that task: You simply speak in soporific tones, and gently rock side-to-side, and the justice will drift off to sleep."

As it so happened, Justice Ginsburg did not need to be awake to vote against my position. But, when the Court handed down its decision, Texas prevailed 5–4. On practically every question before the Court, Texas won, with the Court concluding that the Texas redistricting map should not be set aside merely because the Texas Legislature had made political determinations in drawing it. The Court did strike down one specific district in Texas, which resulted in the map being slightly redrawn, but overall it was a near-total victory.

Many aspects of redistricting litigation are less than ideal. As Chief Justice Roberts wrote in a different case concerning affirmative action, "it is a sordid business, this divvying us up by race." And observers have rightly recognized that gerrymandered districts produce less than ideal representation, and that individual members instead respond to however their specific districts are configured. Some have understandably criticized the process as representatives picking their constituents, rather than constituents picking their representatives.

Those are fair concerns, but they tend to be far more vocally advanced whenever one's party is out of power. When Texas Democrats had a stranglehold on redistricting, not many Democrats spoke out against it. Since Republicans achieved a majority in the Texas Legislature, not many Republicans have spoken out against it.

The process is ugly, but it recalls Winston Churchill's famous adage that "democracy is the worst form of Government, except for all those other forms that have been tried from time to time." Likewise, congressional maps drawn by elected legislators have serious flaws. But the Framers of our Constitution entrusted those decisions to elected legislatures because they believed in democracy. Unaccountable federal judges drawing our maps would ultimately deprive the people of control over those crucial decisions.

The decision in *LULAC v. Perry* was 5–4. And when it comes to ensuring that We the People—the actual voters—control our elections, we are once again just one vote away.

◆   ◆   ◆   ◆

There were stark similarities between *Bush v. Gore* and Texas redistricting. I was reminded of those in January of this year, during the impeachment trial of President Trump. Both *Bush v. Gore* and redistricting were complicated legal battles, interwoven with political knife-fighting. Both were directed at multiple audiences simultaneously—not just the judges or justices making the legal determinations, but also, in a very direct sense, at the American people. When the House of Representatives voted to impeach President Trump, and the Senate was required to carry out its constitutional obligation to conduct a trial on that impeachment, I resolved to lead the effort in the Senate to make the legal case and the public case for why the conduct alleged did not satisfy the constitutional standard of "high crimes and misdemeanors."

There is a unique species of litigation which occurs only rarely and is sometimes separated by decades, where politics, public messaging, and persuasion are all entirely enmeshed with the legal arguments. Having been through now three such major battles—*Bush v. Gore*, redistricting, and impeachment—I am particularly grateful to be serving today in the United States Senate, where the responsibilities of defending the Constitution, of drafting the law, and of overseeing the Executive are so often interconnected with the realities of politics, the battle in the media, and the needs of public persuasion.

GETTING JUDICIAL NOMINATIONS RIGHT GOING FORWARD

Republicans have, historically speaking, been absolutely terrible at judicial nominations—especially nominations for Supreme Court justices. To borrow from baseball, Republicans at best bat .500. Once confirmed as justices, at most, half of Republicans' Supreme Court nominations actually behave as we hoped they might behave in terms of remaining faithful to their oath of office and the Constitution.

Democrats, on the other hand, bat nearly 1.000. They are almost perfect in that almost every single Democratic Supreme Court nominee, on virtually every major case that is a hotly contested, votes exactly as the Democrats who appointed them would have wanted them to vote. Perhaps the most notable exception was Byron White, who was John F. Kennedy's only Supreme Court nominee. Justice White's great apostasy was that he was one of the two original dissenters in *Roe*, and sometimes he would also side with the more conservative justices on criminal cases. Aside from Justice White, Democrats' Supreme Court justices, almost without exception, vote precisely as they would want them to.

It's also not random or bad luck. There is a clearly definable pattern among Republican nominees, differentiating those justices who remained faithful to their oath, who stood strong and followed the Constitution, from those who did not.

Remember, if a judge changes on the bench, he or she always changes in the same way. Republican nominees only shift in one direction: they shift to the left. "Evolving" is the polite term. And it is because the pressure on a Supreme Court justice to move to the left is enormous. The press coverage consistently praises justices who vote with the left, heralding them as courageous heroes. Indeed, this past year, there were two separate movies that came out within months of each other, chronicling the life of Ruth Bader Ginsburg in hagiographic terms better suited for Mother Teresa or George Washington. Somehow Hollywood has never produced the film, *Nino, The Extraordinary Justice Scalia*.

So when Republican nominees side with the left on the Court, they're praised in the newspaper, lionized as statesmen, and fêted publicly. This is so true that the former longtime Supreme Court reporter for the *New York Times*, Linda Greenhouse, had an entire syndrome named after her. Dubbed the "Greenhouse effect," it was used to describe how justices like Anthony Kennedy and Sandra Day O'Connor gradually move ever more leftward in order to receive adoring praises from Greenhouse's coverage in the *New York Times*.

It's not just the press coverage; it's also the entire dynamic of Washington, D.C. Justices who move to the left are welcome at cocktail parties. They are treated with respect, with deference, even with praise and adoration. They are among the "cool kids." Republican-nominated Supreme Court justices who do not do that are barely acknowledged in polite society.

If you look back at the history of Republican nominations, there's a clear difference between the Republican picks who stuck to their guns once they made it to the bench and those who backed down. And presidents and senators should examine that pattern before nominating or confirming anyone to the Court. The justices who have been most faithful to the Constitution include Justice Scalia, Justice Thomas, my old boss Chief Justice Rehnquist, and Justice Alito. All of them share important characteristics: Before they were nominated, each of those justices had a long and demonstrated record. Each had served in the executive branch, each had defended conservative or constitutionalist positions, and, critically, each had been roundly criticized for doing so.

Indeed, I believe there's no better predictor of whether a Supreme Court justice will remain strong and faithful to the Constitution than whether he or she has a long record of being excoriated by the press, mocked by the legal academy, and ridiculed by polite society, and holding his or her ground nonetheless. Only by looking for stoic and adamant resistance to the "Greenhouse effect" can we reliably deduce that a prospective nominee has the mettle and the fortitude to stick to his or her convictions when confronted by Washington, D.C.'s proverbial storm of locusts.

We should also expect nominees to have real, demonstrated track records across the spectrum of constitutionalism. We don't need jurists who are only sound on structural issues, or who are only sound on certain key Bill of Rights provisions, or who are "good" on criminal-justice issues while failing to uphold the Constitution in other domains. Rather, we need judges and justices who are committed to the full panoply of constitutional issues—and who have demonstrated their commitment and bled for those ideals over the course of their careers.

Incidentally, the flip side of these criteria is true, as well. Those justices who have been faithless, who have been willing to join the activists in imposing liberal policies regardless of what the Constitution might provide, often fall in a similar pattern: Typically, they have little to no record, they have assiduously avoided controversy, they have refrained from taking difficult stands, and they have avoided subjecting themselves to the harsh light of criticism. They have been timid where they could have been bold or assertive.

For seven decades, Republicans have gotten this wrong, starting in the 1950s. Two of the most liberal justices of the twentieth century were picked by the Republican President Dwight Eisenhower: Earl Warren and William Brennan. It was a time when the Supreme Court was not believed to be all that important. It was still, to borrow the Framers' term, the "least dangerous" branch, and so nominations to the high court were seen as appropriate to use as political bargaining chips or for currying favor with needed electorates.

Warren had been the Republican governor of California and a formidable candidate for president. Going into the 1952 Republican convention in Chicago, Democrats had held the White House for two decades, since FDR's election in 1932. As it so happens, two chief justices would arise from that convention.

Ideological divides in the party were present then, as now. Most of the Northeastern moderate Republicans supported General Eisenhower; most of the conservative Republicans supported Ohio Senator Robert Taft. On the first ballot, Eisenhower received 595 votes, 9 short of the 604 required for the nomination. Taft received 500 votes. Warren was in third, with 81 votes. Rounding out the field were former Minnesota governor Harold Stassen with 20 votes, and General Douglas MacArthur with 10.

Richard Nixon, then a forty-three-year-old fiery, anti-communist senator, was supporting his fellow Californian Earl Warren. Eisenhower ultimately would offer Nixon the vice presidency (which of course he accepted). Warren's delegates initially refused to support Eisenhower, hoping that in deadlock the convention would settle on their candidate as a compromise. So all twenty of Stassen's delegates switched to Eisenhower, giving him the majority needed to win. Warren Burger was the leader of Strassen's convention supporters, delivering the critical votes, which set the stage for future President Nixon to later name him our fifteenth chief justice.

Earl Warren was more cagey in giving his own support. He demanded in exchange—and Eisenhower gave—a promise that he would be nominated for the next Supreme Court vacancy that occurred. What nobody knew was that, on September 8, 1953—just nine months into Eisenhower's first term—Chief Justice Fred Vinson would die suddenly. Eisenhower sent his attorney general to California to meet with Warren, who had just returned from a hunting trip. He asked Warren whether he understood the promise to include the chief justice-ship, rather than merely an associate justice position. "The first vacancy," Warren replied.

And so the Warren Court was born.

Eisenhower's second nomination to the Court was William Brennan, a New Jersey Supreme Court justice and a Democrat. Appointing him was seen as helpful to shoring up Eisenhower's support with Catholics and Irish Americans.

Warren, of course, went on to preside over one of the most activist courts in history, and William Brennan single-handedly led the left on the Court for almost thirty-four years. A small man with a sparkling wit and an easy smile, Brennan excelled at persuading his fellow justices to join him in reshaping America. He was well known for describing the most important legal principle at the Supreme Court as what he would call, with a grin while holding up five fingers, the "Rule of Five." As he would say, "with five votes, you can accomplish anything"—no matter what the law or Constitution said otherwise.

Eisenhower's biographers reported that, in 1958, Eisenhower observed that he had made two mistakes as president, "and they are both sitting on the Supreme Court." Alas, Warren and Brennan were hardly the only Republican mistakes.

When he became president, Richard Nixon did slightly better: overall, he got 25 percent of his nominations (who were confirmed) right. Nixon started his presidency with the historic opportunity to replace Chief Justice Warren, who had announced his retirement the year earlier. He first offered the chief justiceship to former New York governor Thomas Dewey, who turned it down. Dewey was an upper-crust aristocrat with a thin pencil mustache; Alice Roosevelt Longworth (Teddy's eldest daughter) famously, and witheringly, described him as "the little man on the wedding cake." He was the leading voice of the "moderate" Republicans—he described his own governing philosophy as "pay-as-you-go liberalism"—and, remarkably, he had turned down the very same offer of becoming chief justice previously from Eisenhower. Dewey, like Warren and Burger, had played a pivotal role at the 1952 convention, helping both Ike and Nixon secure their respective nominations; four years before that, in 1948, Dewey had been the (losing) Republican presidential nominee against Harry S Truman. Dewey's running mate? Earl Warren.

When Dewey turned him down, Nixon then nominated Warren Burger to become chief justice. Burger had a white mane of hair right out of central casting, but he was a pompous, dull, and mediocre court of appeals judge, who did little to turn around the liberal lurch of the Court. That being said, he was relatively effective in the political game of Washington, exerting real influence on presidential decisions. And, had history played out differently, his tenure on the Court might have been quite short. Nixon's memoirs reveal that he asked Burger to be prepared to run for president in 1972 if the Cambodia invasion went badly. Then, when Spiro Agnew resigned in disgrace in 1973, Burger was on Nixon's short list for VP, along with John Connolly, Ronald Reagan, and Nelson Rockefeller. Of course, the appointment went instead to Gerald Ford, who then succeeded Nixon as president. Had the choice gone otherwise, we could have ended up with President Warren Burger.

Nixon also nominated Lewis Powell, an aristocratic and genteel Virginian who had been the president of the American Bar Association. Powell turned Nixon down when he was first offered the Court in 1969 but accepted it when offered again in 1971. A corporate lawyer and member of the board of directors of tobacco giant Phillip Morris, he was a lifelong Democrat who loved to find "middle-ground" policy compromises regardless of what the law might say. Powell joined the majority in *Roe v. Wade*—as did Warren Burger—and the most notable opinion he authored was his controlling concurrence in *Regents v. Bakke* (still followed today) that upheld race-based affirmative action by public universities.

By far his best appointment, Nixon also nominated William Rehnquist (or "Renchberg," as Nixon called him repeatedly in the

Watergate tapes, misremembering the name of the very conservative lawyer then leading the Office of Legal Counsel in the Department of Justice). For years as an associate justice, Rehnquist earned the nickname "the Lone Ranger" because he dissented alone, over and over again, from decisions moving the Court further and further left.

The year I clerked for him happened to be his twenty-fifth anniversary as a justice and his tenth as chief; at our annual dinner, all of the clerks (seventy-five in all) chipped in to get him three gifts, each of which was thereafter displayed in his office: a Lone Ranger adjustable doll, a full-size Indian headdress, and a ship captain's wheel. The former reflected his tenacity in dissenting alone, year after year, and sticking to principle. The second memorialized his ascension to Chief. And the third symbolized how he had carefully steered the Court, building majorities and transforming many of those lone dissents—in criminal law, religious liberty, and federalism especially—into the law of the land.

Nixon also had two failed nominations: Clement Haynsworth and Harrold Carswell. Haynsworth, for a variety of reasons, was defeated by a bipartisan vote of 55–45, becoming the first Supreme Court nominee rejected by the Senate since 1930. Carswell was an appellate judge from Florida who had been a vocal defender of segregation. In 1948, he had given a shameful speech while running for office:

> I believe the segregation of the races is proper and the only practical and correct way of life in our states. I have always so believed, and I shall always so act.... I yield to no man as a fellow candidate, or as a fellow citizen, in the firm, vigorous belief in the principles of white supremacy, and I shall always be so governed.

In addition to his atrocious record on civil rights, Carswell also happened to be a lousy judge. Responding to the charge that Carswell was "mediocre," Senator Roman Hruska gave the following defense, which famously backfired: "Even if he is mediocre, there are a lot of mediocre judges and people and lawyers. They are entitled to a little representation, aren't they, and a little chance?"

The Senate rightly rejected Carswell's nomination 51–45. (Years later, in 1976, Carswell was convicted of battery for sexual advances he made to an undercover police officer in a Tallahassee men's room.)

After Haynsworth and Carswell were defeated, Nixon nominated Harry Blackmun, who would prove to be the worst justice he appointed. Blackmun, of course, became the author of *Roe v. Wade* and, over time, a staunch liberal. Blackmun and Burger had been best friends for decades, ever since grade-school, and Burger had lobbied Nixon to appoint his friend. In fact, Burger had been the best man at Blackmun's wedding. They were dubbed the "Minnesota Twins."

Blackmun had an undistinguished judicial record, before which he was the outside counsel for the Mayo Clinic. Quickly, he found himself overwhelmed by the responsibility of the Court. At first, he simply followed Burger wherever the Chief would lead. Over time, he grew bitter and resentful, not wanting to be overshadowed by the chief justice. Blackmun desperately sought praise, recognition, and adulation. And the firestorm he ignited (unwittingly, it appears) with *Roe v. Wade* changed him profoundly. Encountering criticism he had never faced before made him more and more angry. In response, he galloped steadily further to the left.

Next, Gerald Ford nominated John Paul Stevens. Although brilliant (he had earned the highest GPA in the history of Northwestern Law School and was himself a former Supreme Court clerk), Stevens had spent only five years as an unexceptional court of appeals judge with no discernible record of taking strong conservative positions. He was a Midwestern Republican, an antitrust lawyer, a leader in the bar, and he seemed a safe and easy choice. Suffice it to say that calculation proved to be a disaster, as Justice Stevens served for three and a half decades and became one of the liberal lions of the Supreme Court.

Even the great Ronald Reagan got half of his Supreme Court nominees wrong. As towering a conservative hero as Reagan was, of the four appointments he made, only two—William Rehnquist and Antonin Scalia—stayed faithful to their oaths. The first justice Reagan named, Sandra Day O'Connor, had been a state court of appeals judge in Arizona and, before that, an Arizona state legislator. Raised on a ranch, she was a Westerner through and through. Her autobiography describes how when Sandra Day brought young John O'Connor home to meet her family, her dad took John out on the ranch with him while he was castrating calves. "I wonder if Dad was trying to tell him something?" she mused.

Reagan had promised to nominate the first woman to be a Supreme Court justice and, with O'Connor, he delivered on that promise. She was friends with Chief Justice Burger (who lobbied hard for her nomination), and she had been law school classmates with William Rehnquist. Indeed, he had been first in the class, and she had been third in the class. I've often wondered: Whatever happened to the poor fellow who was ranked number two? Coincidentally, Rehnquist and O'Connor dated briefly while in law school, and he even proposed marriage (which she declined). By the time each was subsequently married, they and their spouses became close friends, all four socializing regularly for the rest of their lives.

That brief romantic history between them led to my most awkward moment clerking. It was 1996, and the Court was considering the first Internet porn case. At the time, the justices didn't really know what the Internet was, so the Court librarians arranged to show them. They grouped the justices two at a time, and so Rehnquist and O'Connor (both septuagenarians), and their seven young clerks were all squeezed into a small, dark room together while the librarians showed the justices just how easy it was to find explicit pornography online. All of us clerks were exceedingly uncomfortable, but given that they had dated five decades earlier, I couldn't help but wonder what both of them must have been thinking that day. Regardless, I still remember what Justice O'Connor said when the first graphic image appeared on the screen: "Oh my...."

But in 1981, when Reagan appointed her, nothing in O'Connor's record demonstrated a particularly conservative sensibility—a record of standing for the Constitution in the face of withering criticism. O'Connor would go on to become the quintessential swing justice, exquisitely subject to the "Greenhouse effect" and always trying to impose whatever outcome she personally thought was fair or right. Never mind what the law said.

After O'Connor, Reagan nominated Antonin Scalia. That nomination occurred when Chief Justice Burger retired from the bench. Reagan had two nominations to make at the same time. He elevated William Rehnquist from associate justice to chief justice, and he named Scalia to replace Rehnquist as an associate justice. My former boss and dear friend, Chuck Cooper (a former Rehnquist clerk), was a senior official in the Reagan Department of Justice at the time and a major proponent of both nominations; he has likened that day to a "double steal" in baseball. It was perhaps the single greatest advance for constitutionalist judging in the history of the Supreme Court.

A story I was told long ago, when I was clerking for Judge Luttig, captures a bit of Scalia's brilliance, charm, and wit. Luttig was Scalia's very first law clerk on the U.S. Court of Appeals for the D.C. Circuit. At the time, there were two conservative luminaries serving on the D.C. Circuit, Robert Bork and Antonin Scalia. Each had been a legendary academic. Each had staggering intellect and demonstrated courage of conviction. Everybody knew one of the two was likely to be Reagan's next Supreme Court nominee. At the time, Reagan confidant Edwin Meese was serving as attorney general, and he had come to the D.C. Circuit courthouse to speak at an event.

U.S. marshals were holding an elevator in the parking garage when Scalia walked up with Judge Luttig, his law clerk in tow. The marshals stopped Judge Scalia, telling him, "I'm sorry sir, we're holding this elevator for the attorney general of the United States." Scalia pushed past them both, stepped into the elevator, jammed the button, and, as the door was closing, he said, "you tell Ed Meese…that Bob Bork doesn't wait for anyone!"

And so it was. The very next nomination on the high court was Scalia's, who was confirmed in the Senate by a margin of 98–0. It reflected a different time in judicial nominations: Rehnquist took most of the incoming fire, and Scalia—the first Italian-American justice in history—sat at the witness table during his confirmation hearing before the Senate Judiciary Committee, calmly smoking a pipe.

By the next year, 1987, Democrats had retaken the Senate, and Reagan got his third Supreme Court vacancy. He promptly nominated Robert Bork. Bork had the bad fortune of being nominated when Republicans no longer controlled a majority in the Senate. The confirmation hearing was a bloodbath, with Ted Kennedy leading the charge, savaging Bork and painting a frightening picture of what he described as "Robert Bork's America." Bork, at the time, had a scruffy goatee and mustache. I have often joked that if someone had just purchased Bork a razor, he would have been confirmed to the Court, because his scraggly beard made him look a bit frightening—even Mephistophelean—and the Democratic senators' antics only played up that impression.

Bork's nomination was defeated, and he earned a place in judicial immortality by having his name transformed into a verb. Even today, "borking" a nominee, as painfully experienced by Clarence Thomas and Brett Kavanaugh, is used to describe unfair, nasty, personal, partisan attacks and relentless mudslinging designed to destroy a judicial nominee. After Bork, Reagan tried again. Once more he went with a conservative judge from the D.C. Circuit, Doug Ginsburg. Although not the luminary that Scalia and Bork had been, based on his subsequent judicial service, Ginsburg would likely have proven a principled justice.

But the left had been aroused. Blood was in the water from the Bork saga, and the mob was not yet sated. This time they went after Ginsburg's personal habits and, in particular, the poor judgment he had to smoke marijuana, both as a student and as an assistant professor at Harvard Law School. In that circus environment, the admitted charges of pot-smoking were sufficient to derail his nomination.

Reagan's third attempt at that vacancy was then-Judge Anthony Kennedy, a judge on the Ninth Circuit Court of Appeals. A Californian, Kennedy was a lifelong Republican who was amiable and well-liked. His career on the Ninth Circuit had been undistinguished, and he had consistently avoided making rulings that risked subjecting himself to criticism. Conservatives in the Reagan administration fought hard for a stronger nominee, but after the debacles of Bork and Ginsburg, conservatives had spent all their capital within the administration. Kennedy was seen as an easy way out and, indeed, he proved to be that, being confirmed in the Senate by a margin of 97–0.

Shortly thereafter, Justice Kennedy received a note from Harry Blackmun that read, "Welcome to the good old number three club." Blackmun, like Kennedy, had been a president's third choice for a vacancy after the first two nominations had failed. I have to say, the "good old number three club" has not served the Constitution or the American people very well. Kennedy proved exquisitely sensitive to public criticism, deeply swayed by the admiration of D.C. society, the legal academy, and the press. And for three decades, Kennedy enjoyed his role right at the center of the Court's high-profile legal and cultural battles.

When O'Connor served alongside Kennedy, the two of them would vie for who could be the most consequential swing justice. Consistently, there was a bloc of three conservatives: Rehnquist, Scalia, and Thomas. And there was a bloc of four reliable liberals, with Kennedy and O'Connor sitting serenely in the middle. If the left could attract just one of them, they got to five and prevailed in a given case.

That's the reason, I believe, that the Court's docket dropped dramatically. In the 60s and 70s, with a reliable left-wing majority, the Court regularly took more than 100 cases a term. By 1981, that total rose to over 200. But, in more recent decades—with swing votes blowing in the wind—in too many cases neither liberals nor conservatives were confident where five votes would land. Avoiding cases was the more risk-averse path to take, and so the typical docket dropped to about 80 cases a year. But, if we get again a predictable, reliable majority—either liberal or conservative—I think it's likely we'll again see north of 100 cases each year decided at the Court.

On some issues, O'Connor was strong and Kennedy more wobbly; on others, Kennedy held firm while O'Connor blew with the wind. Between the two of them, outcomes were always uncertain. When O'Connor retired, Kennedy enjoyed over twelve years as the lone swing justice. I remember that as law clerks we joked that for criminal cases at the Court, they were decided by the "Greg test." You see, Justice Kennedy has a son named Greg. And if the case was a case where Kennedy could possibly imagine his son might get into particular trouble under the facts of the case, then Kennedy was going to rule for the criminal defendant. But, if the case was something truly horrific, an axe murder or the like, Kennedy knew Greg could never commit such crimes and so was a much more reliable vote for the prosecution. (The test wasn't perfect, as we saw in an earlier chapter, since at times Kennedy was perfectly capable of siding with vicious child rapists, which went far beyond the mild standards of the "Greg test.")

After Reagan came George Herbert Walker Bush. Bush had two nominees to the Supreme Court: Clarence Thomas—who has been extraordinary, ferociously principled, and profoundly consequential— and David Souter, who during his time on the Court traveled from being mildly conservative to becoming the leader of the left wing on the Court.

Souter had served on the New Hampshire Supreme Court and was a Harvard graduate and a Rhodes Scholar. He has high intellect, but nothing in his judicial record demonstrated even a whit of conservative instincts. He had just been appointed and confirmed to the U.S. Court of Appeals for the First Circuit, where he had spent mere weeks before being considered for the Supreme Court.

This nomination was to fill the seat vacated by William Brennan, and at the end of the process, two judges were brought in to interview with President George H. W. Bush: Souter and Edith Jones, a judge from the U.S. Court of Appeals for the Fifth Circuit. Judge Jones was everything Souter was not. She had demonstrated a proven record, had upheld the Constitution, had followed the law, and she had endured brutal press vilification for daring to do so. Yet she remained fearless, principled, and unbowed.

President Bush was risk averse, and New Hampshire Senator Warren Rudman energetically vouched for Souter. Although not a conservative, Rudman told Bush" in effect, wink-wink, nudge-nudge, "even though there is zero paper trail, and there is nothing in the course of his life to prove that David Souter is conservative, trust us, he'll be great."

Nothing better captures the Republican disaster of Supreme Court nominations than that episode. Let me suggest something: If you have lived fifty years of your life and there is nothing whatsoever in anything you have said, written, or done to demonstrate you're a conservative...then you're not. And if by some bizarre miracle, you happen to be, perhaps the Supreme Court of the United States is not the best place for the world to find out.

The Bush White House wanted to avoid controversy, and confirming Edith Jones would have required a fight. Judge Jones actually stood for something—she stood for the rule of law—so nominating her would have cost political capital. So they went with Souter instead.

I remember when I was clerking, there was a tradition at the Court where each of the justices would typically have lunch one day during the term with the clerks from each of the other chambers. It was wonderful tradition, and one I thoroughly enjoyed.

The one justice who refused to participate was (retired) Justice Byron White. He was an extraordinary figure, a legendary athlete and Rhodes Scholar who had been the runner-up for the Heisman Trophy and then led the NFL in rushing in 1938 (as a twenty-one-year-old rookie) and again in 1940—while *simultaneously* ranking first in his class at Yale Law School. That is a feat that was never replicated before or since (to put it mildly).

White left the NFL to serve in the Navy in World War II, and when Patrol Torpedo boat 109 (PT-109) sunk in the Pacific after colliding with Japanese destroyer *Amagiri*, Lieutenant Commander White wrote the intelligence report that transformed Lieutenant (Junior Grade) John F. Kennedy into a war hero. Two decades later, White became President Kennedy's only appointment to the Court.

Although I wasn't a fan of his jurisprudence, I would have loved to have had lunch with Byron White. But he never forgave the law clerks and justices who spread internal gossip and the details of the Court's decision-making to Bob Woodward in his classic insider book, *The Brethren*, and as a result, Justice White resolved not to have lunch with clerks from any other chamber. In prior decades, his games on the Supreme Court basketball court—the highest court in the land—were legendary: a college football hall-of-fame great, with hands seemingly carved from stone, he man-handled pencil-necked law clerks in the paint. Nothing he did (no matter how rough) was ever a foul, but if you so much as touched his arm, he'd call it. Alas, by the time I was clerking, White had retired from basketball, so sadly I didn't get the chance to have lunch or play hoops with him.

I'm thankful all the other justices continued the lunch tradition, and I recall having lunch in Justice Souter's chambers. He told us that each day for lunch he had a small bowl of plain yogurt and an entire apple (core and all). On the weekends, he added fruit to his yogurt. I remember sitting back and finding it curious that Souter apparently liked yogurt better with fruit, but he was enough of an ascetic to deny himself that pleasure five days of the week.

A lifelong bachelor and a slim, reserved man, Justice Souter had primarily known the rural world of New Hampshire. At lunch, he described his time on the New Hampshire Supreme Court, which was his only significant judicial experience prior to his nomination to the Court. In particular, he explained how the complicated and important constitutional questions often before the U.S. Supreme Court never made it to the New Hampshire Supreme Court. Instead, he joked that their cases would "often involve a car that had hit a cow."

I don't think David Souter knew he was a liberal when he was nominated to the Supreme Court. He had simply never confronted those issues—had never thought through them. In his first year or two on the Court, he had a relatively conservative voting record, voting often with Justice Scalia.

Souter's clerks often mirrored the temperament and jurisprudence of the justice. They were reliable liberals, often quintessential Birkenstock-wearing, granola-hippie types. I mean that more figuratively than literally, although some of his clerks fit that description literally as well.

There is no doubt that the world would be profoundly different if President Bush had chosen Edith Jones instead of David Souter. But to truly understand how dramatically things went wrong, we should reflect on what the Court would have looked like had two nomination outcomes been different—had Bork been confirmed instead of Anthony Kennedy, and Jones been nominated and confirmed instead of David Souter.

If those two things had both happened, we would have had a five-justice majority of which *Antonin Scalia would arguably have been the most liberal*: a majority consisting of Chief Justice Rehnquist, Clarence Thomas, Robert Bork, Edith Jones, and Antonin Scalia, with Justice O'Connor floating out there as the possible sixth vote in any particular case. The annals of constitutional history for the last four decades would have been dramatically different.

The constitutionalist wing of the Court would have been strongly fortified at the time when President Clinton nominated Stephen Breyer, a brilliant court of appeals judge and Harvard Law professor, and Ruth Bader Ginsburg, a trailblazing activist lawyer for the ACLU and an extraordinarily successful Supreme Court litigator. Remarkably, in Ginsburg's case, despite her having served as the general counsel of the ACLU and there being no mystery to anyone how leftwing her political ideology was, she was confirmed 98–0.

Despite Breyer's and Ginsburg's confirmations, the constitutionalist majority could have survived had Republicans gotten their picks right. First, Sandra Day O'Connor retired, which presented George W. Bush with a tremendous opportunity to shore up the Court's devotion to the Constitution. Bush nominated Judge John Roberts to take her place. Shortly after that nomination, William Rehnquist passed away from thyroid cancer. Because the nomination was still pending, Bush withdrew Roberts's nomination to be an associate justice and instead nominated him to be the chief justice. And shortly thereafter, Bush nominated Judge Samuel Alito to fill the associate justice position.

With John Roberts, the decision once again came down to two judges sitting in the White House. In one room was John G. Roberts, a brilliant lawyer, a judge on the D.C. Circuit, former deputy solicitor general of the United States, and someone widely considered the finest Supreme Court advocate of his generation. He was a former clerk to Chief Justice Rehnquist. I remember when I was clerking asking the Chief, "Of all the lawyers who appear before the Court, who's the best?" The Chief chuckled and with a wry grin said, "I think I could probably get a majority of the Supreme Court justices to agree that John Roberts is the finest Supreme Court advocate alive." As a twenty-six-year-old young lawyer, I heard that with amazement and, needless to say, paid close attention to every argument Roberts had at the Court. He was a brilliant advocate, but, personally, Roberts kept his cards very close to the chest.

In the Bush 41 administration, when he had been deputy SG, he had signed briefs in some controversial cases, most notably in *Rust v. Sullivan*, supporting the Bush administration policy that restricted medical personnel paid with federal taxpayer dollars from advocating for abortion. But no one who knew him believed those were necessarily Roberts's own views. In his time as a government lawyer, in his years leading the appellate practice at one of the nation's top law firms, and then in his time on the D.C. Circuit Court of Appeals, Roberts carefully avoided controversy. He was someone whom everyone knew wanted to be on the Court, and he lived a life to avoid any of the pitfalls that might derail that nomination.

In the other room at the White House was my former boss, Judge J. Michael Luttig. Luttig was the leading conservative judge of his generation. Appointed to the Fourth Circuit Court of Appeals at age thirty-six, he was fearless, brilliant, and deeply principled. In case after case, he followed the law, explaining the constitutionality of his decision in scholarly detail and enduring the pounding of criticism that inevitably results from standing for constitutional principle.

George W. Bush, like his father, when presented with the choice between a judge with a long, proven conservative record and the battle scars to demonstrate his fidelity and another judge with a much quieter and more opaque record, chose the easier path. But one can be forgiven for asking, what if President Bush had chosen the road less traveled?

To date, John Roberts has proven a somewhat more conservative chief justice than many of the activist judges described in this chapter. His first glaring deviation consisted of his two decisions upholding the Obamacare legislation. In both of those decisions, he engaged in legal gymnastics to achieve what I believe was a political outcome. In the first Obamacare decision, plaintiffs challenged the law and, in particular, the individual mandate that imposed a penalty on Americans if they did not purchase private health insurance. That law was challenged as exceeding the federal government's constitutional authority to regulate commerce between the states. The plaintiffs argued that forcing someone to purchase a product they do not have, which they do not want, and which they may not be able to afford, is not constitutionally permissible "regulation of interstate commerce."

The Supreme Court's majority opinion in *NFIB v. Sebelius* authored by Chief Justice Roberts, agreed. I still remember well sitting down and reading that opinion the day it came down. The first 80 percent of the opinion is strong, principled, and consistent with the Constitution. The jurisprudential holdings on the Commerce Clause and the Spending Clause are important and faithful to the limitations on federal power.

Then, at the end of the opinion, Chief Justice Roberts engages in a quick little sleight of hand. Although the individual mandate would have been unconstitutional if it were a "penalty" (which is what the statute called it), Roberts instead decided to transform it into a "tax." A tax is an imposition of a duty by the federal government to pay money to the federal government. It is governed by a different clause of the Constitution, the Taxing Clause.

The Court's jurisprudence had long held that there is wide discretion for the federal government to design taxes. But here's the rub:

The individual mandate was not a tax. Nowhere in the thousands of pages of that mammoth bill did Congress describe it as a tax. Not only that, but the Democratic members of Congress who advocated for Obamacare repeatedly argued on the floor, and in the press alike, that it was *not* a tax. Barack Obama himself repeatedly argued that it was *not* a tax.

And notably, the U.S. Department of Justice did not make their principal argument that the mandate was a tax; DOJ raised it only as a secondary, alternative argument. And there was a reason that the Obama administration devoted little time and energy to this argument: because it was simultaneously arguing that the mandate was *not* a tax. A separate statute, called the Anti-Injunction Act, prohibits the Court from considering legal challenges to taxes until after they are paid. DOJ wanted the Court to consider and reject the challenge, so they argued that the mandate was *not* a tax under the Anti-Injunction Act, while claiming at the same time that it *was* a tax under the Taxing Clause. On the first day of the three-day oral argument, Justice Alito called them out on that contradiction:

> Today you are arguing that the penalty is not a tax. Tomorrow you are going to be back and you will be arguing that the penalty is a tax. Has the Court ever held that something that is a tax for purposes of the taxing power under the Constitution is not a tax under the Anti-Injunction Act?

The Obama solicitor general admitted that, "no," the Court had never done that. But that didn't stop Chief Justice Roberts. Writing for himself and the four liberal justices, he concluded that Obamacare was not a tax under the Anti-Injunction Act, and yet, remarkably—at the very same time—it was a tax under the Constitution.

This was not a minor distinction. Obama had campaigned in 2008 promising the American people he would not raise taxes on Americans earning less than $250,000 a year. If the individual mandate were a tax,

Obama would have brazenly broken that promise. Indeed, the individual mandate, when it was in operation, typically resulted in the IRS's fining over six million Americans each year because they could not afford to purchase health insurance. Of those the IRS fined, roughly 80 percent earned $50,000 a year or less and roughly 40 percent earned $25,000 a year or less. Single moms waiting tables and working sometimes two, three jobs—who couldn't afford health insurance because they earned less than $25,000 a year—nonetheless found themselves subject to an IRS fine. It was one of the factors that later led former President Bill Clinton to describe this scheme as "the craziest thing in the world."

Obama and the congressional advocates for Obamacare were quite deliberate and emphatic in arguing that the mandate was not a tax. One can understand why. Taxes are visible, taxes are out in the open, and taxes are readily subject to democratic accountability. If politicians want to raise taxes, voters can decide if they agree with that decision. But it is not the role of unelected judges to impose taxes upon a sovereign people from the bench.

Long after the Obamacare decision came down, multiple reports emerged from within the Court that, at a conference shortly after the Obamacare oral argument, Roberts had initially voted to strike down the individual mandate. I have no independent confirmation of that, but I also have no reason to doubt those widespread reports. The reports go that Roberts, after conference, changed his mind and so circulated an opinion ruling the opposite way from how he had voted in conference. I know John Roberts well. He's a friend, and he was an incredibly talented Supreme Court advocate, but he also knew precisely what he was doing.

Here's what I think happened. Roberts believed that striking down Obamacare would subject the Supreme Court to political criticism. He wanted to avoid that criticism. He wanted to shield the Court from being attacked in the course of a presidential campaign. As a clever lawyer, he thought carefully about a way to do so. He could write an opinion where virtually all of the holdings were principled, sound, and constitutional. With one little trick, transmogrifying the mandate into a tax, he could uphold the law and do, he believed, no lasting damage to the Court's jurisprudence.

I suspect he viewed that decision as fulfilling a role, much like the role Chief Justice John Marshall played in *Marbury v. Madison*, where Marshall established the power of judicial review and for the first time struck down a statute enacted by Congress. He did so at a time when the Republic was new, when his political enemy Thomas Jefferson was in the White House and James Madison was secretary of state, and when the executive could easily have defied an order of the newly established Supreme Court.

Marshall was clever. He wanted to protect the legitimacy of the Court, and so *Marbury* was decided in such a manner (on jurisdictional grounds) that there was nothing Jefferson or Madison could do to defy the Court. I don't think malice motivated Chief Justice Roberts in *NFIB v. Sebelius*. I think he was motivated by a genuine desire to protect the Court from political conflict. But that is not the job of a Supreme Court justice. As Roberts himself famously said at his own confirmation hearing, a judge's job is like a baseball umpire: simply to call balls and strikes. With Obamacare, Chief Justice Roberts took off his umpire's cap, picked up a bat, and swung hard at the pitch.

Had George W. Bush nominated Judge Luttig instead of Judge Roberts, I have complete confidence that five justices would have ruled according to the law and struck down Obamacare as unconstitutional. That would have presented a complicated political outcome for elected politicians, but it would have been an outcome consistent with the justices' oaths of office.

The person I believe George W. Bush most wanted to nominate to the Court was Alberto Gonzalez. Gonzalez had been a corporate lawyer at a major Texas law firm, Vinson & Elkins, when then-Governor Bush appointed him to be his general counsel. He next appointed Gonzalez Texas secretary of state and then a Texas Supreme Court justice. When Bush became president, he made Gonzalez White House counsel and then U.S. attorney general.

If appointed, Gonzalez would have been the first Hispanic justice in history, a milestone that Bush would absolutely have loved to set. But national conservatives didn't trust Gonzalez. They repeatedly made clear to Bush that they would have serious problems with his nomination; the phrase often repeated was, "Gonzalez is Spanish for Souter."

When I was on his 2000 presidential campaign, I was the policy staffer advising Bush on the issue of judicial nominations. He told me then that his father had made two mistakes as president: promising not to raise taxes and appointing Souter. George W. didn't want to repeat those mistakes.

So instead he nominated Harriet Miers, the successor to Gonzalez as White House counsel. Harriet is a talented lawyer and fiercely loyal to President Bush. But she had no record whatsoever as a judge and virtually no background or experience in constitutional law. And, according to the public reports, she did not perform well in her meetings with senators. As each day passed, conservative leaders began expressing more and more concern, and, remarkably, Bush decided to withdraw her nomination. When that happened, I sent her a quick email, telling her something to the effect of "Heidi and I know you're hurting right now; we're thinking of you and praying for you." I figured, in the wake of her nomination's being withdrawn, that she'd be pretty shell-shocked, but whenever she returned to her email it might give her some comfort. I was astonished when, just a couple minutes later, Harriet replied with something like "Thanks so much. I'm doing fine, just back at work!" It was a response that demonstrated grace and class and exceptionally strong character.

Both Gonzalez and Miers lacked any discernable proven record of defending conservative principles or paying a real price for doing so. And history teaches that, without such a record, the odds are overwhelming that they would not have become good justices. Maybe they'd have been David Souter, maybe they'd have been Sandra Day O'Connor, but there was no reason on earth to think they'd be Antonin Scalia.

And so, after a bumpy few weeks, the second justice that Bush appointed ended up being Sam Alito. Alito had been a judge on the U.S.

Court of Appeals for the Third Circuit for many years. Prior to that, he had been in the solicitor general's office and in the Office of Legal Counsel. Indeed, he had been a deputy to my former boss Chuck Cooper when Chuck ran the Office of Legal Counsel in the Reagan administration. Then-Judge Alito had a long, demonstrated record of following the Constitution and had endured the criticism that such fidelity necessarily entails. Indeed, his nickname on the Third Circuit was "Scalito." Justice Alito was a terrific choice, and in his time on the Court he has proven a strong, principled, constitutionalist jurist.

Barack Obama had two nominees: Elena Kagan, the brilliant former dean of Harvard Law School and former solicitor general of the Obama administration, and Sonia Sotomayor, the first Hispanic justice to serve on the Court who had been a reliably liberal judge on the U.S. Court of Appeals for the Second Circuit. In almost any given case, the four liberal justices—Ginsburg, Breyer, Sotomayor, and Kagan—today vote in near-lockstep with one another. That lockstep, of course, is exactly how Democrats and the political left want them to vote, and so their opinions on any major issue are more or less predictable.

President Trump has also thus far had two Supreme Court nominees. Trump's first nominee, Neil Gorsuch, had a solid record on the U.S. Court of Appeals for the Tenth Circuit—including multiple robust opinions in defense of religious liberty—although it was a record not nearly as lengthy, distinguished, and conservative as those of Rehnquist, Scalia, or Alito.

Justice Gorsuch's first two terms on the Court were mostly good, but only time will tell what kind of Justice Neil Gorsuch will ultimately become. History, alas, has shown that these questions are measured in decades, and not merely in a few years.

Sadly, this past June—in the most notable decision of his short tenure—we've already seen Justice Gorsuch joining Chief Justice Roberts and voting with the four liberals in a landmark decision, where the Court concluded that the Civil Rights Act of 1964, which prohibits discrimination "because of . . . sex," also covers sexual orientation and gender identity. As a policy matter, you might believe Gorsuch's position isn't unreasonable.

Indeed, legislation to protect sexual orientation and gender identity has repeatedly been introduced in Congress, and at different times it has passed both the House and the Senate. But rather than allow elected legislators to make the policy decisions—and to address whatever compromises might be needed to protect free speech, religious liberty, and other fundamental rights—the Court just decreed the law was changed. Justices Thomas, Alito, and Kavanaugh dissented. Justice Alito put his disapproval in no uncertain terms, writing that "the Court's opinion is like a pirate ship. It sails under a textualist flag, but what it actually represents is a theory of statutory interpretation that Justice Scalia excoriated—the theory that courts should 'update' old statutes so that they better reflect the current values of society."

President Trump's second nominee, to replace Justice Kennedy, was Brett Kavanaugh. Judge Brett Kavanaugh had a record much like that of John Roberts. Indeed, when then-presidential candidate Trump put out his initial list of eleven judges, and subsequently his expanded list of twenty-one judges, Kavanaugh's name was deliberately omitted. The reason for this was simple; Kavanaugh, on the D.C. Circuit had written an opinion in a case called *Seven-Sky v. Holder* arguing that the Obamacare individual mandate was a tax; it was an opinion that many saw as a roadmap for Roberts's subsequent decision upholding Obamacare in *NFIB v. Sebelius*.

Kavanaugh had been a law clerk to Justice Kennedy, and the Washington rumor mill churned with the belief that Kennedy wanted Kavanaugh to replace him and that Kennedy agreed to retire only after the Trump White House made that promise. I don't know for certain if those rumors are true, but they are certainly plausible.

Kavanaugh, like Roberts, has often sought to avoid controversy. It is no small irony, then, that his confirmation hearing was transformed into a brutal and vicious personal smear, driven by the Democrats.

Judge Kavanaugh was previously a senior staffer in the George W. Bush White House, and he was very much a D.C. insider. He's smart, affable, and gregarious. Had Jeb Bush won the 2016 presidential nomination and become president, Brett Kavanaugh almost certainly would have been Jeb's first nominee. Personally, I like Brett, but when President Trump nominated him after the urging of many longtime voices in Washington, I worried about the jurisprudential consequences.

So I raised serious concerns. My preference, which I urged energetically for both of Trump's vacancies, was nominating Senator Mike Lee. Mike Lee, the senior senator from Utah, is my closest friend in the Senate. He's brilliant and the son of Rex Lee, President Reagan's legendary solicitor general who is considered one of the finest Supreme Court advocates ever to have lived. Mike was a law clerk for Justice Alito. He is a constitutional scholar who is a deeply committed conservative. Over and over again, he has stood for the Constitution and has endured relentless, pounding criticism for doing so. As I explained, I believe that is the single most important criterion for a Supreme Court justice.

Critically, Mike doesn't give a damn what D.C. thinks of him. He doesn't go to D.C. cocktail parties. That's a very good test for Supreme Court nominees: whether they have any interest in (or tolerance for) going to D.C. cocktail parties.

With both vacancies, I urged President Trump and I urged Vice President Pence that the administration should nominate Mike Lee. Trump had promised to nominate justices "in the mold of Scalia and Thomas," and Mike fit that bill perfectly. Of all of the potential choices, he was the one I was absolutely certain would remain faithful to the Constitution, no matter what. But Mike, in the 2016 presidential election had not supported Donald Trump, even after he was the nominee. And each time I pressed the case to the president and the vice president, that was deemed a disqualifying factor—even though, at my urging, Mike was one of the twenty-one names on the list of potential justices that then-candidate Trump had put out.

Shortly after Kavanaugh was nominated, Vice President Pence joined the Republican senators for our Tuesday lunch, as he often does. I pulled him aside and told him directly, "Mike, if, a decade from now, a 5–4 majority of the Court reaffirms *Roe v. Wade*, this week may well be the reason why." I very much hope and pray that does not prove to be the case.

Kavanaugh's nomination appeared to be headed for an easy confirmation until the now-infamous bombshell allegations from Dr. Christine Blasey Ford arose. Dr. Ford alleged that when she and Judge Kavanaugh were both in high school, at a drunken party, he had sexually assaulted her. These allegations had been privately raised months earlier in a letter to Senator Dianne Feinstein, the Democratic ranking member on the Senate Judiciary Committee. But Dr. Ford, at the time, asked that the allegations not be made public.

The Judiciary Committee has a mechanism for assessing allegations of this kind. The Committee can ask the FBI to conduct an investigation to ascertain what actually happened. The Committee also can meet in closed session to consider sensitive information or charges in a confidential setting. But Senator Feinstein did not ask for an FBI investigation— nor did she ask for a confidential hearing to consider these allegations. Instead, she sat on the allegations for months until the week before a high-profile Supreme Court confirmation vote, when suddenly Dr. Ford's claims were leaked to the press.

Chaos erupted, and I believe the Senate Democrats callously took advantage of Dr. Ford and used her in a political effort to stop Judge Kavanaugh. Shortly after the allegations arose, all of the Senate Republicans on the Judiciary Committee met together in Mitch McConnell's conference room. We discussed what to do. I urged my colleagues that we needed to have a public hearing, quickly, that Dr. Ford needed to be given a full and fair opportunity to present her allegations because the allegations were serious, and that Judge Kavanaugh, likewise, deserved a full and fair opportunity to defend himself.

Some of my colleagues were reluctant to hold a hearing. We had already had one confirmation hearing for Judge Kavanaugh. But I argued, along with several other members of the Committee, that the only way to resolve this issue and move forward with the confirmation was to allow the public to decide. When Clarence Thomas's Supreme Court nomination likewise faced the explosive charges of sexual harassment from Anita Hill, it was the public hearings where Professor Hill and then-Judge Thomas both testified that allowed the American people to make their own assessment of the veracity of the charges.

Although today's media and legal academy desperately want to erase this from the public record, at the time, polling showed roughly two-thirds of Americans believed Judge Thomas and did not find Professor Hill's allegations to be credible. I urged my colleagues that if Judge Kavanaugh were to become Justice Kavanaugh, the American people likewise would have to have an opportunity to listen to and to see Dr. Ford and to listen to and to see Judge Kavanaugh address these allegations. Oftentimes, Republicans, as a political matter, are slow to make the decision that needs to be made, and we end up getting battered in the press and public opinion for days or weeks, only to reluctantly do what should have been done in the first place. I urged my colleagues, rather than endure the public beating, to announce the hearing now. It was the right thing to do, I argued, and it was also the only way to move forward with the nomination. My colleagues agreed.

Secondly, I urged my Judiciary Committee colleagues to bring in an outside counsel to question Dr. Ford. The Democrats' political plan was not complicated to surmise. They planned to bring Dr. Ford before the Committee and, at the hearing, they hoped the questioning would feature Republican senators on the Committee—primarily old white men—sternly questioning an alleged sexual-assault victim. Had that transpired, the public reaction would have been swift and harsh. No Republican senator, I argued, wanted to vigorously cross-examine Dr. Ford—myself included. At that point, one of the more senior Republican senators volunteered, "I'll do it," to which several of us said, "uh, no thank you." Instead, I argued, we should bring in an experienced prosecutor, a woman, to lead the examination. My colleagues once again agreed with me.

The Senate Judiciary Committee reached out to a number of respected female former prosecutors in the Washington, D.C., area. Even though they had been senior officials in Republican administrations and knew and respected Judge Kavanaugh as a person, they were unwilling to step into the maelstrom of political criticism that would be visited upon any lawyer taking that position. So, we hired an outside counsel, an experienced lawyer from Arizona, who had been recommended to the Committee. She did an able job.

During the course of the hearing, I and other members of the Judiciary Committee gave her extensive guidance as to how she should approach the questioning. My advice was, "Be incredibly gentle. Be respectful. Bend over backwards to treat Dr. Ford with the utmost respect." Your job, I told her, is not to be Perry Mason. It's not to deliver a withering cross-examination showing weaknesses or inconsistency in the testimony. Instead, your job is to gently elucidate her testimony and gently press where any inconsistencies might lie.

Given the choice between being aggressive or being respectful, I urged her, "Lean in the direction of respect." She did so. She gently cross-examined Dr. Ford—so gently that, in the course of the hearing, several friends texted me asking, "What on earth is wrong with your lawyer? She's not beating up the witness." But that, of course, was not her job.

After Dr. Ford testified, Judge Kavanaugh came next. With Judge Kavanaugh, I told our counsel, "You no longer need to be gentle. Lean into him. Ask difficult questions. Press on him. He's a big boy, and he can take it." She did so and pressed on his story. Judge Kavanaugh adamantly, passionately denied the allegations.

As the hearing progressed, Senate Democrats became more and more angry. They became steadily more vicious, attacking and smearing Judge

Kavanaugh personally. They were frustrated, I believe, that their political plan of letting Republican senators stupidly attack an alleged sexual-assault victim had not materialized. Their frustrations spilled over into bitter and nasty personal attacks. At that point, our role in the hearing changed. We instructed our outside counsel, "You've done a good job. We can take it from here." Countering partisan attacks from Democrats was something that Republicans on the Judiciary Committee felt more than capable of doing.

At that point, we took over in the hearing, engaging directly. I tried to systematically lay out the facts, pointing out how even though Senate Republicans had treated Dr. Ford with nothing but respect, Senate Democrats cynically responded without providing Judge Kavanaugh with a proper opportunity to defend himself. Instead, they (and the media) just presumed him guilty. I also pointed out how each of the three witnesses Dr. Ford referenced had stated on the record, under penalty of perjury, that they did not remember the incident that she alleged.

Perhaps the most memorable exchange of the hearing came from my colleague, Senator Lindsey Graham, who angrily exploded at the blatant hypocrisy of the Democrats. "What you want to do," Lindsey bellowed at the Democrats sitting across the Judiciary Committee dais, "is to destroy this guy's life, hold this seat open, and hope you win in 2020." Not content to leave it there, he continued: "This is the most unethical sham since I've been in politics."

My eighty-five-year-old mother, who is very conservative and had not previously thought highly of Lindsey Graham, immediately sent me a text: "Okay. I love Lindsey Graham." In the hearing, I walked over and showed Lindsey the text, which caused him to laugh heartily.

Once the allegations came to light, the FBI conducted a supplemental investigation into Dr. Ford's claims. They interviewed the witnesses identified by Dr. Ford and prepared detailed reports on the results of those interviews. I sat in the secure basement of the U.S. Capitol and read every page of that FBI investigation. Each of the alleged witnesses disagreed with Dr. Ford's account. At the end of the day, the facts alleged by Dr. Ford sharply contradicted the facts alleged by Judge Kavanaugh. Both could not be true. In our legal system, when we have contradictory testimony, we regularly look to corroborating evidence—whether additional testimony or evidence can shed light on what actually occurred.

In this instance, none of the potential corroborating evidence supported Dr. Ford's allegation, and all of the witnesses who had been identified contradicted the claims. Given that, I voted to confirm Judge Kavanaugh, as did a majority of my fellow senators. The experience of that confirmation hearing was no doubt searing and personal, and it was made all the more painful because Judge Kavanaugh and his wife have two young daughters. I've known Brett Kavanaugh for nearly twenty years, from the early days of the Bush administration. And I've known his wife Ashley (a native Texan) even longer, since our work together on the 2000 George W. Bush campaign. I consider them friends; both are good and honorable people, and it's a travesty that their family was dragged through the mud the way they were.

What kind of Justice Brett Kavanaugh will be is a question that will take many years to assess. John Roberts has already become the new Sandra Day O'Connor, and some observers fear Kavanaugh may join him as the new Anthony Kennedy, together as the swing justices and arbiters in the middle of the Court. And, as the recent Title VII case illustrated—just as it would vary whether it was Kennedy or O'Connor siding with the liberals—it could also sometimes be Gorsuch doing so. It's too early to make that conclusion, but time will tell. I fervently hope that's not the case.

Both nominees will no doubt prove better than the nominees Hillary would have put on the Court. But, Republican presidents must do better than our record the past seventy years.

Going forward, there will be additional vacancies either for President Trump to fill or for the next Republican president to fill. The most important criteria that I believe should be applied is whether that individual (1) has a demonstrated proven record of being faithful to the Constitution and (2) has endured pounding criticism—has paid a price for holding that line. Had I been able to choose between Edith Jones and David Souter, I would readily have chosen Judge Jones. Had I been able to choose between John Roberts and Mike Luttig, I would have enthusiastically chosen Judge Luttig. Had I been able to choose between Brett Kavanaugh and Mike Lee, or Neil Gorsuch and Mike Lee, I would have unhesitatingly chosen Mike Lee.

All for the same reason. The stakes are too high—too many critical issues are hanging in the balance. Every single time, without exception, the Republicans nominate a justice who lacks a serious proven record of going through the crucible, that justice has proven a disappointment.

Clerks often emulate their justices. We need more former Scalia and Thomas clerks, and fewer Kennedy clerks. On Trump's list of twenty-one, Fifth Circuit Judge Don Willett has a decade-long record as a fearless conservative (and he would be the only Evangelical Christian on the Court). Not on the list of twenty-one, Fifth Circuit Judge (and former Thomas clerk) Jim Ho likewise has amassed a very strong record, as has former U.S. solicitor general (and Scalia clerk) Noel Francisco (either of whom would be the first Asian-American on the Court).

Justices "in the mold of Scalia and Thomas" should mean just that.

In the world of Washington, there are always trusted insiders, gray-beards who will tell a president, "I know so and so," and even though their record doesn't demonstrate it, "trust me," deep down in their heart, they're going to be conservative. History teaches us that those siren promises are always, always, always wrong. If a judicial nominee does not have a demonstrated proven record, if we cannot be confident he or she will withstand the praise and punishment, the carrot and stick of the press and the academy, then they should not be named to the Supreme Court. The stakes are simply too high. After all, we're just one vote away.

ACKNOWLEDGEMENTS

Writing this book, my second, has been a joy. For nearly two decades, my professional life revolved around the Supreme Court, and it is an extraordinary institution. Living legends have walked those marble halls. The victories they have won for Justice and Rule of Law—and, at times, the damage they have inflicted on our Nation—have been incalculable.

I am grateful for all those who assisted in writing. Josh Hammer, a young lawyer and talented and rising opinion journalist, helped research and write the entire manuscript. I wrote much of the book during the coronavirus lockdown, and Josh and I spent hours and hours on the phone and on email going chapter by chapter. He did a superb job.

As always, I am immensely thankful for Heidi and our two daughters, Caroline and Catherine. They were on lockdown with me, all four of us together 24/7 in our house: Heidi working upstairs in her office, Caroline doing distance schooling to finish sixth grade in her bedroom, and Catherine finishing third grade at the kitchen table. They put up with me, ensconced in the living room, papers and legal briefs lying everywhere, writing day after day. I suspect they'd tell you they put up with a lot more than that.

And I appreciate the many people who helped review early drafts. Steve Chartan, Sam Cooper, Lauren Aronson, Andrew Davis, Omri Ceren, Jeff Roe, David Polyansky, Jason Johnson, and both my parents read parts or all of the book, and generously shared their insight and suggestions.

My book agent Keith Urbahn provided his predictably wise counsel, and my editor Paul Choix—and the entire team at Regnery—exercised a (thankfully) light touch, but they made the draft significantly better.

I'd like to say any errors in this book are Jeff Roe's fault. But, speaking more fairly, the responsibility for any mistakes is mine.

INDEX